W9-DER-527

THE NEXT BATTLEGROUND

THE NEXT
BATTLEGROUND

■ ■ ■

JAPAN,

AMERICA,

AND THE NEW

EUROPEAN

MARKET

■ ■ ■

TIM JACKSON

Houghton Mifflin Company

BOSTON   NEW YORK   1993

For information about permission to reproduce selections
from this book, write to Permissions, Houghton Mifflin Company,
215 Park Avenue South, New York, New York 10003.

Library of Congress Cataloging-in-Publication Data

Jackson, Tim.
The next battleground : Japan, America, and the new European
market / Tim Jackson.
p.   cm.
Includes bibliographical references (p.   ) and index.
ISBN 0-395-61594-1
1. European Economic Community countries — Foreign economic
relations — Japan.
2. Japan — Foreign economic relations — European
Economic Community countries.
3. Investments, Japanese — European Economic Community countries.
4. Investments, American — European Economic Community countries.
5. Competition, International. I. Title.
HF1532.5.Z4J34   1993   92-41918
337.4052 — dc20   CIP

Printed in the United States of America
HAD 10 9 8 7 6 5 4 3 2 1

Excerpts from *Rivethead: Tales from the Assembly Line*,
copyright © 1991 by Ben Hamper, are reprinted
by permission of Warner Books, Inc.

For Emily Marbach

CONTENTS

INTRODUCTION

A S 1993 APPROACHES, a great change is taking place in Europe. After a century of trying to compete with the larger populations of the United States and Japan as a disparate group of a dozen nation-states, Western Europe is at last turning itself into a single economic force. With the change complete, firms as far apart as Edinburgh and Naples will share one domestic market, with more consumers and more economic output every year than either the United States or Japan. But new opportunities bring new dangers. Even before the twelve member states of the European Community had committed themselves to forming a single market, Japanese companies had begun to invest heavily inside it. Since then, every year from 1986 to 1992, the stock of Japanese investment in Europe has grown; and as the last trade walls fall, hundreds of Japanese companies stand ready to start local production in their new factories.

There is therefore the risk that what European business executives have thought of for decades as a dream may in fact turn out to be a nightmare. In a number of important businesses — notably the computer, electronics, and car industries — it may be not European firms that take the greatest advantage of the single market but firms from Japan. Just as American firms were more successful during the 1950s and 1960s at negotiating the complexities of a dozen different sets of national rules than the Europeans themselves were, Japanese firms could in the coming decade emerge as the only ones to display the breadth of vision necessary to succeed in a newly unified market. There would, however, be a price for that success: Japanese businesses installed in Europe would be taking away profits, sales, and eventually jobs from locally owned businesses.

What is less often noticed is that a Japanese economic take-over of Europe would be disastrous for the United States too. American firms have already been bloodied by competition from Japan in their own back yard. For many U.S. businesses, the standard pattern in which companies tend to make big profits at home but fight more competitively abroad has been turned inside out: to keep afloat in the U.S. market, they now rely on profits from Europe. Expensive and difficult to get into, the European market is now a rich source of profits with which the U.S. firms subsidize their mainstream activities. But it is unlikely to remain so for long. With a single market in Europe, competition must intensify. And if Japanese firms gain a decisive advantage, the threat they pose to American businesses will be vastly greater than at present. There is a danger of a vicious downward spiral: driven out of Europe, American firms could see lower sales volumes and thus higher costs, which in turn could weaken them in their fight for survival at home. The very same economies of scale that helped them succeed in Europe a generation ago would then be working against them. And the only nation whose industries span all three of the world's big markets would be Japan.

This book is about these twin threats, to Europe and to the United States, and how to prevent them from turning into reality. Over the past few years, discussion of Japan has been dominated by two conflicting theories. One, which has come to be known in the United States as the "revisionist" view, argues that things in Japan are not what they seem. Businesses do not seek profits like those in the West; people prefer to sublimate rather than celebrate their individuality; consumers would rather pay more than less; and even the way the government makes policy is impossible to pin down. On the strength of this view, influential people in both the United States and Europe want their governments to treat Japan as a pariah state: to suspend the rules of international free trade from which it benefits, and to start treating issues previously thought of as business issues instead as political ones. Another, more sympathetic, view insists that Japan is a victim of misunderstanding. Not much about the country is different from anywhere else, say its adherents; Japan has simply had a bad press from people who know nothing about it and never bothered to learn its language. If it ever practiced unfair trade, the country certainly does not do so now; and the problem Japan poses to the West is nothing more or less than that adversity and defeat in war have trained the Japanese to work harder than anyone else.

The starting point of this book is less stark than either of these views. Japanese society is indeed very different from Western society; it is impossible to live in Japan for any length of time and not see that. So far, Japan has managed to avoid some of the malaises — bad industrial relations, crime, and the poverty and instability that sometimes result from the decline of the family — that have infected Europe and the United States since the Second World War. These things are an undoubted advantage to Japanese companies as they compete for markets all over the world. But they are changing too: as shareholders demand more profits, consumers more bargains, and workers more leisure, Japan in the year 2000 will be almost unrecognizably different from what it was in 1970. It is now possible to imagine a time when Japan will look no more strange to the United States than Germany does today.

But Japan itself has been the object of study by too many great experts already, so that theme, unfolded in chapter 2, is not developed far. Rather, the central aim of this book is to look at the battleground itself: the European market, and what businesses are doing there. Its purpose is to see where European and American firms are losing, and to try to identify in those cases what the Japanese are doing right. It deals in turn with the financial sector, with the car industry, with the computer business, and with consumer electronics.

The results are surprisingly varied. As chapter 3 argues, Japan's banks and stockbrokerages pose no threat at all to Europe. Both went through a period of giddy expansion in the 1980s which was the temporary result of the financial rules and economic conditions of the time. Their growth was not sustainable. In their rush for growth, banks picked up lots of bad debts; today, they show no sign of being able to carry out the core business of borrowing and lending any more efficiently than competitors in Europe or the United States. Japanese securities firms, likewise, grew to the size of leviathans as their highly protected domestic stock market went skyward. As share prices have fallen, the stupidities and dishonesties that accompanied their expansion have been revealed. And from now on, the gradual process of deregulation is certain to make their domestic trade less profitable. The Tokyo stock market and the Japanese investor are no longer a mine of money for export.

Embarrassing though Japan's financial sector is, it should not lead the West to become complacent — for there are other areas where the threat is terrifyingly real and immediate. Chapter 4 looks at the shock that is waiting to happen in the European car industry. Japanese companies sell one car in three in the United States, but only one in nine in Europe. Many Europeans (some of them in the car industry, who ought therefore to know better) argue that the European car makers can avoid the same "fate" as the Big Three U.S. makers if only governments will give them the protection they ask for. But Toyota and Nissan did not win the market share they now have in the United States only because of policy mistakes in Washington; they did so because they were able to make cars more efficiently than were the existing American makers. Over the past decade, the U.S. firms have done a great deal to catch up; it is now Europe that is the laggard of the three. The coming decade is likely to see a bloodbath as efficient Japanese firms attack the mass market in Europe where Ford and General Motors are dominant, and then move upmarket to attack the luxury car business, which is the only segment where Europeans still make the best products.

In the computer industry, examined in chapter 5, European companies have always been weak. Despite the pioneering work done by a handful of European inventors, the industry's history is largely one of American innovation and marketing. In world terms, the Germans, French, Italians, and British are marginal. Companies like Olivetti, Bull, and Siemens are dependent on subsidies, trade protection, favored sales to the public sector, or all three. One thing is clear: their future is uncertain at best. At worst, it will consist in merger or contraction, or in absorption by sturdier American or Japanese firms. Whether Japanese firms can beat the Americans remains hard to predict; as computers become more and more like off-the-shelf electronics goods, the Japanese advantages will come to weigh more heavily. But there is no sign yet of any slackening in the inventiveness that is at the root of American competitive advantage.

The position is reversed in consumer electronics, as chapter 6 shows. American companies are now effectively out of the industry. It was in radios, tape recorders, and televisions that the first Japanese threat to U.S. industry came, and American firms were driven out before they had time to realize what was hitting them. Scores of U.S. firms mistook Japan as nothing more than a place where labor was cheap, and tried to respond by moving their operations to Mexico or Singapore; but the real problem was that Japanese firms were making their products better, smaller, cheaper, and more reliable, and were bringing them to market more quickly. There are still some European electronics firms left, and one in particular is the guardian of a treasure trove of technology. But to avoid the fate of its American predecessors, it needs to squeeze every last penny from each of its inventors' good ideas or technical advances, and it needs to rediscover the marketing expertise that helped it to expand in the first place. Whether it will succeed or not remains to be seen.

How can the government — whether in Washington, in Brussels, or in the different national capitals of the European Community — help? Some things are straightforward. The government can help to foster good human capital, by turning out a highly educated and skilled work force from national schools. It can provide a reliable infrastructure of roads, telephones, postal and delivery services, computer networks, and information. It can pursue stable economic policies, so that companies can plan for the future without unnecessary worries about wild fluctuations in their wage bills or input costs, and without jeopardizing their position in overseas markets by tinkering excessively with the exchange rate. But whether the government can do more to foster so-called strategic industries remains unclear. Chapter 7 shows that one notorious attempt to intervene directly in one European industry proved sadly unsuccessful. Industrial policy brings with it more dangers than opportunities for success.

So businesses that are facing hard times in Europe cannot look outside for a scapegoat. Having given up hope that government can bail them out of their difficulties, no longer able to convince themselves that their problems are entirely the result of "unfair" competition from Japan, they are then forced to look inward. Chapter 8 assesses in turn the advantages that companies from the United States, Europe, and Japan face in this imminent battle for dominance of the continent, and then goes on to look at the sort of things lagging firms need to do to catch up with the leaders. They need to think again about how to deal with their employees and with their suppliers; they need to go back to some old-fashioned notions about profit and loss and about products. They must also throw off their fears about competing in Japan itself. Far from being a closed citadel, the Japanese market is now the world's most demanding. It has supplanted the United States as the place where the leanest and most efficient maker of each product must be in order to stay abreast of developments. So European firms, and some American ones too, need to do more to sell in Japan. But above all, they must stop worrying about what Japan is doing wrong and start concentrating on what it is doing right. In short, they must either turn Japanese themselves or give up.

This book could not have been written without the help of the hundreds of people in Japan, the United States, and Europe who talked to me about their work or their area of special expertise as I was doing my research. They include analysts, business leaders, consultants, diplomats, economists, government officials, historians, journalists, politicians, and factory workers. Some of them are named in the text or in the notes; to others, identified by pseudonyms or altogether nameless, I am equally in debt.

I must thank Andreas Whittam Smith, the editor of *The Independent*, who has given me permission to make use in this book of research I carried out in the course of writing articles for the paper, and who generously allowed me to take time off between my old job in Tokyo and my new job in Brussels to get a head start on the writing of the book. Rupert Pennant-Rea, the editor of *The Economist*, is responsible for kindling my interest in Japan by sending me there in the first place as a young and untried foreign correspondent. Nicholas Valéry, who arrived soon afterward for his third period of residence in the country, proved an untiringly kind and patient teacher of his craft, and an oracle of experience and precedent. Taeko Kawamura, Yasuko Furukawa, and Hanabusa Midori (the latter being the only exception to the practice followed elsewhere in this book of writing Japanese given names before family names) proved not only skilled assistants and researchers but also loyal friends and advisers.

The months I spent on the road were punctuated by weekends during which I stayed at the houses of friends. Daniel

Jackson and Claudia Marbach were particularly kind hosts in Boston; David Rosenfeld, with his experience of Japanese newspapers, offered fascinating new insights into the issues while putting me up in Palo Alto; Terra Brockman regaled me with stories of her own literary struggles in Japan when I was her guest in New York.

Essential work and fact checking was done at the New York and San Francisco public libraries, at the Library of Congress in Washington, at the British Library in London, at the Bodleian Library in Oxford, and at the libraries of Stanford University, the Tokyo Foreign Correspondents' Club, and the International House of Japan.

Chalmers and Sheila Johnson offered valuable criticism when the book was only in outline. Ashley Summerfield, Nigel Savage, Hamish Macrea, Peter Miller, Martin Edelshain, and Toshiaki Yasuda were all kind enough to plow through draft chapters and to save me from inconsistencies and mistakes. For those that remain, some of them against their advice, only I am responsible.

William Miller in Tokyo was the first to see my plans, and helped guide them with great skill and good humor toward their eventual home in Japan. Gill Coleridge, my agent in London, was a patient and warm adviser on scores of practical details, and Esther Newberg served staunchly on my behalf as agent in New York. Michael Fishwick and Richard Wheaton in London, Barbara Luijken in Haarlem, John Sterling in New York, and Hiroshi Hayakawa in Tokyo all worked untiringly as excellent editors and publishers without jeopardizing the daunting goal of simultaneous release in three different languages and four countries.

As hosts, chefs, long-distance advisers, stylistic critics, and proofreaders, my parents provided a reassuring haven halfway between San Francisco and Tokyo to which I returned before, during, and after my research. As writers themselves, one just having finished a book and the other just having begun one, they were understanding of my ignorance and patient with my impetuousness.

Emily Marbach, who followed me from Tokyo to Brussels, was present at both the conception and the delivery of this book. She has heard all the jokes before, pretends to have forgotten them, and laughs every time. That is why this book is dedicated to her.

NEW YORK
SEPTEMBER I, 1992

THE NEXT BATTLEGROUND

ONE

The World's Biggest Market

L IKE BREWERS AND DISTILLERS all over the world, the Burgundian producers of the French blackcurrant li- queur known as *cassis de Dijon* would like people to believe that drinking their sweet, dark mixture is good for you. Who could disagree? A *kir royale* — a glass of cham- pagne tinted pink by a drop of *cassis* at the bottom — is one of the most pleasant preludes to a meal. A generation from now, however, people looking back may well argue that *cassis* played a crucial part in the shaping of the world economy of the twenty-first century. It is only a slight exaggeration to say that no drink has ever brought so much prosperity to so many people.

The story begins in a court case in the late 1970s, with one of those pettifogging disputes that Europeans ought to have grown out of. The makers of *cassis* found that although hun- dreds of thousands of Germans were quite happy to down a *kir* or two when on vacation in France, their concoction could not be sold in Germany. With a characteristic insistence on keeping to the rules, the German government had insisted that *cassis*, delicious though it might be, did not conform to its national standards for alcoholic drinks. With regret, it explained to the German firms that had imported *cassis* that they would be forbidden to sell it to the public.

To many Europeans the idea seemed preposterous. Here were two countries that had successfully put behind them the bitter history of the Second World War, the First World War, the Franco-Prussian War, and generations of conflict before that. Since 1950 the former enemies had put their coal and steel industries in common hands. Seven years later they had signed a treaty in Rome to create a European Economic Community with Italy, Belgium, Luxembourg, and the Netherlands. They had set up a special European Court to settle disputes among them. Together, those six countries — later to become nine, and then twelve — had undertaken to remove all the barriers between their markets in a dozen years or at most fifteen. And yet in 1978, more than twenty years after the Treaty of Rome, Germans could still be forbidden by their government to buy a French blackcurrant drink. Cynics seized on the story with glee; how, they demanded, could anybody take seriously a group of countries that claimed to be trying to come together, if a mere cocktail ingredient was enough to separate them?

This time, however, the cynics were to be proved wrong. For the Burgundians took their case to the European Court of Justice — and won it in 1979. In awarding them the right to export their product to Germany, the court issued a landmark judgment that proved to be a turning point in the history of the European Community.

> *Cassis de Dijon* . . . established the general principle that all goods lawfully manufactured and marketed in one member country should be accepted also by other member countries, while also recognizing the need for some exceptions related to "the effectiveness of fiscal supervision, the protection of public health, the fairness of commercial transactions and the defense of the consumer"[1]

— or, to put it less accurately but more bluntly, a drink that was good enough for the French ought to be good enough for the Germans, unless there was a good reason why not. Good reasons might include many things, but the Germans could not just point to their regulations and declare the matter closed.

In coming to their *cassis* judgment, the members of the European Court were recognizing something with much broader application. The entire process of European integration, they saw, was being held up by hundreds of such tiny problems. The different countries of the European Community had removed the formal tariffs that guarded their borders; they had expressed their commitment to closer economic cooperation; they were even meeting with increasing frequency to try to determine a single response to major problems facing the world.

But the thousands of government regulations in different countries across Europe, each of which was a small obstacle to trade, added up to daunting barriers that effectively prevented companies in one country from doing business freely in another. As a result, the French car company Renault could have a 30 percent market share on the west bank of the Rhine, but only 3 percent in the European market east of the river. The two biggest makers of chocolate for the Spanish market could be absent from the top ten in Italy. Milk prices could rise fast in Britain, but fail to attract a single pint of imported milk from France.

In short, Europe was squandering its advantage. With a densely packed population almost half as big again as that of the United States and more than double the size of Japan's, it remained a patchwork of fragmented markets. To make matters worse, it also seemed to be in economic decline. With the exception of Germany, which had continued its smooth and apparently unstoppable path of growth since the end of the Second World War, the other members of the European Community suffered in common from high unemployment, high inflation, and low economic growth. For years, they had lagged behind the United States and Japan; at the end of the 1970s, the four "dragons" of East Asia — Hong Kong, Singapore, Taiwan, and Korea — suddenly began to look as if they might begin to outstrip the poorer countries of Europe if things carried on for another decade.

The decision handed down by the European Court of Justice over *cassis*, however, raised a vision of a very different Europe: a Europe that really was a common market, and that could develop economic and political power to rival both the established dominance of the United States and the increasing weight of Japan.

More than a decade later, in 1992, the continent was almost unrecognizable. Under the charismatic presidency of Jacques Delors, who had moved to the top job in Brussels in 1984 after a stint as France's finance minister, the Community actually appeared to be putting that vision of 1979 into effect.

It had happened in an unobtrusive way. Less than a year after Delors arrived in Brussels, he and his colleagues presented the Community's member governments with a bland-looking white paper called *Completing the Internal Market*, which set out 279 different measures and a timetable for putting them into effect, and which would demolish one by one the myriad barriers that had kept Europe fragmented. With unthinking enthusiasm, the different national governments accepted it. Only later were they to realize that building a truly single market involved not just restraining the zeal of customs officers but also ceding much of their power to Brussels. For firms could not compete on equal terms in the new Europe with other firms that paid lower taxes, profited from an undervalued currency, gave their workers fewer days off, were able to subsidize foreign sales with high profits from their domestic markets, and benefited from government subsidies. In all these areas, creating the single market turned out to be a slippery slope toward ceding power to Brussels.

Margaret Thatcher realized early on that the process would end in a much tighter European Community than she wanted to see. Her suspicions were confirmed when Delors predicted in a speech at the European Parliament in 1988 that the power to legislate in 80 percent of economic matters, and more than half of social and fiscal matters, would in effect be transferred from the national parliaments to the institutions of the Community within a decade. The incensed prime minister hit back in a carefully crafted speech at Bruges in September of that year. "I am the first to say that on many great issues the countries of Europe should try to speak with a single voice," she said.

> But working more closely together does not require power to be centralized in Brussels, or decisions to be taken by an appointed bureaucracy . . . We have not successfully rolled back the frontiers of the state of Britain, only to see them recognized at a European level, with a European super-state exercising a new dominance from Brussels.

A year later, Thatcher showed that she meant business by declining to send Lord Cockfield, the Briton who had been responsible for the internal market program on the Commission, back to Brussels for a second term.

True to her roots in a small grocery in a provincial British town, the prime minister had sensed something that other political leaders in Europe were much slower to grasp: ordinary people were still highly suspicious of the idea that the continent's nation-states should pool their power in a political union. The governments of the EC's twelve member states had started out the negotiations firmly intending to limit their discussions to the economic sphere. A single market would bring immediate and tangible economic benefits, they thought, while the benefits from political union were much harder to sell to voters. Yet little by little, it became clear that creating an absolutely seamless single market would involve much more than they first had in mind. All over the continent, newspapers began to write about how unelected bureaucrats in Brussels were issuing edicts on everything from the cleanliness of beaches to the flavor of potato chips.

The bubbling public discontent only boiled over in spring 1992, when the voters of Denmark went to the polls in a referendum on the 1991 Maastricht treaty on political union. Under the treaty's provisions, the EC's members proposed to forge a single foreign policy, to move in clearly defined steps toward a single currency and a single monetary policy, and eventually even to join in common defense. For a mixture of contradictory reasons — ranging from conservatives' fear of immigrants and anger at having to sacrifice aid to Africa for subsidies to Spaniards and Irishmen, to socialists' fears that Denmark's high-tax, high-welfare social system would be regulated out of existence from Brussels — the Danes voted by a margin of less than fifty thousand votes against Maastricht. Politically, nothing would ever be the same again. Although the other EC countries worked hard to drum up support for the treaty and have it ratified everywhere else, the Danes had revealed that the politicians had gone too far ahead of their people. Europe was in for a decade of much slower integration; Jacques Delors would never live to see his dream come true.

Political union may be on hold, therefore; the single market, however, was a juggernaut that could not be stopped once it had begun to move forward. Its first victim was Thatcher herself. The prime minister's stance had come to seem increasingly incompatible with the economic realities of the new Europe even in her own country; in 1990 her authority shaken when her own chancellor of the exchequer resigned over the same issue, she was challenged when she stood for re-election as leader of her party. Barely winning the first round of the contest, she withdrew in order to avoid the humiliation of possible defeat in the second, and thus gave up hope of continuing as prime minister. Her successor, John Major, reasserted the skeptical British view when the countries of the Community met in Maastricht at the end of 1991 in order to amend the Treaty of Rome to fit the new Europe. He insisted that Britain should have the right not to join the planned single European currency toward the end of the decade if it did not want to. But his victory was a hollow one: Britain was already so closely tied to the rest of Europe by its exchange rate that it could not set interest rates without one eye on decisions already taken by the Bundesbank in Germany.

By the end of 1992, it was clear that the far-reaching program, begun in 1985 and made possible by the 1979 court decision on *cassis*, would be a success. Here and there, undoubtedly, there would be areas in which Lord Cockfield's 279 measures had not yet all been put into practice. Certain barriers would therefore remain between the markets of the twelve members of the Community. Denmark's position remained unclear, as did the future of the proposed European Economic Area, encompassing the EC and seven industrial countries to its east. And the argument over Europe's broader future — how many new members it should admit, and how much power the existing members should surrender to Brussels — was certain to continue for decades. But by and large, Europe was most of the way to becoming a single market. Its deadline of December 31, 1992, was about to be met.

More than eight years earlier, on a wet day in April 1984, a nondescript Japanese businessman, probably in the regulation single-breasted suit and conservative haircut, presented his small red passport at the immigration counter at London's Heathrow airport. He can hardly have attracted much attention. Even then, before the flow of Japanese investment in Britain had become a flood, those in charge of immigration and customs were used to seeing large numbers of Japanese. Most of them were men: to the intense disappointment of the local tourist board, Japanese women did not yet consider the shopping good enough to want to come in any great numbers to Britain. But on the whole, they were polite and well-behaved, and usually gave (albeit in halting English) satisfactory answers to the questions put to them by those whose job it is to guard Britain's borders against rabies, drugs, smugglers, and illegal immigrants.

Yet Toshiaki Tsuchiya was probably the most important visitor who passed through the airport that day in 1984. He was a senior executive at Nissan, Japan's second-biggest car maker, and he had come to settle down in Britain in order to set up the first Japanese car factory in Europe. A man with a reputation at the company's head office in the Ginza district of Tokyo for getting things done, Tsuchiya must have known what a task he had ahead of him. The company's first expansion into manufacturing abroad — in the United States — had been so far only a mixed success. What could he do in Britain? It was to be five years before the answer was clear.

Nissan's plan to open a factory in Europe had a precedent: the company was already making cars in the United States. The members of the advance team from Nissan that arrived in Britain knew that their new home was full of companies, workers, and managers experienced in the car industry. But their reading of the newspapers and their knowledge of the competition made them far from enthusiastic about making use of local resources. The very last thing they wanted to do was to make expensive, unreliable British cars in dirty factories where uncooperative workers and class-conscious managers fought over trifles.

After identifying a handful of key British managers who they thought might be willing to make a fresh start, the members of the Nissan team sent them over to Tokyo to see how their new employer wanted its British factory to be run. As if treading on glass, they held delicate negotiations with different British labor unions to see whether they could satisfy British law and tradition by having a union in the plant, but prevent that union from hijacking the management of the factory and obstructing the managerial innovations that would be a key part of its competitive advantage.

Living and working in Britain was something of a shock for the expatriate Nissan managers. There were many good points, of course: land was cheap, so they were able to live in comfortable houses near their work for far less than the price of a boxy little apartment at home, and to join a golf club for a year for little more than the price of an afternoon's play at home. But to many of them, Britain was a difficult place: it seemed dirty and undisciplined by comparison with home. Both assembly line hands and managers had to be reminded constantly to turn out work of top quality, rather than work that was merely acceptable. And for the Japanese managers, a period of extended duty abroad was doing nothing for their careers back at the head office. The more relaxed manners they picked up in Britain seemed insubordinate and selfish to their former colleagues, and their children routinely had problems trying to get into Japanese universities after years away from the strict regimen of schools in Japan.

All the same, the factory began production in 1986 with the assembly from kits of a modest sedan that was one of the less technically complicated of the Nissan line. The factory made some ninety thousand cars in its first year. Within five years, the factory had worked up to a regular tempo: the quality of the cars made at the Sunderland factory was ahead of that of the cars made in Tennessee, and could stand comparison with the quality at any Nissan plant in Japan; in terms of productivity, each worker at the factory was turning out almost twice as many cars per year as workers at other British factories only a few hours' drive away.

By then, Tsuchiya had already returned to Japan. But the legacy he left behind him was a car factory that was, despite its short history, the most efficient in Europe. What was more, it was a factory that had built up from nothing a network of local components suppliers trained in Japanese methods. And even if the factory's European competitors were unremittingly hostile, the British government was ready to show its thanks for the way in which Nissan had shaken up the British car industry. With the blessing of Margaret Thatcher, Nissan's chairman, Takashi Ishihara, was awarded an honorary knighthood.

Tsuchiya did not go home empty-handed, however. Although Nissan is no more willing than other Japanese companies to give prominence to its stars, his colleagues knew very well that he had impressed the chairman when he chose to pay a visit to Britain. Tsuchiya's reward was discreet but unmistakable: he is now at the head of Aichi Machine Company in Nagoya, a company in which Nissan has a substantial shareholding.[2]

To see why Tsuchiya had come to Britain in the first place, however, we have to look at the wider economic conditions that were facing his firm. For a long time, the government in Tokyo had made a policy of keeping the yen undervalued in order to encourage the country's exporting industries. As the fledgling economy strengthened, though, Japanese workers had become more productive. By the mid-1980s, a soaring trade surplus had signaled that it was time to allow the yen to rise to a stronger exchange rate against the dollar.

Most of Japan's leading exporting companies saw which way the wind was blowing. They knew that European firms had used foreign investment as a way of seeking new markets at lower risk. Almost exactly a century before Tsuchiya came to Britain, hundreds of British engineers had been hard at work in Japan, building bridges and lighthouses, railways and telegraphs, never suspecting that the technology they transferred there would take root and return to their own country in their grandchildren's days. Early in the twentieth century, the superior methods of American car manufacture had produced exactly the same phenomenon when Henry Ford brought his approach to mass production over from Michigan to Britain. He had earned himself great personal unpopularity by appearing ambivalent between the German and the British sides during the war; but his company's European operations survived unscathed and continue to this day.

As its current account continued to rise, Japan therefore came under growing pressure from its leading trading partners to revalue. In 1985 it gave in: at a meeting held in the New York Plaza Hotel, the government conceded that the yen should be allowed to float upward. In little over three years, the Japanese currency rose to a value 80 percent higher against the dollar than before. The government knew that if its exporting companies were to survive this dramatic deterioration in their international competitiveness, they would have to carry out a massive program of restructuring, cutting costs, and moving production offshore to places where labor was cheaper. So it kept domestic interest rates very low in order to encourage companies to invest in new, high-tech equipment.

This had an unexpected side effect, however: a speculative boom the like of which the world has rarely seen. By April 1990 the price of shares on the first section of the Tokyo stock exchange had risen to the point where the average price-earnings ratio for the shares on the exchange's first section was 48, compared with 13 for New York. Land prices in the capital and in several other towns more than quintupled in four years. Consequently, anyone who had substantial holdings of shares or property made a killing — and newly rich Japanese suddenly began to make their appearance on the international circuit: betting heavily in the casinos of Las Vegas or Monte Carlo, buying up the best duplexes on New York's Upper East Side, spending heavily on anything that took their fancy as they traveled through Europe, the United States, and Asia. The Seibu-Saison Group, a Japanese leisure and hotel chain that benefited hugely from the run-up in land prices, took advantage of this trend by buying into the 104 hotels of the Intercontinental chain.

Some Japanese investors appeared to have lost their heads altogether. Ryoei Saito, for instance, head of a family that owned one of the country's largest paper companies, bought a pair of pictures, a Van Gogh and a Renoir, for $160 million in a single week. (He later scandalized the art world by saying that he proposed to have the paintings buried with him when he died, an intention that he hastily denied when a tidal wave of international anger broke over his head.) Another Japanese consortium acquired Pebble Beach, the most prestigious golf course in the United States, with the intention of financing the $1 billion it had paid by selling off memberships to Japanese businessmen at rates that would have been considered optimistic even in Tokyo. Sadly, the plan did not work: in early 1992 the deeds were handed over to a rescue group organized by its bankers for half the price paid little over a year earlier.

Such tales were one of the reasons that Japanese investors suddenly began to look menacing from abroad. But beneath the speculative froth there was a second factor at work. Japanese companies had made a dramatic jump in the decade before the 1985 Plaza Accord. They had turned from being merely successful exporters from a little-understood developing country into powerful companies with valuable interests and markets all over the world. They had seized the initiative in the car industry; they had driven the Americans out of consumer electronics and the memory chip business; and they were posing a worrying threat to Western computer makers. More broadly, Japanese firms were on the way to world technological leadership in the growing number of businesses in which they chose to compete: by the end of the 1980s, the four top holders of new patents registered in the United States were all Japanese.

By making it clear that producing things in Japan would gradually but unavoidably become more expensive, the finance ministers who met at the Plaza Hotel forced many leading Japanese firms to look at their operations and to rethink them fundamentally. Business leaders in Tokyo began to see that for the size they had grown to, with the customers they had spread across the world, they were too exposed to shocks in Japan's relationship with the rest of the world. They had to become more global.

Three things in particular pushed successful Japanese firms toward investing overseas. First was the desire to be closer to their customers in markets all over the world, but particularly in the United States and Europe. Second, the firms had to cut costs: with the yen 80 percent higher than in 1985, they were finding in 1988 that many of their more basic products would be ruthlessly undercut by the competition if they failed to find cheaper places to produce them than Japan. And third was the danger of protectionism: with big market shares in

Europe and the United States, they were vulnerable to trade frictions. It did not need to be anything so specific as a threat to keep a particular company out of a particular country: many companies realized — far earlier than politicians were to — that if Japan continued to run big trade surpluses, pressure would increase to reduce exports of goods from Japan no matter how little economic sense there might be in doing so. Products made in the markets where they were sold, on the other hand, would undoubtedly prove less controversial.

But the focus of overseas investment was changing. After concentrating its export efforts on the United States for year after year, Japan appeared suddenly to have discovered Europe. Earlier in the 1980s, Japan's growing trade surplus had become a source of international trade friction. It rose from $2 billion in 1980 to $31 billion in 1983, and then to $56 billion in 1985; in 1987 it appeared to have peaked at $96 billion, but then after three years of decline it began to rise again in 1991. The trade imbalance with the United States was bad enough, but by the turn of the 1990s it was proving a headache in Brussels as well. At first, the Japanese government unwisely encouraged the surplus to be underestimated: its published trade statistics counted as imports from Europe the paintings by dead European artists which Japanese billionaires bought at auctions in New York. But soon the figures became irrefutable: in 1991 alone, the bilateral trade surplus with the European Community shot up by 48 percent to a total of over $27 billion. Even the hordes of Japanese tourists abroad — dismounting with admirable discipline from their tour buses to take photographs, stream through the department stores, and find their way to the best Japanese restaurants in every town they visited — were unable to spend enough money to recycle that imbalance.

Not content with merely selling things in Europe, the Japanese appeared to want to buy things there too. Earlier in the 1980s, Japanese investors had started to pile into vacation homes in Hawaii, golf courses in California, office buildings in New York. They had shocked the public by buying into what many thought of as the very icons of American culture: Columbia Pictures, for instance, which Sony bought in 1989 for over $2 billion; or Rockefeller Center in Manhattan, control of which was acquired by Mitsubishi Estate in a transaction worth an inflated $846 million in the same year.

After watching for a while from afar, Europe, too, now found itself being courted. Bruised by the hostility they had elicited in the United States, Japanese investors were much more discreet in the Old World. But they still managed to pick up Château-Lagrange, a grand old Bordeaux vineyard that lay next door to the prime property of Léoville-Lascases and had fallen on hard times. They bought into luxury hotels in the south of France, and into golf courses in Spain. They won control of a handful of prestigious English brands, such as the English Aquascutum raincoat label and Simpson's, the department store in Piccadilly. They even acquired Bracken House, the London office building recently vacated by the *Financial Times*, Europe's leading business newspaper.[3]

It was not a matter only of tangible purchases. For years, the electronics firm Sony cultivated Herbert von Karajan; when he died, the firm was able to obtain exclusive rights to the pictures and the sound of almost all the work of his last years by coming to a speedy agreement with his widow. When Sony consolidated its control of CBS Records and Columbia, *Newsweek* complained that it was buying "the soul of America." What price the soul of Europe, nationalists in Paris and Rome might have asked?

Perhaps surprisingly, however, it was not these cultural icons such as golf courses, vineyards, and impressionist pictures that caused the most worry to the bureaucrats of the European Commission in Brussels. What scared them was the fact that Japanese companies were busily establishing an aggressive business presence in Europe to take advantage of the freedom to sell across national boundaries that would come after 1992.

Japanese banks, securities houses, and insurance companies were setting up branches in the City of London, and trying to buy into the financial sectors of Germany, France, Italy, and Switzerland. Japanese manufacturers too were arriving in growing numbers. Toshiba, the company that dominates the world market for portable computers, opened a new factory in Regensburg in 1990; it hopes eventually to supply the entire European market from Germany as a result. In 1991 Sony acquired a prime site on the Potsdammer Platz in Berlin, the city destined to be the economic center of Europe; from 1996 or thereabouts into the next century it expects to be running its entire European operations from a new regional headquarters there. Toyota, the world's most efficient car maker, was in 1992 putting the finishing touches on a vast new factory complex in central England where it plans to build 200,000 cars a year. And these are just the most prominent examples. Until 1984, Japanese manufacturers had been establishing European affiliates at a rate of roughly 20 a year. In 1985 there were 25 new European plants. In 1986 the number rose to 36; in 1987, 58; in 1988, 70. And in the single year of 1989, no fewer than 118 new Japanese manufacturing operations were started in Europe — more than the total number established between the end of the Second World War and 1979. By January 1991 a survey conducted by the Japan External Trade Organization was able to count some 676 Japanese manufacturers operating in Europe.

What made all this frightening was partly the suddenness of Japan's move across the Atlantic. But it was also the fact that the sectors in which Japanese companies appeared to be investing most aggressively — the car industry, computers, and electronics — were precisely the same as those in which Europe felt itself most acutely lagging behind both the United States and Japan. There was also the fact that the investment was so skewed: fully one-third of all the Japanese manufacturing investments inside the Community were focused on a single country, Britain, where a welcoming free-market government, a language they had already learned in the United States, and an island-nation mentality made the Japanese feel very much at home.[4] As a result of this concentration, the economic effects of the wave of new investment was certain to be uneven: even if it had no effect on total employment, the arrival of the Japanese appeared set to create jobs in Britain but to take them away in France, Italy, and elsewhere.

As the single market project got under way, the prospect of a Japanese invasion began to raise fears in Brussels. Willy de Clercq, the member of the European Commission from Belgium responsible for external relations, staked out an unyielding position. "We see no reason," he said in a statement that was later to be quoted frequently against him, "why the benefits of our internal liberalization should be extended unilaterally to third countries."

But it was in Paris that fear turned to hysteria. Jacques Calvet, the man at the head of the Peugeot cars group, demanded that the invaders be kept at bay and branded Britain alternately as "Japan's fifth island" and as a "Japanese aircraft-carrier" off the coast of Europe. Edith Cresson, the French prime minister, attacked the Japanese as "ants," and accused them of "sitting up all night thinking of ways to screw the Americans and the Europeans." (One of her colleagues felt obliged to explain during a later visit to Tokyo that the prime minister's reference to "ants" was merely a mark of her great respect for the Japanese work ethic.)[5]

That fear now seems laid to rest. There was a period when de Clercq's views seemed likely to find their way into the heart of European trade policy — for instance, in the discussions over banking, in which Brussels for a while said that a foreign bank would be allowed to operate inside the new Europe only if European banks were given identical privileges in its home country. (That would mean, for example, that the legal line drawn between the United States' banking and securities industries, and the federal restrictions on interstate banking, would result in discrimination against American banks in Europe.) After strenuous lobbying from Washington, however, the bureaucrats decided to relent. Foreign banks in the new Europe, they said, will be given "national treatment": they will receive the same privileges and the same obligations as

European banks. And the banking compromise turned out to be a foretaste of wider policies up to the end of 1992. Broadly speaking, at least, the new Europe will not be a fortress.

What is more, the Japanese have far fewer investments in Europe by value than the Americans do — and they have also invested far less in each European country than businesses from other EC countries. A study by Stephen Thomsen and Phedon Nicolaides, two economists at Chatham House, a London think tank, shows that in Germany, investment from Japan accounted for only 7 percent of total inward investment in the 1970s and 1980s; during that period, the United States and the rest of the EC each accounted for about five times as much of Germany's inward investment.[6] And in Britain, despite its reputation as the Japanese aircraft carrier off the coast of Europe, money from Japan was only 4 percent of total inward investment. Some 26 percent of the money that flowed into Britain during the 1970s and 1980s came from elsewhere in Europe, and a full 47 percent of it was American.

And all this was against a background in which investments in all directions were flowing faster. The Chatham House analysts found that in 1984 foreign direct investments in Europe were worth 0.3 percent of all the goods and services Europe produced in that year (that is, its gross domestic product, or GDP). By 1989 they accounted for 1.5 percent of Europe's GDP — five times as high a proportion of a pie that had grown sharply in any case.

These, then, were the reasons behind the sudden explosion of Japanese investment abroad and the greater sensitivity of Westerners to it. But as the factories began to be built and the distribution networks cemented, Japanese firms became aware of a mismatch. In the United States, the country that had been their first and their most lucrative export market, Japanese businesses were well placed. But the world was changing. With its new single market, Europe suddenly began to look like an El Dorado of opportunity, a place where companies that got in early and managed to establish low-cost manufacturing centers and distribution networks sensitive to the different demands of customers in Düsseldorf or Dijon would make a killing.

Yet compared with their progress in the United States, the Japanese were far behind in Europe. A sign of their backwardness could be seen from the car industry, which accounts in most industrial countries for a tenth of the jobs in manufacturing and the same proportion of industrial output. In the United States, Japanese companies sold almost one car in three. In Europe, they could barely claim one car in nine.

The result was a scramble for new investment and new activity by Japanese firms in Europe, exaggerated as all such scrambles are in Japan by the mob mentality that makes a hundred businesses follow as soon as one leads. To Europe, as a decade earlier to the United States, the sudden arrival of Japanese investors looked so swift and so purposeful that it seemed organized. Had it been done by Western firms, such an operation could only have been carried out under governmental orders. Seen from Tokyo and Osaka, it looked rather different. Far from being a disciplined army, the businesses flocking to Europe were like a group of huntsmen, each following a distant horn in competition with hundreds of others, not quite sure what was going on at the front of the pack but all the same desperate not to fall too far behind.

As the Reagan years drew to their close, a growing number of experts in Washington began to complain about the faults of American trade policy toward Japan. The United States had been too slow to force the Japanese to open up their markets for cars and computers, they argued, though admittedly that was partly because American car and computer companies had dismissed Japan as an unimportant and alien place for far too long. The United States was also too slow to wake up to the damage being done to its semiconductor industry in the mid-1980s, when Japanese firms that had invested far too heavily in chip production responded to the resulting glut with predatory pricing. Only when most of the American competitors in the industry had already been forced to withdraw did Washington come in heavy-handedly and force Japan to sign a deal that raised chip prices, thus benefiting the Japanese firms that now controlled the market and harming the American computer companies that relied on cheap chips to keep turning out newer and better computers.

By contrast, the United States had been far too quick to wield the big stick in trying to get Japan to import American rice. Short-grained white rice has been Japan's staple food for a thousand years and more; although Japanese farmers are almost comically inefficient at growing it — their costs are at least eight times those of farmers in Thailand, and farms in Japan are the size of pocket handkerchiefs — the political power of the farm lobby and the conservatism of the Japanese public has meant that there is only a modest domestic lobby in favor of opening the market and cutting the price of rice on the supermarket shelf in Tokyo. But prompted by California farmers, many of whom benefit already from underpriced water and export subsidies, Washington chose to devote a healthy proportion of its negotiating good will to the problem of Japan's rice market. That store of good will was used up unexpectedly fast: in 1991, a diplomatic incident was narrowly avoided when Japanese officials threatened to arrest American rice farmers for breaking the law by importing sample bags of their produce to a trade show outside Tokyo. By 1992, as the Uruguay round of trade talks was inching to its close, the Japanese had drawn back from even their modest earlier hints at removing the import ban and allowing imports equivalent to 5 percent of demand subject to a high tariff. Japan's rice market seemed as closed as ever, while exports of Japanese industrial products continued to flood into the United States.

American trade negotiators later told how the circumstances in which they were forced to work stacked the deck in Japan's favor.[7] The U.S. trade representative's office had to rely on staff who were liable to leave for the private sector at any moment, and who had often come to the job only a couple of years earlier. The structure of American trade law only allowed the administration to get involved if prompted by complaints from U.S. business. And even the small details were to the detriment of the Americans. They would often fly to Tokyo in small groups to negotiate, bleary-eyed from jet lag, with urbane bilingual Japanese teams that fielded ten well-briefed officials against every harassed American. It was no wonder that the Japanese were able to string the negotiations out over years, offering concessions after repeated discussions that turned out on inspection to be little different from concessions they had offered before.

All these criticisms fade into insignificance, however, when compared with the way the European Community made policy on Japan. To be fair, Europe started from far behind. While the United States was able to draw on the knowledge of the large population of naturalized Japanese Americans in California and in Hawaii, Europe had no Japanese ethnic minority. With the exception of Britain, which was effectively allied to Japan between the two world wars but then fought it in Asia in the 1940s, the continent remained largely unexposed to Japan's military and industrial strengths for years after Americans were discussing it. And Japanese studies in European universities, as well as being more narrowly historical and literary than in American schools, remain even now miserably funded and relatively unpopular compared with the subject in the United States.

One of only a handful of people at the European Commission in Brussels who have lived in Japan and speak its language, Endymion Wilkinson has argued eloquently in a recent book that relations between Japan and Europe have been a story of embarrassing mutual incomprehension.[8] The Japanese put it differently. At a press briefing in Tokyo in 1991, foreign correspondents were surprised to see Kaoru Ishikawa, head of the international economics division of the Japanese foreign ministry, depart dramatically from his prepared script. Leaning forward earnestly on his reading desk, he complained bitterly that his country was unappreciated. For the past century, he said, Japan had looked admiringly toward Europe.

"On the other side," he concluded sadly, "they didn't even notice that someone was loving them. That reflects the fact of our bilateral relationship." His point was underlined by the impeccable English in which it was delivered. Despite his command of the language, Ishikawa spoke with an unmistakable French accent: he was educated by French missionaries.

Another feature of the relationship can be seen from the fact that, with a few honorable exceptions, European companies have been much slower than American firms to see the benefits of doing business in Japan or investing there. In 1983 statistics recorded that there were more French missionaries than French businessmen resident in Japan. Between 1950 and 1989 American firms invested ten times more in Japan than any European Community country did.

Given this lack of knowledge and experience in Europe, it is no surprise to find that Europeans were much slower to wake up to the advances that were being made in Japan after the Second World War than were Americans. While management gurus from the United States were poring over Japanese manufacturing methods and Japanese technology, while American sociologists were looking at Japan's labor relations and its education system, while American economists and financial specialists were examining Japan's industrial structure and the way Japanese businesses raise money, European politicians and business leaders persisted in believing that the challenge from Japan was the same as that from any other developing country with low wages, an undervalued exchange rate, and working conditions that no European would tolerate.

Even today, Europeans who ought to know better continue to allege that Japan's market is protected by high tariffs — whereas in fact whatever informal barriers there might be, Japan levies lower average duties on imports, and restricts the quantity of fewer products, than either the United States or Europe. It is ironic that Europeans should have had so much less curiosity about the sources of Japan's success than Americans have, and as a result less understanding of them, for the Japanese system is at least in part a cocktail of many things that can be seen at work in Europe. The role of banks in the German economy is one example; another is the way France is run by a homogeneous elite spanning business, politics, and the bureaucracy.

What brought matters to a head in Brussels was a change of policy toward Japan in Washington which took place in 1990. After years of unsatisfactorily trying to bludgeon Japan into submission, the United States found itself forced to embark on a dramatically different approach.[9] The two sides sat down, alternately in Washington and Tokyo, to discuss not specific bilateral trade issues but the "structural impediments" to trade between them. This initiative, known as SII for short,[10] has had startling results. For in the negotiations, each side began to pick up complaints being made by the other's domestic opponents, and to delve into matters that had traditionally been considered the exclusive preserve of domestic policymaking.

The Americans told the Japanese that they ought to reform the restrictions that prevent the spread of supermarkets and department stores in Japan (and thus the spread of imported goods); that they ought to beef up their feeble enforcement of antitrust law; that they should spend much more money on roads, sewers, airports, and other infrastructure projects that might bring business to U.S. firms. The Japanese, on the other hand, told the Americans that their schools were a disgrace: if the United States wants to continue to be a world economic power, it must make sure its work force is literate and skilled. Tokyo also added that Washington should eliminate its budget deficit; abolish the quarterly reporting of financial results that is thought to force the managers of U.S. public companies to think short-term; prevent the abuses that allow the barons of big business in the United States to make millions of dollars a year while their companies go to the dogs; and adopt the metric system, which has now taken root almost everywhere else in the world but to which American firms remain stubbornly resistant.

Two things were significant about the SII talks. First, the

shift away from sector-by-sector complaints to discussions of the broader economy encouraged the negotiators to spend less time worrying about Japan's bilateral trade surplus with the United States. In the past, that had encouraged Americans in the misapprehension that the entire problem was a matter of barriers in Japan rather than of a mismatch between two rather different economic systems. And second, SII changed the debate in a more profound way still: for the first time, it moved discussion partly onto the uncomfortable ground of what was wrong with the United States, rather than the traditional one of what was wrong with Japan.

Meanwhile, Europe was still carrying on with its old methods. As early as 1988 Britain had been pressing its partners in the Community to take a broader view of relations with Japan; after long years of pressure, Britain had succeeded in getting most of the trade concessions that it wanted, and was now ready for more mature relations with the Asian superpower. Other European countries, however, were more willing to put their names to declarations of good intent than to change the day-to-day way in which they dealt with Japan. Despite widely publicized promises for cooperation, little was done except in science and technology. Officials continued to fly from Brussels to Tokyo to demand the reduction of quotas on leather handbags or fish — demands that, even had they been met, would never have reduced the Japanese trade surplus with Europe by more than a tenth. And as the SII negotiations progressed, the European Community found itself unable to do anything but stand on the sidelines bleating that it hoped Japan would be sure to accord to all its trading partners any concessions it might give to the United States during the negotiations. (This last hope proved to be unfulfilled. Many companies responded just by transferring contracts from their European suppliers to American ones. And in the early stages of the 1992 U.S. presidential election, a brief rise in protectionist feeling in the United States prompted the Japanese bureaucracy to put the word out to big business to buy American at all costs: some Japanese firms even went so far as to admit that they would buy an American component even if it cost half as much again as an equivalent domestic one.)

In May 1991 Jacques Delors paid his first official visit to Tokyo in five years. That in itself was a revealing thing. Japan had long been the single most important external economic issue facing the European Community; yet it was proof of how far Brussels was from taking the problem seriously that Delors, visionary though he was, had been allowed to neglect for so long such an important part of his job. Later, Japan and Europe issued a "high-level political agreement" — a vague document in which the two sides applauded each other's belief in freedom, capitalism, and democracy and promised to send various of their officials to meet twice a year. The document had been issued at Tokyo's request, after Brussels had negotiated a similar one with the United States in November 1990. Significantly, however, the Europeans held up the talks for some time as factions in Brussels bickered over what to say about the trade surplus in the agreement's section on international economic relations.

At the same time, the Community seemed to be repeating the most egregious mistakes of the United States. It struck an agreement with Japan to set minimum prices for computer chips in an attempt to protect the European semiconductor industry, despite the evidence from the United States that floor prices had hurt computer makers but failed to keep chip makers in business. And it negotiated a joint declaration with Japan on the subject of car sales in the single European market which tried to appease the different interests of the European car industry but succeeded only in leaving unanswered every one of the questions that really mattered.

As the Japanese and American economies have become more intertwined and as both sides have become more familiar with the other, mistrust of Japan in the United States might have been expected to fall away. Sadly, things did not work out quite like that. As the Cold War drew to its close, American mistrust of Japan's motives was inflamed by the Toshiba incident, in which a subsidiary of the Japanese electrical and electronics conglomerate was found by the CIA to have contravened COCOM rules by selling sensitive technology to the Soviet Union that allowed Soviet submarines to be propelled silently and thus to evade American detection. It was increased further by the circulation in Washington in 1990 of a pirated translation of a book by Akio Morita, the chairman of Sony, and Shintaro Ishihara, a maverick novelist-turned-politician, which argued that Tokyo had for too long apologized to visiting Americans and promised to accede to unreasonable demands. What was needed, as the two insisted in their title, was "a Japan that can say no" — that would be prepared to be more assertive. Ishihara even went so far as to assert that the United States was dependent on Japanese semiconductors for its weapons technology,[11] and to propose that Japan should teach Washington a lesson and sell a chip or two to the Soviets for a change.

With the Soviet Union and its former empire in Eastern Europe collapsing visibly on the world's television screens, it was no wonder that some Americans should seek a new enemy to replace it. Opinion polls showed that the American public, despite its apparently insatiable appetite for Japanese products and despite the growing popularity of Japanese design and Japanese food, consistently considered Japan more of a threat than the Soviet Union. When a pair of writers, a Pennsylvania professor of politics and an Australian poet, teamed up to write the book *The Coming War with Japan,* the response in Tokyo was immediate. Although one of the book's authors admitted that the title had been dreamed up by the publishers, and insisted that their aim was more to point out that the two industrial superpowers had economic interests that were fundamentally conflicting than to predict the outbreak of hostilities any time in the coming twenty years, some thirty thousand copies were snapped up in the book's first week on sale in translation in Japan. Japanese readers evidently relished the thought that Ishihara's uncharitable view of the United States was mirrored by similar suspicions across the Pacific.

Underlying these apparently worrying trends, however, policymakers in the United States have long been aware of the challenge posed to the international order by Japan's new economic power. With the exception of Saudi Arabia and Kuwait, the two countries most directly interested in the outcome, Japan was the world's biggest contributor to the war chest that financed the U.S.-led military action in the Persian Gulf. Japan's overseas aid program, which grew by leaps and bounds in the 1980s, has made Japan the biggest donor of grants and low-interest loans to no fewer than twenty-five developing countries — and hence a country that may well have influence over them in the future. In Asia, Japan holds an overwhelming position in a big trade bloc of fast-growing economies. It has already won more influence at the International Monetary Fund and the World Bank. Its latest aim is to win a permanent place on the United Nations Security Council, from which it was excluded in the early postwar years when it was still considered an "enemy nation."

The rhetoric of American diplomacy already reflects these facts. Mike Mansfield, a U.S. ambassador to Tokyo, liked to talk of dealings between the two countries as "the most important relationship in the world, bar none," a shibboleth that is regularly repeated whenever an American politician visits Tokyo. The fact that the reality of international relations bears little resemblance to the rhetoric is as much Japan's fault as anyone else's: the government proved itself miserably inept and vacillating during the Persian Gulf war, demonstrating clearly that while Japan may already be the United States' most important interlocutor in international economic discussions (for instance at meetings of the Group of Seven industrial nations), it remains a political minnow when war and diplomacy are at the top of the agenda.

While their colleagues in Washington spend much of their time thinking about Japan, the leaders of the new Europe in Brussels find it puzzlingly distant. Except at the top of a few foreign ministries and a few businesses, Japan's new importance in the world remains largely unappreciated in Europe. Europeans have been absorbed by the drama of the collapse of the Soviet Union and the breathtaking progress of its former satellites in turn from subservience to revolution to radical economic reform and, in the sad cases of Yugoslavia, Armenia, and Azerbaijan, to war. They have spent precious years arguing over the details of how to turn their disparate markets into a powerful single force, over the dramatic transfer of power from national capitals to Brussels that was implied in the treaty signed by the Community's twelve members at Maastricht in 1991. And they have jointly fretted over the Uruguay round of international trade talks, trying to preserve the lavish subsidies paid to European farmers without drawing the world's blame for sabotaging the talks.

Not one of these concerns can be dismissed as trivial. Europeans have good reasons for looking inward — or even when they look outward, for concentrating on problems that seem close to home. Yet paradoxically distant though it may be, Japan offers the key to many of the world's biggest international problems. With the United States mired in its own federal debt, Japan is the only power that has the money to help the European Community with the mammoth task of trying to keep economic reform in Russia on course — something that Japan has so far been highly reluctant to do, because of a territorial dispute between the two nations over the ownership of a string of windswept islands stretching out from Hokkaido into the cold waters of the North Pacific.

Japan could also help to quiet the clamor from the countries of Eastern Europe to join the Community, by offering them a market for their exports and the managerial and technological help they will need if they are to use trade to escape from their present poverty. So far, Japanese companies have been as hesitant and fearful about investing in Europe's eastern half as they have been impetuous in its western half.

It would be a mistake, however, to believe that Europe and the United States are the only parts of the world in which Japanese business is seriously interested. Japan already dominates the lucrative and fast-growing markets of Asia. Its companies have invested so heavily in East Asia that cynics are beginning to observe that the country has achieved by commerce what it failed to do by military conquest with its ill-fated Greater East Asian Co-Prosperity Sphere. And as companies in Thailand and Indonesia forge ever tighter links with patrons in Japan, political leaders in Singapore and in South Korea are beginning to say openly that it is to Tokyo, rather than to Washington or to Brussels or Bonn, that they look for ideas on how to develop their societies in the future.

It is not hard to see why. Over the past two decades, Japan's formula has delivered consistently higher economic growth than those of its key industrial competitors. In the boom years of the late 1980s, its workers won higher real wage increases than those in Britain, despite the apparent docility of Japanese trade unions. In the bust years of the early 1990s, Japan's economy was slower to move into recession than were those of both Europe and the United States. So fast did the Japanese economy grow between 1986 and 1991 that the increase alone in the country's gross national product in that five years was greater than the total of France's GNP.

But it is not only economically that Japan is a place that works. It is also a remarkably safe and peaceful country, with a capital city in which visitors can wander late at night with little more to fear than crowds of tipsy office workers who do not know how to hold their liquor.[12] By comparison with Europe and the United States, Japan has little illiteracy, little crime, few single-parent families, a tiny underclass. What is more, Japan's problems appear much easier to solve than those of other industrial countries. Its people work too hard, but they are getting used to taking more holidays. Its schools are too strict, but they are beginning to loosen up. Its companies are too obsessed with brawn, as measured by sales, market share, and stock price, but they are paying increasing attention to brain, as measured by profits, dividends, creativity, and high margins. One of the striking outcomes of the SII trade negotiations with the United States is that Japan has committed itself to a list of things that will make life easier for its inhabitants, and prices lower for its consumers. The same set of negotiations has produced a set of prescriptions for the United States that will be almost universally painful: less government spending, higher taxes, harder work, stricter schools.

Even today, Japan is a very different place from the grim workaholism imagined in Europe. Tokyo and Osaka, the cities that have for a century absorbed foreign influences fastest and been the harbingers of trends for the rest of the country, are full of fashionable new Italian restaurants — where, contrary to the popular impression abroad, a prix fixe lunch of fresh pasta, crusty bread, green salad, and espresso coffee can be had for less than ten dollars. The 1980s property boom has given Japan a crop of innovative buildings unrivaled elsewhere in the world. Among scores of other leisure booms, Western classical music is becoming a staple of the middle class: all over the country, stylish new concert halls are popping up, where well-dressed couples and their children listen to Haydn string quartets and nibble on delicate pastries in cafés in the intervals. Much of the money spent by Japanese consumers never appears in their salaries, because it is disguised as business spending; according to official statistics, Japanese companies spent more on entertaining in 1990 than the entire output of Ireland.[13]

Europe needs to pay more attention to Japan. But the arrival of Japanese business on European shores makes the questions more urgent still. Japanese firms that have succeeded in Europe — as in the United States and elsewhere in the world — have done so mostly because they are flexible, innovative organizations that have earned the commitment they get from their work forces. The place they come from — the way its market disciplines firms, the relations it has promoted between work force and management, the limited penetration it has allowed foreign competition — has something to do with it. But management is the key, and the best proof of that is the fact that Japanese firms have continued to prosper after transplanting their operations to Europe and the United States and using European and American workers to make products in the markets where they are to be sold.

Twenty-five years ago, European business faced a similar dilemma from across the Atlantic. On that occasion, the invaders were from the United States. Then too the new arrivals seemed to be invincible, and seemed to benefit from special weapons unknown in Europe, such as cheaper sources of finance and better relations among industry, government, and universities. So great was their fear then that Europeans began to talk of an "American challenge" that raised fundamental questions about their societies, their methods of governance, the way their businesses worked. They saw in the United States

> not the unfettered workings of competitive capitalism but something very different: a highly organized economic system, based on enormously large units, nourished by an industrial-academic-governmental complex and stimulated, financed and directed by the national government . . . To speak of a "managerial gap" is really too superficial: the real gap is institutional and cultural.[14]

They complained in particular about the way in which American firms seemed to be targeting deliberately the sectors of Europe's economy that were most technologically advanced, and the "systematic and organized assistance" the federal government in Washington gave them.[15]

As fashions in management theory have changed, fewer and fewer specialists any longer believe that the links between the U.S. Department of Defense and the United States' high-technology industries are the key to the nation's future.

Commentators such as John Zysman of the Berkeley Round-table on the International Economy talk not of "spin-off" (the 1960s idea that military R&D and the space program would yield huge dividends for civilian American industry) but of "spin-on": the notion that technology now flows in the other direction, with products that have been simplified, improved, and made cheaper for the mass consumer market increasingly becoming useful tools for military scientists.[16] It now seems clear in retrospect that it was the straightforward energy of American managers and the skill of American workers that accounted for the international successes of American companies. Far from colonizing and ultimately taking over Europe, as the Jeremiahs predicted, American businesses found that their competitors in Europe began swiftly to imitate their advantages. The United States continues to invest in Europe, but it is no longer seen as a threat.

This, therefore, is the key question facing Europe in the 1990s. Is the Japanese challenge any different? Wrong though it may have been to attribute American success to a secret weapon, to some formula involving the links between business and government, may it not all the same be right to do so in the case of Japan? Consequently, is Europe not justified in being far more suspicious of Japanese business in general and Japanese investment in particular? To these three questions, the answer is certainly not. The very distance of Japan from Europe — and the fact that so few European companies employ managers who can speak Japanese and who have lived in Japan — makes it tempting to look for conspiracies to explain Japan's success. But as the pages that follow will show, it is actually due to far more familiar factors. And the quicker European firms realize this, and start to imitate the practices of Japan's most successful firms, the quicker the gap will close.

In a recent book on European integration, an American journalist named Daniel Burstein predicted that the United States is in danger of finding itself outflanked in the world economy by an alliance between Europe and Japan — a trend, he argues, that has already begun with the wide-ranging strategic alliance struck at a secret meeting in Singapore in March 1990 between Daimler-Benz, the biggest industrial company in Germany, and the Mitsubishi Group, the biggest industrial group in Japan.

> Even if Herr [Edzard] Reuter and [Shinroku] Morohashi-san [the two chairmen] were loath to say publicly exactly what their strategy was, it was self-evident. The two corporations were teaming up to outflank American industry in its last bastions of global leadership, particularly aircraft manufacture. The capital resources, productive excellence, and long-term planning capacities of both Japan and Germany would be structurally linked and optimized.[17]

At first sight, the idea seems tempting. With their high population densities, their nostalgic defense of inefficient farmers, their history, and their formality, Japan and Europe appear to have more in common culturally than Japan and the United States. The two Old World economic blocs also share an instinctive fondness for economic regulation above the unpredictability of the free market's invisible hand. (When I moved from Tokyo to Brussels in 1992, I was struck by how similar the languages of Japanese and European bureaucrats are. In a set of negotiations about allowing road haulers, shipping firms, bus services, and airlines to compete equally in a single market, a number of top officials from Germany, France, Spain, and Italy pleaded for "transitional periods" on the road to free competition to avoid the "market disruptions" that would result if more efficient companies were to be allowed to undercut less efficient ones. Such sentiments were exactly the same as those voiced by Japanese officials when faced with demands for market opening from the United States.)

Apart from this vague similarity of approach, however, there is almost no reason to think that Europe and Japan might team up at the expense of the United States. Officials at the European Commission in Brussels chortle at the idea.

"If only!" says one. As we have seen, European-Japanese political relations are a missing side of a crucial triangle: both
Europeans and Japanese have underestimated each other fa-
tally for years.[18] Shintaro Ishihara, the co-author of *The Japan
That Can Say No*, expends his venom on the United States
primarily because he believes that Europe is a decadent civi-
lization that is utterly past it.

The business links are weak, too. Keidanren, Japan's leading
business organization, has for long years neglected its European counterparts; only in 1992 did it begin to invite the leaders of UNICE, the international federation of European business associations, to Tokyo for talks. The Daimler-Mitsubishi
alliance, widely hailed though it was at the time as the "deal
of the decade," has so far failed to deliver any startling results:
as we shall see later, the German company has not even managed yet to use Mitsubishi technology to raise the tempo of
its thorough but lamentably unproductive car factories.

To make things worse, there is also a technological mismatch: Japanese firms need alliances with American businesses much more than they need those with businesses in
Europe. The web of cross-licensing in the chip industry is
mostly across the Pacific, for instance; the same is true of the
car business, and also of the powerful pairing created by American music and movies when combined with Japanese electronic hardware skills.[19] So it is likely to be some years before
American politicians and business leaders are kept up at night
by the thought — which would do credit to Edith Cresson —
that the Japanese and the Europeans together are combining
to do down the United States.

All the same, the arrival of the Japanese in Europe poses
one of the greatest challenges to the United States since the
Second World War. To see why, recall that American competition with Japan is taking place against a background of increasing Japanese domination of third markets all over the
world. In East and Southeast Asia, the fastest-growing region
of the global economy, Japanese car companies and electronics firms already hold impregnable positions. Computer mak-

ers, machine-tool manufacturers, shipbuilders, and steel firms are not far behind — so much so that it is Japanese, rather than American, machine tools that the backstreet factories of Seoul and Taipei are attempting to reproduce by reverse engineering.

Losing a market to a competitor is never cheering, even at the best of times. But it brings with it a more profound danger than the immediate loss of profit. The position of Japanese companies in Asia gives them not only a cheap production base but also the opportunity to build up economies of scale unchallenged — which will eventually bounce back to the United States, when spreading the same costs over much higher production volumes allows Japanese firms to cut their prices in the markets where they do compete with American makers. So far, Japanese firms in the automotive and electronics industry have largely kept competitors out of their domestic market.[20] The danger that faces the United States in Europe is this: if Japanese companies succeed in winning large market shares in Japan, in Asia, and in Europe too, they will be able to fight in the United States with a tremendous advantage.

This loss of grip is particularly acute when the region in question is Europe. The Community is more than just a market for American firms: it is the world's largest and perhaps also its most lucrative market. Since their arrival in force in the 1960s, American firms have paradoxically benefited from the fact that Europe has been fragmented into a dozen different markets. Harmful though it has been for consumers, this fragmentation has allowed prices, and thus profits, to be kept high — for although distributing across Europe imposes significant extra costs on business, it also allows businesses to charge with impunity different prices for the same product in two towns that may only be fifty miles apart. Firms that have managed to establish the sales networks required have done very well out of this cartelized system. To many an American business, selling in Europe is a far more lucrative prospect than selling at home. Compaq, the American computer firm, survived hard times in the United States thanks to the fat profits remitted to it by its European subsidiaries; likewise, in 1991 General Motors made half as much money in European profits as it made in American losses.

Weakened by the frenzy of leveraged buyouts in the late 1980s, battered by the recession of the early 1990s, hesitant about their ability to continue to lead the world in technology, American firms are dependent as never before on their interests in Europe. As the prospect of much stiffer competition in Europe becomes a reality, however, U.S. businesses that have big investments on the continent face their biggest challenges in years. Firms that never quite managed to achieve the same efficiencies in Europe as they did in their home markets, will begin to disappear. (Federal Express, for instance, announced in early 1992 that it would be withdrawing from much of the European market and handing over the delivery of its packages to subcontractors. The company had failed to master the land-based distribution networks inside the European market and was hemorrhaging money.) Firms that have managed to build profitable and efficient European operations, on the other hand, will see their cozy positions under attack not only from Japanese business but also from Europeans themselves seeking to take advantage of the single market.

Predicting the outcome of this battle royal, which will certainly shape the future of the world economy in the next century, is something no wise commentator would attempt. It will be a three-cornered fight: American, Japanese, and European business methods will slug it out in the newly created arena of the world's biggest market. For Americans, it will be the first time that their challengers for leadership of the world economy have fought them on the neutral ground of a third party. For the Japanese, it will be the ultimate test of whether the exporting successes of the 1990s can be turned into the IBMs and Unilevers, the General Motors and the Shells of the twenty-first century. For Europeans, the stakes will be highest of all: it is over their turf that the battle will be fought.

Before assessing the situation in four of the most important industries, let us turn first to the threat from Japan. What does it consist of? What precisely is it that makes Japanese firms so competitive?

TWO

A Glimpse Inside
the Japanese Miracle

MAKE NO MISTAKE: Japan really is very different from other industrial societies. Many of the social forces that Europeans and Americans take for granted operate in very different ways in Japan.

The Tokyo subway is a good place to glimpse this. During the morning rush hour, almost two thousand people every two minutes get on the Marunouchi line at Shinjuku station to go eastward into the city center. They allow themselves to be marshaled by the blue-suited station staff into neat lines on the platform — two by two, like animals boarding the ark — in front of the exact points where the doors will open when the train arrives. As it pulls in, the platform men make a path for the passengers who want to get off, and then politely usher the waiting passengers onto the train. Meanwhile, a reserve line has been been formed by new arrivals. When the loaded train moves out of the station, the railway men gently lead the reserve lines three steps to the right so the entire process can begin again. It is a piece of choreography of the utmost elegance, carried out with remarkably little fuss. Yet the truly astonishing thing about it is that unlike a corps de ballet, the passengers have never been formally rehearsed. Even the English, who used to be renowned as a people who loved to queue, never reached such heights as these: if the number of people pressing to get onto a train grew too large, panic would ensue and the social order would break down. These extraordinarily patient commuters of the Marunouchi line are the descendants of the Japanese villagers who in earlier centuries were expected to evacuate their homes at an orderly walking pace, rather than in a rush of hysteria, at the first sign of an earthquake.

While the citizens of most Western industrial countries shrink instinctively from crowds, except at sporting events or stock exchanges, the Japanese are much less worried about having their individuality subsumed in a group. They complain superficially about the crowds in Tokyo, but choose to export the crowds with them when they go on tour bus vacations in California or Hawaii. On weekends, they queue for half an hour for a cup of tea in a Tokyo department store but leave deserted the mountains and forests an hour away by train. They accept a degree of guidance that would be intolerable anywhere else: all over their cities, loudspeakers are meekly listened to as they give advice, warning, instruction. In school, the Western tradition prizes native wit: students prefer to be thought of as clever but a bit lazy, rather than hard-working but a bit dull. In Japan, the opposite is true: children are told they will pass their exams with four hours' sleep a night, but will fail with five. While Westerners strive to be different, Japanese strive to be average. While Westerners argue furiously about politics at dinner parties, the Japanese see politics as a television spectator sport in which they can be gripped by the progress of the latest political-financial scandal but fail to see any contradiction between disapproving of the corruption of the prime minister and voting his party straight into power again at the next election. The Japanese buy more newspapers per capita than anyone else in the world, but the quality of public debate inside them is low. In the late 1980s, a woman leader of the Japanese socialist party told her country that the position of women was changing, but newspaper advice columns continued to tell battered women not to leave their unfaithful alcoholic husbands. Tokyo's inhabitants know that they sit above the junction of four of the earth's tectonic plates, in one of the world's most seismically dangerous spots, yet they participate happily in misleading earthquake preparedness days and put their faith in an official committee that promises to warn them beforehand of natural disasters — despite the reminders from tremors every few months that when disaster hits it will probably be unexpected and will certainly be impossible to escape. "The Japanese were the most alien enemy the United States had ever fought," said the American anthropologist Ruth Benedict in her book *The Chrysanthemum and the Sword.* "In no other war with a major foe had it been necessary to take into account such exceedingly different habits of acting and thinking."[1]

These puzzling features of Japan — a society that is outwardly a modern parliamentary democracy, but which provides frequent and worrying flashbacks to its three centuries of modern history as a centralized military dictatorship and police state — have given rise to a school of American analysis that has come to be called "revisionism." Its founder, Professor Chalmers Johnson of the University of California at San Diego,[2] has insisted persuasively for twenty years that Japan is neither a free market nor a centrally planned economy, but an unprecedented hybrid beast that lies between the two. Karel van Wolferen, an influential Dutch journalist in Tokyo, argues in his devastating 1989 study *The Enigma of Japanese Power* that all the important institutions in Japanese society — from the prime minister and the bureaucracy to big business, the political opposition, the union movement, schools, priests, lawyers, and gangsters — have been subsumed into a single sinister System with no accountable center of power. In such a view, mere companies are too narrow a canvas: Japan, the entire country and all its 123 million people, are a problem for the world. Clyde Prestowitz, a former U.S. trade negotiator, and James Fallows, an American journalist, argue that Japan needs to be "contained" by policies of special severity. This is a provocative thesis and, particularly in the case of van Wolferen, one that has been too carefully documented to be dismissed out of hand. Yet the truth is that by many measures Japan is not an unmixed success. International business surveys sometimes claim that Japan is "the world's most competitive country," but anyone who has lived there knows that such a judgment is far too sweeping.

Actually, in terms of labor productivity — a measure of how efficient companies are at converting the work of their employees into goods or services — it is the United States that is the world's most competitive economy. It was no wonder, therefore, that Kiichi Miyazawa raised anger in Washington when, in answering a parliamentary question in February 1992, the Japanese prime minister accused the United States of losing its "work ethic." Lazy or not, Americans were able to riposte, we are still more efficient workers than you.

Proof of that can be seen in many different sectors of Japanese industry. Japanese retailing is lamentably inefficient, with millions of tiny neighborhood shops offering customers a very limited range of goods at high prices. Japanese retail banks provide an extremely polite but miserably inefficient service, in which personal checks are almost unknown and a basic bank transfer to pay a household electricity bill can cost ¥600 ($4.99); their sophisticated automated teller machines are a welcome response to the time that otherwise has to be spent sitting in the banking hall, waiting for one's number to be called. Road repairs in Japan are an almost comical affair, in which one often sees three people guarding an empty hole in a deserted city street in the middle of the night, carefully directing nonexistent traffic with their electrically lighted sticks. Japanese offices are usually woefully overmanned; many of the apparently zealous employees who can be seen through the windows of office buildings in central

Tokyo late at night are in fact passing the time until their boss is ready to go home by reading the newspaper or watching television. (They are overwomaned too, with "office ladies" condemned to a career of tea-making and elevator-operating, culminating in compulsory retirement at marriage or at age twenty-five, whichever is the earlier.) Japanese trains run on time, but the national railway company had more excess workers when its privatization began than the entire payroll of Toyota Motor Corporation. Above all, Japanese farmers, protected from more efficient competitors abroad because of their political clout, grow their rice in paddies averaging a ludicrously tiny 2.7 acres. By the time it gets to consumers, it is between six and ten times the world free-market price.[3]

It is both Japan's strength and its weakness, therefore, that it does only a few things well — but those it does well, it does very well. Toyota, Japan's most important company, is on its own responsible for a fifth of the country's trade deficit with the United States. Three-quarters of Japan's entire exports are classified in international trade statistics under "machinery and equipment," a category that is dominated by three products and the machines used to make them: cars, computers, and electronics. Any attempt to trace the rise of Japan in relation to the rest of the world, or to predict the effects of Japan's investments overseas, must start with these businesses.

The rise in awareness of Japan in the United States — and the more extensive coverage of it in American newspapers — has made many American businesspeople familiar with what their Japanese competitors are doing. One consequence of this can be seen in the productivity statistics: according to the Japan Productivity Center, American companies actually raised their productivity faster than Japanese companies between 1980 and 1986 in seven out of twelve major manufacturing sectors. This was at least partly because they began to respond to the challenge from Japan early in the 1980s. But in Europe, myths about the secrets of Japanese success remain prevalent; I was surprised at how many half-truths and outdated impressions were repeated by senior European business executives I met in the course of researching this book in 1991 and 1992.

One myth, which was the first response of many Western businesses when they found traditional markets under attack from Japan, is that Japanese companies benefit from being able to pay their workers low wages. That was certainly true in the 1960s when Japan was still a developing country. It was less true, however, in the 1970s; and by the 1980s, it was plain wrong. International Labor Office figures show that straight hourly wages in manufacturing in 1988, converted into dollars at the current rate, were already higher in Japan than in the United States, Britain, Canada, France, Germany, Italy, and Sweden. (When indirect labor costs such as health care are added in, however, Japanese workers count as about the same price as many European workers — a point discussed in more detail later in this chapter.)

A second myth is that Japanese exports benefit from an undervalued exchange rate. In April 1949 the value of the yen was fixed by the American occupying forces at ¥360 to the dollar. That became an official exchange rate when Japan entered the IMF three years later, and it remained fixed under the Bretton Woods system until August 1971, when the United States unilaterally decided to take the dollar off the gold standard. The yen strengthened to ¥175 to the dollar in 1978 but spent most of the first half of the 1980s in the ¥230s. In 1985, however, the most dramatic change in the world currency system since the end of Bretton Woods took place: following a secret agreement at the Plaza Hotel, the yen began to rise steadily against the dollar. By 1988, when a dollar bought only ¥128, the yen had appreciated 85 percent against the U.S. currency.

Over those three fateful years, Japanese companies were ruthless in paring their export profit margins in a desperate attempt to hold on to market share in the United States, their biggest market. With the help of the rigged domestic distribution system, they also succeeded in riding out the rise of the yen without facing much competition from imports: although wholesale prices in Japan fell by over 8 percent between 1985 and 1988, reflecting the availability of much cheaper goods from abroad, none of the saving was passed on to the long-suffering public: the Japanese consumer price index actually *rose*, by 1.4 percent, in the same period. The inefficient retail sector had gobbled up the difference.

Those dubious techniques should not distract attention from a more important point, however. If it was undervalued against the dollar before 1985, the yen has certainly not been undervalued since; and what is more, Japanese industry managed to avoid a high-yen slump by carrying out a miraculous restructuring in the space of only three years.

A third myth is that Japanese firms are able to hammer their foreign competitors because they have access to a bottomless well of cheap capital. With very low interest rates to pay on their borrowings, the argument runs, Japanese companies now and in the future will have the unfair advantage of being able to tolerate much lower rates of return, and hence lower profits and prices, when they invest in new equipment or research and development. It is certainly true that real interest rates fell to an all-time low in Japan while the yen was rising. The Bank of Japan and the Ministry of Finance wanted cheap money, to help companies finance the restructuring that would be necessary to survive a higher yen. Many big firms took advantage of the authorities' generosity to bolster their profit-and-loss accounts by borrowing cheaply and then using the money they had raised to invest in the stock market.

When the financial authorities saw the size of the bubble that had been created by the excesses of this *zaiteku,* or "financial engineering," as it was euphemistically known, they began to raise interest rates in order to bring things back to earth. By 1991, after five successive increases in the bank's official discount rate, Japanese companies found themselves paying about the same for money as their U.S. and European competitors; and although the bank began to take its rate down a notch or two in late 1991 as it saw tighter money having the desired effect, foreigners could no longer complain that they suffered a long-term disadvantage against their Japanese competitors. Proof of that came with big cuts in planned 1992 investments by the electronics and computer companies: not even Japan, they proved, could continue investing in new plants without thinking about what benefits it might derive in return.

Perhaps the most pervasive myth about Japan, however, is that its markets are protected with high tariffs. They were, it is true: in the 1960s, the bureaucrats saw protection of "infant industries" like steel, cars, and computers from foreign competition as a key part of the job of nurturing them. Today, though, Japan has the world's lowest tariff rates. Cars and computers, for instance, come in tax-free; in the United States and Europe, both are subject to tariffs of 10 percent or more. Whiskey and wine, which were until 1988 subject to a discriminatory tax treatment that kept out imports, are now on equal terms with *shochu*, the domestic Japanese spirit. Japan's greatest embarrassment remains agricultural protection: figures from the Organization for Economic Cooperation and Development show that in 1989 Japan was subsidizing its farmers more, and forcing its consumers to pay more for their produce, than either of the other two big economic blocks.

All the same, those barriers, too, are coming down. Under pressure from the United States, Japan started to dismantle its quotas on beef and oranges at the end of the 1980s, and was even talking about opening its rice market at the end of the Uruguay round of international trade negotiations. The emotional significance of the issue can be gauged from the fact that, under pressure from the powerful farmers' lobby, the Diet has passed no fewer than three resolutions reaffirming its opposition to the importing of even a single grain of rice.

Naturally, Japanese big business has been rather successful at holding back the arrival of competitive products even after tariffs have been done away with. Despite the incursions of BMW and Mercedes, which have helped foreign makes to account for almost one in three luxury cars in Japan, the foreign market share of basic models is ten times smaller. IBM, the biggest computer maker in most of the world's industrial countries, has a market share of less than 10 percent in Japan, thanks to the web of bureaucratic controls in which it was tied up in its early days. But it is not only Japanese companies that are to blame. The distributors of Scotch whisky chose deliberately to keep prices and margins high and sales low long after the barriers to the Japanese market came down; they judged that they would make more money by restricting supply than by cutting prices.

A better place to look for what has made firms like Toyota or Sony so successful is surely inside the firms themselves. One thing that jumps out at the visitor is their attitude toward costs: while European and American firms are often keen to impress customers with their financial might — a case in point is the stunning corporate architecture of New York City — the big Japanese exporters are keen to appear poorer than they really are.[4] The Toyota Motor Corporation, known familiarly in Japan as the Toyota Bank because of its ferociously powerful cash flow, has its head office in the center of Toyota City, a vast complex of assembly and component factories belonging to the firm and its suppliers. Toyota City, the modern equivalent of Henry Ford's famous River Rouge complex in Michigan, is probably the world's most efficient industrial machine. Yet the corporate head office of the company is in a slightly dowdy low-built concrete building dating from the 1960s. As we shall see later, Matsushita Electric Industries, the world's biggest consumer-electronics company, is more cheese-paring still.

Are these merely outward signs, helpful in trying to drive down a supplier's price during negotiations? No. For inside the building as well, successful Japanese companies are not just keen on cutting costs per se — that, like motherhood, is something everyone approves of — but they make it their business to *know* far more accurately than most of their foreign competitors how expensive it is to hold stocks of spare parts, which components are priced too high or too low, which product lines yield most profit, and what the financial effects would be of a myriad of different tiny organizational changes in the factory.

A good example of this was reported by the management consultants James Abegglen and George Stalk in *Kaisha,* their book on the internal workings of Japanese corporations.[5] At the beginning of the 1970s, one of their Western clients found that its European forklift truck business was being overwhelmed by cheap imports made by Toyota. What was the secret, the Western firm wondered? It could not be dumping: Toyota was selling the forklifts at the same price in its home market as in Europe. A careful study of the company and its competitors revealed that Toyota had identified the broadness of the Western firm's product lines (it made some twenty different product families of forklifts) as a factor that raised its costs sharply. This was because the company's factory had to stop production every time it changed from one type of forklift to another: while it did so, its workers had to stand around idle, and stocks of components for other kinds of trucks continued to clock up interest payments as they sat in the storeroom. When Toyota entered the market, it chose to offer only six product families; the result was that its materials costs were 14 percent lower, its overheads a third lower, and its labor costs only half those of the Western competitor. (Labor costs did not matter much in any case, for they accounted for only 4 percent of the Western firm's total costs.) Altogether, the study revealed that Toyota's costs appeared to be 79 percent of the Western firm's; Toyota was therefore making more money than the Western firm even when it undercut its prices by 20 percent.

In that particular case study, the Western firm was able to hit back when it realized what was happening to it. More often, though, Western firms respond to this kind of price competition by making things worse: they actually increase product variety, and try to offer more specialized products in order to find market niches where they will be sheltered from competition. Such a strategy is usually doomed to fail; after achieving a cost advantage like the one Toyota did, a new competitor can then start to expand its product range as its market share rises.

As well as keeping a gimlet eye on costs, Japan's best companies have invested tremendous effort in their manufacturing processes. As we shall see in chapter 4, American car companies perfected (or so they thought) the process of mass production at the beginning of the 1920s, and made few important changes to their system until competition from Toyota forced them to in the late 1970s. This is partly because in Europe and the United States engineers and technical specialists prefer to work on the more prestigious job of designing products, rather than on getting someone else's design into production — or, worse still, on finding ways to improve the manufacturing process of a product already in production. Not so in Japan: its most competitive factories are organized specifically to make it as easy as possible to identify inefficiencies in the production process and then to correct them. This is true not only of the way work is done on the factory floor, with quality circles and teams given full responsibility for the way they organize their own part of the assembly process; it is also intrinsic to methods of new product design, and to relations with suppliers.

Abegglen's study showed convincingly that the businesses in which Japanese companies had the strongest labor productivity lead over their American competitors were those in which the number of manufacturing steps were highest. Technical complexity is an issue as well: the biggest Japanese industrial success story of the 1980s was the market for computer memory chips. In 1980 the United States dominated world supply, providing about three-quarters of all the memory chips used. By 1986 Japan's big semiconductor makers, Hitachi, Fujitsu, Toshiba, and NEC, had succeeded in overturning that lead: Japan came to account for almost 60 percent of memory sales, leaving the United States with barely half its earlier market share. The key to their success was not only a highly aggressive pricing strategy, which involved selling below cost for a while to keep the factory at full output while it learned to make the chips more efficiently; it was also a question of mastering a highly complex and unstable production process, in which an open door, a few grains of dust, or an unexpected change in the humidity of the "clean room" in which the chips were being made could cause a sharp drop in the yield ratio, or the proportion of manufactured chips that are usable at the end of the production process. By 1992, when the latest product in computer memory was a 4-megabit DRAM,[6] Japan held over 80 percent of the market.

By the mid-1980s Japanese firms were able to wield a different weapon in world markets: flexibility. Having earlier competed on price, and then by focusing their efforts on a smaller number of more economical products, they are now able to produce an increasingly wide range of products without suffering the traditional penalty of higher costs. This new flexibility has advanced furthest in the car industry, where it has been dubbed *lean manufacturing*. In essence, it consists of reducing the time it takes to change over the factory machinery from one product to another and cutting out stocks all the way through the production process, so that the factory can produce five or six different products at the same time on the same production line — and with even higher quality than before.

Robots are an interesting indicator of the problem of managing a manufacturing process. Japan has more than 220,000 industrial robots, almost twice as many as the rest of the world put together. This is only partly because of labor costs; high though they are, Japanese wages are nowhere near high enough to justify such a disparity. The real reason for the robotics gap is that successful Japanese companies know far more precisely which jobs their employees are doing inside the factory, and how much value those employees are adding. It is precisely because their production processes are stable that they have been able to respond to higher labor costs by picking out the processes that can be most easily automated. In the car industry, the United States and Italy are the only two countries that have experimented with large-scale automation: the results have been disappointing, with high maintenance costs and almost embarrassingly inflexible factories that prove to be very hard to change over from one product line to another. Introducing robots, it seems, is the best way to expose weaknesses in the production process.

Since the spread of flexible production, another trend has become clear. After years of acting as "followers," Japan's big companies have now become technological leaders. This may sound surprising — are the Japanese not, after all, the great "copycats"? The answer is no. In the 1960s and 1970s, as they tried to catch up to the American and European lead in the automobile, computer, and electronics industries, Japanese companies had a simple job: they had to scour the market for promising technologies that their competitors had not yet put to good commercial use, and beat them to it. Time and time again, Western firms kicked themselves for allowing Japanese companies to pinch their own good ideas from under their noses: the videocassette recorder, the fax machine, the audiocassette, four-wheel steering in cars, multivalve engines, even the fundamentals of large-scale integration in the manufacture of computer chips. In all of these cases, and more, Americans or Europeans could claim the glory of invention but just failed to see a market.

With a few exceptions, such as new materials technology, Japan continues to be weak at the basic, blue-skies research that underpins future advances in scientific knowledge. But apart from that, everything has changed. Japanese companies are now pushing outward on the borders of technology. In the car industry, Honda has come up with a revolutionary "lean-burn" engine that promises to bring in a generation of cleaner, more economical vehicles. In electronics, companies like Toshiba and Sharp rule the world in developing the flat-panel color screens that seem destined to take over from the old-fashioned cathode-ray tube in computers and televisions. In submicron computer chip development and in optical storage technology, companies like Hitachi and Canon have left the United States and Europe behind. Such changes are already showing up in the statistics. By 1990 the top four recipients of American patents were all Japanese companies. And there was a dramatic change in Japan's "technology balance of payments" — that is, the difference between the money it received and the money it paid for patents, intellectual property, and other license fees. In 1973 the country paid out 4.5 times as much as it received. By 1988, although the total paid out had risen (reflecting both Japan's economic development and the broader fact that higher R&D costs are making it harder for anyone to go it alone), its payments were only 1.27 times its receipts. By the mid-1990s, Japan is likely to be an exporter, not an importer, of technology.

The trouble with such fast changes, not just in technology but also in factory organization, is that they impose tremendous strains on the work force. Employees who have been used to doing something one way find themselves asked to do it another; worse (or better, depending on how you look at it), they are asked not just to do different things but to do a wide range of different things flexibly. One of the greatest advantages that competitive Japanese firms have is that they have found a way to make their employees embrace change rather than reject it. How?

One way is well known: Japan's famous "lifetime employment" system. Yet this is rather different close up from the way it is often portrayed. Only a small elite — about a fifth of Japanese workers, most of them male workers in big manufacturing companies — have a real expectation that they will be kept on by their firms through thick and thin. For the rest, different arrangements apply. Women, as we have seen, have hitherto been excluded from serious responsibility in Japanese industry; they are expected to make tea and photocopies and to retire gracefully, preferably by marrying one of their colleagues, at twenty-five.[7] Temporary and part-time workers are treated as a periphery: they receive far fewer benefits (no subsidized holiday cottages or company junkets abroad, for instance) than the full-time workers at the next desk, they are largely uncovered by Japanese employment protection legislation, and they are liable to lose their jobs as soon as the company faces financial difficulties.

Inside that group of core workers, however, Japanese firms have managed to create a climate of extraordinary stability and mutual advantage. Most core employees join the company straight from high school or university: they arrive like clean slates, waiting to have the company philosophy written onto them. Pay and promotion is by seniority, so there is none of the leapfrogging that tends to alarm and anger older employees in American firms. Heavy investment is made in training, because the firm can be confident that few of its core employees will leave to work elsewhere. And the prevailing ethos is that effort, rather than innate ability, is the thing that helps one get ahead.[8] In return for their unthinking loyalty, the employees get two important returns: an understanding that they will not put themselves out of work by cooperating with progress; and an understanding that the company's shareholders, suppliers, and top management will all suffer if hard times have to be shared. This probably began in 1950, when Toyota tried to sack a quarter of its eight thousand workers — its president had to go, too. But the practice continues: in early 1992 the president of the Yamaha musical instrument company was forced to resign for the very same reason.

There is a price, however. European and American firms are often driven to laying off their employees because that is the only way to cut their wage bills. In Japan, workers buy their continued employment by being flexible on pay, too. They get bonuses twice a year, worth on average a total of about five months' salary. If the company's performance slips, it can cut its wage bill painlessly by reducing the bonuses. But the principle is a fine one: it encourages the employees to realize the ultimate truth that their own fate is tied up inextricably with that of the firm. In most firms, employees also receive on retirement a lump-sum payment rather than a pension.

Two things have made it possible for Japanese companies to bring such a system into being. One is the docility of the work force. Although Japanese factories in Europe and the United States are renowned for their egalitarianism — the same gray tunics for everyone from cleaner to general manager in the United States, for instance, or the abolition of the ludicrous British habit of providing separate dining facilities for workers of different seniority — workers in Japan are in fact extremely conscious of hierarchy. Fewer signs of it are visible to outsiders, but that is partly because no signs are necessary: status is inherent in the Japanese language, which uses a different vocabulary depending on whether you are speaking to your betters or your inferiors.[9] Most big Japanese companies have their own trade union. Some unions stage token lunchtime strikes once a year, in which the employees don red headbands bearing blood-curdling slogans before returning to work demurely afterward; but for the most part, they have effectively been incorporated into the company's personnel department. They are part of the system rather than an opposition to it.

European trade unionists should think twice before condemning such submissiveness. The statistics show that obedience to the company appears to pay handsomely: in each of the years between 1985 and 1990, Japanese workers received pay raises that were worth 3 percent after inflation — a record of remarkable consistency that no other industrial country can match.

The other thing that has allowed Japanese firms to forge such a relationship with their workers is the structure of the work force itself. With an unusually young population — and therefore relatively few people of management age — Japanese companies have never had much of a problem in dealing with employees who fail to make top management as they get older. The first division run the firm; the second division are farmed out to subsidiaries; the third division stay at the level of *kacho*, or section chief, until retirement; and the fourth division are known as the *madogiwazoku*—the tribe who sit in front of the windows, as a sign that they are being kept on but have few responsibilities. As the population gets older, however, this system is coming under pressure: not only are firms having to pay out more to workers who retire, but the traditional seniority principles are coming under pressure as there are just too many workers in their forties and fifties.

"Are Japanese customers fair?" This is the bizarre question posed by T. W. Kang, a Korean businessman who lives in Japan, in a recent book telling American firms how to get into the Japanese market.[10] But it is an interesting one all the same. The buying public in Japan has expectations of quality in everything it buys which are more exacting than in any other world market, and this has a dramatic effect on the way Japanese companies do business.

For instance, over the past few years American cherry farms have exported impressive quantities of fresh fruit to Japan. When they began to do so, however, several of them found that the buyers in big Japanese supermarket chains were routinely rejecting produce that customers in the United States would unquestioningly accept. It was not until the Japanese firms sent representatives to the West Coast of the United States to walk up and down the packing lines, picking out cherries one by one that were too small or too underripe, that the farms got the message.

Filofax, a British stationery firm, had a similar experience. When it started exporting its pocket organizers to Japan, its local distributor told the company that the organizers could be priced well over double the going rate in the European or American market. To achieve that price, however, the organizers had to be both perfect and beautifully displayed. So the Japanese distributor provided top-quality cardboard cases, costing about sixteen dollars apiece, for Japanese Filofaxes. The distributor also thought that the plastic bags surrounding the packages of refill paper looked cheap, so it arranged to have them opened on arrival in Japan and then repacked one by one in better-looking clear plastic bags.[11]

Kang argues that the formula for success with Japanese customers is QCDS — quality, cost, delivery, and service. With a few consumer goods, it is debatable whether cost comes even as high as second on the list: sometimes, as with the absurd melons that sell in Tokyo department stores for ¥10,000 ($80) or more, the only thing that matters is an appearance of unblemished perfection. But there is no doubt that in general, competition in Japan is a bracing cold bath that provides excellent training for winning in the other markets of the world. Companies that have succeeded in Japan, ranging from DisneyWorld to BMW, from Procter & Gamble to United Distillers Group, from Virgin Atlantic to McDonald's, all have in common a reputation for quality.

Quality alone is not enough, however; agility counts too. Numerous foreign companies have introduced a new product into the Japanese market, and found to their dismay that a rash of competitors sprang up with lightning speed as if from nowhere, offering a similar product either at a slightly lower price or with some other advantage. McDonald's, for instance, was the pioneer of mass-produced fast food in Japan; pundits insisted on its arrival in the early 1970s that the idea would never catch on among the fish-eating, health-conscious Japanese. They were absolutely wrong. But McDonald's soon found its sales being eaten into by smaller competitors, such as Mos Burger and Lotteria, which were offering McDonald's-type menus with modest alterations to suit changing Japanese tastes. McDonald's is now the biggest restaurant chain in Japan, but it has kept its place only by constantly innovating, and by abandoning the shibboleth of a single world menu that has been behind the success of McDonald's in every other market. The turning point was when it introduced the Teriyaki McBurger in 1989. By 1991 it was even offering McChow: Chinese-style rice dishes.

This is not a pattern that is unique to new products introduced by foreign firms. Within a few months of the first home fax machines' coming on the market in Japan in 1987, there were twenty different models jostling for space on the shelves of the discount stores in Akihabara, Tokyo's electronics district. Half a year after Toshiba launched the first real notebook computer in Japan, it had half a dozen competitors. And the same can be said for countless innovations in the car industry. The point is that the intensity of competition in Japan's domestic market — a market, incidentally, that is bigger than the markets of France, Britain, and Germany put together — makes the winning companies lean and practiced before they even start to do business abroad. One of the ironies of Japan's postwar industrial history has been that often firms that were second or worse in the domestic market had the earlier successes abroad. In the car industry, Honda expanded abroad to escape from Toyota's powerful embrace of sales and distribution at home; in computers, Toshiba overcame NEC's dominance of the Japanese PC market and sold machines in the United States; in electronics, Sony sold abroad when faced with the problems of trying to beat Matsushita's twenty thousand tied retailers.

Given the furious competition in its consumer markets, it might seem paradoxical that the other important feature of Japan's industrial landscape appears at first sight fundamentally anticompetitive This is the *keiretsu* system of industrial groupings. Today's industrial groups in Japan have their origins in the Edo period, when powerful merchant families like the Mitsubishi and Mitsui began to build up conglomerates of different businesses. By the 1930s these families accounted for some two-thirds of Japan's economic output; ten years later, they were single-mindedly behind the Japanese war effort. A special law was promulgated in 1943 to assure a stable supply of capital for more than one hundred firms deemed important for the war effort by forging links between them and specific authorized banks.

The occupying U.S. forces did their best to break up the family conglomerates, but they were not altogether successful. Forced to divest their holdings and step down from their posts, the heads of many of the families simply found more subtle ways of carrying on the same approach to business. The majority of the shares of the group companies were discreetly distributed among the other firms in the same group, resulting in a handful of loose groups with no parent company but with a web of cross-holding between tens, or even hundreds, of firms in the same group. A group usually contained a bank, an insurance firm, a trading company, a real estate company, and an array of manufacturers and heavy industrial businesses.

As Japan developed after the war, these *keiretsu* did a highly efficient job of spreading technology from outside through the companies of the group, and helping group companies first to finance and then to distribute and sell the goods they made for export. Today, the Mitsubishi group has a combined turnover of $300 billion, and the group centered around the Dai-Ichi Kangyo Bank a total of $400 billion: were they forced to issue consolidated accounts, these two would easily count as the world's two biggest businesses — far ahead of General Motors' paltry $135 billion. Most of the companies in the big groups do about a fifth of their business in-house; their cross-shareholdings amount to about the same. They account for over 15 percent of the Japanese economy, and almost 2 percent of the entire world economy.[12]

The extent to which such relationships govern business in Japan can be seen at corporate parties. When the guests of Mitsubishi Electric ask for a beer, they are most likely to be served a brand called Kirin. Kirin is not the only beer in Japan (though it does have a market share of almost 50 percent), nor is it by any means the tastiest; but Kirin, unlike other brands such as Asahi, Sapporo, and Suntory, is a member of the Mitsubishi Group.

One of the things that has allowed this form of industrial structure to survive is the feeble way in which Japan's antitrust rules are enforced. The Japanese Fair Trade Commission, a body modeled on its U.S. counterpart and set up by the American occupiers under a law almost identical to their own, has done nothing to restrain the power of the groups. (Nor has it been notably effective in stopping Japanese industries from forming cartels: the construction business is notorious for its *dango*, or bid rigging. And under severe political pressure the FTC even went so far as to authorize the setting up of more than two hundred local retailing cartels in April 1989 when the government brought in a new consumption [sales] tax but wanted to allow small shopkeepers to foist its cost entirely onto consumers.)

Membership in an industrial group provides one important protection to a Japanese firm: it makes it harder for the firm to be taken over, since most of its shares will be distributed among friendly companies. But apart from that, the development of the Japanese economy has meant that the remaining motivations for continuing the groupings are conservative and risk-avoiding. The groups were born in an era when the biggest problem for companies was a shortage of capital. There was a reminder of the old days in 1990 and 1991, when the crash of the Tokyo stock market in 1990 and the high interest rates that persisted the following year made it hard for Japanese companies to raise capital either by issuing shares or by borrowing. But in the long term, with Japanese firms increasingly able to raise money on foreign capital markets and with a corporate-bond market fast taking shape at home, such shortages are likely to be reduced sharply. The corporate links come in handy, though, when a group company runs into trouble. Then, like the Meiwa Trading Corporation in early 1991, it can rely on a friendly group of stable shareholders to provide funds and management advice for a restructuring. Yet it is striking just how many of Japan's most successful exporting companies — Honda, Sony, Matsushita, Sharp, and Ricoh, to name but a few — do not belong to these groups.

That is not to say that they operate entirely on their own.

Japan's big manufacturers have evolved a quite different structure, which is confusingly known as a *kigyo keiretsu*, or enterprise group, and consists essentially of vertical groups of suppliers, distributors, and subcontractors based on a dominant manufacturer. Just as with the old-style horizontal groupings, the firms are linked by the umbilical cord of cross-shareholdings and long-term business dealings. But here, the aim is different; the firms are in business together to turn out products in a single industry at the lowest possible cost. Toyota Motor Corporation, for instance, has less than one-seventh as many employees as General Motors. This is because it stands at the apex of a pyramid of supplier groups ranging from vast high-tech firms quoted on the first section of the stock exchange which supply electronic engine management systems, to back-yard family widget-making businesses.

It was this system that came under attack in 1990 and 1991 when T. Boone Pickens, an American corporate raider, picked up more than 20 percent of the shares of Koito Manufacturing, a Toyota supplier, from a notorious greenmailer and stock market operator in Tokyo. Pickens asserted, quite correctly, that Koito was virtually a dependent of Toyota: the assembly firm had seats on its board, routinely interfered in its management, and was quick to demand lower prices for its components than those the firm was able to get from outside customers. Yet it was far from clear that this had done the firm harm. In accepting its subservient role to Toyota, it had agreed (as do hundreds of other Japanese supplier firms) to accept worse conditions for its workers than Toyota workers themselves receive, and to act as a buffer for the bigger company in times of slack demand by laying off part of its work force. But the relationship has its positive side as well. Supplier and assembler cooperate in finding ways to make car parts more efficiently than outside Japan, and share the profits of that endeavor. The arm's-length relationships common in the United States and Europe have not produced a notably healthier — or comparatively more profitable — components industry.[13]

One thing is missing, surely. So far, little has been said about the role of the government. What about Japan, Inc.? What about the Ministry of International Trade and Industry (MITI)?[14] What about the methods of *gyosei shido,* or administrative guidance, which Japanese government officials use to tell big business what to do? Of all the aspects of the rise of modern Japan, this produces the most furiously partisan opinions in the West: on one side, a view that this is the "secret weapon" responsible for all Japan's industrial successes, which Europe and the United States would do well to adopt; on the other, a view that Japanese industrial policy never existed — or if it did, it is part of Japan's history and ended in the 1970s.

The second of these views is particularly hard to defend. A striking reminder of the power that the Japanese bureaucracy continues to exert came in September 1990, when the Ministry of Finance and the Bank of Japan judged that the sluggish performance of the Tokyo stock market was damaging business confidence. Representatives of a handful of big securities firms were summoned one day to the ministry for an informal chat over a cup of green tea, and sure enough, the market later rose a staggering two thousand points in a single day — its biggest jump since the Second World War. A further illustration of the power of the bureaucracy can be seen in the persistence of the practice of *amakudari,* in which hundreds of retiring senior civil servants "descend from heaven" to lucrative jobs in the private sector from which they can continue to further the aims of their former employer.

Yet Japanese bureaucratic power has its limits. After having enthusiastically urged Japanese electronics firms to enter the market for computer memory in the early 1980s, MITI decided in late 1990 that firms like Hitachi, Fujitsu, Toshiba, and NEC were now investing too much money and were in danger of provoking a world semiconductor glut. Despite MITI's earnest advice, however, the companies continued to try to outdo each other in the size of the new investments in plant and equipment they announced week by week; it was not until the downturn hit in 1992 that the market pressure of declining profitability forced the firms to draw back. And some firms, particularly those that do not belong to *keiretsu* and are little beholden to the civil servants, have always been more independent still: Honda, for instance, entered the car business against the express wishes of the government, which thought that Japan already had too many car companies.[15] Since then, it has been the only car company that has dared to decline the honor of receiving a retired bureaucrat on its board of directors.

The ministries tend to intervene most actively in four well-defined sets of circumstances. First, just as in many European countries, they are keen on looking after industries that have particular social significance or where free markets would drive many inefficient firms out of business. The economic activity most dependent on the government lead is agriculture, where productivity is lamentably low and Japanese farmers rely on the Ministry of Agriculture to keep competitors away from the country's shores. Also protected are small shops, whose owners could until recently count on MITI to stop supermarkets from opening nearby,[16] and, perhaps bizarrely, public bathhouses, or *sento*, where the health ministry regulates everything from the fees to the temperature of the water. In the 1950s and 1960s, a minority of Japanese households had baths at home; as the standard of new houses has risen, the bath owners have come under threat.

Second, the bureaucrats move in when they think an industry is in structural decline and needs to be rationalized. This has happened with shipbuilding (in which the government promoted the building of new, high-technology yards, a policy that bore sweet fruit at the end of the 1980s as ship prices rose and order books filled to bursting); and also with the steel industry, which under careful government guidance has become more efficient and automated, and has diversified into everything from biotechnology to notebook computers.

The MITI specialty, however, is "infant industries": using tax breaks and publicly funded joint R&D projects to promote sectors of the economy that it thinks are going to be important in future, and nurturing them with high tariffs. In the main, it has been spectacularly successful, though perhaps with hindsight one could doubt the wisdom of trying to exclude from the car industry the company that led the way for others in moving production overseas and getting a foothold in global markets. Yet there have certainly been slip-ups. In the computer industry, for instance, MITI promoted the development of a computer mainframe industry in Japan just in time to see mainframe computers overtaken by the newly arrived personal computer. And in the memory chip business, arguably the speediest and most spectacular hijack of a world industry in history, there are grounds for hesitation: so successful have Japanese companies been at dominating the world supply for DRAMS that they themselves are beginning to question the wisdom of carrying all the supply risk for such a vast industry. The turn of the 1990s saw Japanese companies trying to reduce their exposure by sharing risk in strategic joint ventures with competitors overseas; many top executives in the industry think that such moves are only the beginning.

The final area in which the bureaucracy exercises great power is in industries or markets where world trade is managed, rather than free. The semiconductor industry is a case in point, in which a secret side-letter in the 1986 U.S.-Japanese semiconductor agreement promised that foreign chips would achieve a 20 percent market share of the Japanese market during the term of the agreement, thus giving the bureaucracy new powers to allocate purchases among domestic companies. This power has been extended by the continued demands from Washington for the government in Tokyo to ensure that foreign firms achieve a fixed market share. A similar situation has arisen from the so-called voluntary export restraints (VERS) in the car industry, in which both the

United States and different countries in Europe have asked Japanese firms to restrain "voluntarily" their car exports. One of the consequences of these arrangements is that they give renewed power to MITI by virtue of requiring it to allocate export quotas among the firms.[17] Even a small reduction in next year's export quota is a threat that can be used by the bureaucracy to pressure a car maker in any way it likes.

Yet the key question is whether the industrial policies that can be observed in Japan are responsible for the export successes of the country's best companies. As mentioned earlier, many European policymakers believed that the secret of the United States' success was the close relationship between the U.S. government, the military, the universities, and big business. At the time, it was fashionable to talk of the importance of "spin-off," in which military technology was expected to lead to the development of new consumer products. A generation later, there is little to show for this view except for Teflon and instant coffee.[18] With the scaling down of the U.S. military after the end of the cold war, much of that government-funded defense R&D now appears to be wasted. And cooperation between the government and big business is no longer seen as the quick fix that it once was.

In some ways, however, Japanese firms have a lot to thank their government for. Most important, Japanese economic policy has avoided the more egregious errors of the West. Japan does not have absurdly low gasoline prices, as the United States does; nor does it have a ballooning public sector deficit, as does Italy; nor did it fail altogether, as British governments did during the 1970s, to deal with inflation. Perhaps because Japan's political system is so unresponsive to public opinion, macroeconomic policy is remarkably stable. The most startling departure from good economic management was the increase in land and share prices at the end of the 1980s, but that was followed by a year and a half of ruthless tight-money policies that solved the problem without lasting damage either to the Japanese financial system or to the wider economy. There is also the fact that, even after taking into account its misleadingly optimistic statistics,[19] Japan has still had consistently lower unemployment than any other industrial country.

Moreover, from a broader view Japanese governments have been surprisingly limited in their interference in the economy. The public sector embraces fewer industries than in almost any other country: only water companies are nationalized, while the rail and telephone networks are at least nominally private companies. And rather than run up public sector deficits, Japan has often made politically painful decisions. One example of this, for all the dishonesty of the way it was introduced, was the long overdue consumption tax of 1989, which adjusted a long-standing distortion between direct and indirect taxes in the Japanese economy. Another was the financing of the country's $13 billion contribution to the military and nonmilitary costs of the Persian Gulf war, long before any other country had done so, by the immediate imposition of higher taxes on tobacco and petroleum products.

In one sense, the revisionists are unquestionably right about Japan: much of its industrial strength does, in fact, come from the ways in which Japanese society is different from the West. But is that so unusual? It has long been commonplace to talk of the way in which American business has been stimulated during the twentieth century by the country's constant supply of new immigrants, or about the role of individualism in Britain's Industrial Revolution in the nineteenth. Japanese society, too, has features that have proved a recipe for business success.

The first may perhaps be the most unexpected to outsiders, given how badly most Japanese speak English and how strange the city of Tokyo seems to a visiting foreigner: the country's ability to assimilate ideas quickly from outside. European and American businesses get a vivid reminder of this when they see the astonishing speed with which locals imitate a new product introduced into the Japanese market. But it is deeper than merely a me-too business sense. It began more than a century ago, after Commodore Perry's black ships steamed into the bay at Yokohama in 1853 and dispelled forever the idea that Japan could just banish the "southern barbarians" as it had before. But the assimilation of foreign ideas only took firm root with the restored Emperor Meiji on the throne, when the samurai behind him decided that what their country needed was to catch up quickly with the West — and promptly set to the task of transplanting European industry and technology. After the reversal of the militarist 1930s and the war, the Japanese were once again greedy for ideas — this time those of the United States. It is no coincidence that W. Edwards Deming, the American prophet of quality in business, was recognized much earlier and much more widely in Japan than in his own land.

Signs of Japan's openness to foreign ideas abound today. The Japanese language has been infiltrated by far more foreign words in the past century than has any European language; they are written in a special syllabary called *katakana*, used only for transcribing foreign words and for the issue of military proclamations.[20] Foreign fashions and crazes strike young Japanese more profoundly than perhaps any other young people in the industrial world. In 1990 the fad was for Italian food (particularly *tiramisu*, the dessert made with espresso, cocoa powder, and Mascarpone cheese) and for British Minis; by 1991 Japanese teenagers were increasingly to be seen on the streets of Tokyo dressed in the style of New York Puerto Ricans. The success of magazines like *Hanako*, which offers its readers every week updates on the most fashionable restaurants, clothes, music, and holiday destinations, is proof of the insatiability of the thirst for the new of young Japanese. There is no doubt that this curiosity, sharply selective though it may be, is the source of much of Japan's commercial energy.

At the same time, there is a passion for order underlying the appearance of chaos. In every commercial act, the Japanese are governed by a ritual: do it *right*. This is evident in the way a businessman hands over his business card,[21] and in the way a clerk in a department store wraps up a purchase, putting a package first inside a high-quality paper carrier bag and then into an outer plastic cover to protect it from the drizzle outside. Despite its ferocious orderliness, the Tokyo subway system actually employs no more workers per station than London's does; the difference is in their attitude toward the work they do.

In business and private life, promptness is the rule, not the exception; people think of themselves as late if they arrive later than five minutes before the appointed time. A socialist member of the Diet was forced to resign in 1989 after causing a two-minute delay to a *shinkansen*, or bullet train, as a result of asking its conductor to make an unscheduled stop so that he could get to a public meeting on time. (The Japanese often find Western attitudes to timekeeping puzzling. A public relations man from Toshiba once revealed to me his Theory of the Intelligent Quarter — the regulation fifteen-minute delay with which, in his experience, all Europeans and Americans demonstrate their status to their hosts.)

A symptom of this passion for order is a willingness to obey and to conform that goes far beyond what Europeans or Americans would consider acceptable. In subway stations, tourist spots, and restaurants, the Japanese submit meekly to orders from people in uniform whose sense of military discipline is only slightly masked by the exquisite politeness with which they issue the instructions. In business meetings, at least, young people do not speak unless they are spoken to. At home, people are shamed by the risk of earning angry glances from the neighbors into separating their household garbage into different categories and putting it out on specified days of the week. Even the teenage dancers in Tokyo's Yoyogi Park demonstrate, by the iron regularity of their disco routines, their view that youthful rebellion is best done in an orderly way.

Of course these things have both a good and a bad side. The bad side is evident more broadly in Japanese society and politics. The country has been ruled for a generation by a party that now no longer even bothers to deny its corruption. The

Japanese have allowed themselves to be left behind in their own country's economic development; housing in particular remains miserably poor, with 42 percent of Japanese households in 1990 unconnected to the sewers and 13 percent without a bath. Japanese society is also repressive to those who are different from the average, and it offers little protection for those who get on the wrong side of the law. Spiritually, one sometimes gets the impression that the country's inhabitants have given up worshiping the emperor only to worship consumer durables instead. Alarmingly, many Japanese answer, "I don't know" when asked their opinion on anything of importance; every year, the nation's readers buy more than a billion *manga* cartoon books, shocking in their violence and absence of intellectual content, which make even the quiz shows and soap operas of Japanese television seem demanding by comparison.

But from the companies' point of view, there is a good side too. They can usually count on thoroughness and unquestioning loyalty from their workers (to the point that a growing number of workers are actually dying of overwork).[22] Also, partly because it is so hard to change jobs in Japan, workers are willing to put their best efforts even into work they do not like. They tend to respond when asked to meet apparently impossible goals. At Sony, engineers were told to produce a video camera smaller than they actually believed possible; they succeeded. At Komatsu, the company slogan was *maru-C* ("Encircle Caterpillar," the firm's U.S. competitor); it did. At Honda, when the firm's motorcycle division was threatened in 1982 by an upstart competitor, the company president declared: *Yamaha o tsubusu!* (We're gonna smash Yamaha). Less than a year and a half later, after a flood of new Honda products had warded off its challenge, Yamaha was forced to declare a loss, cut its dividend, lay off workers, and replace its president.[23]

Behind many of these observations is the Japanese education system, which may seem superficially to be similar to the American system (in whose image it was remade by the occupying forces after the Second World War), but it is actually quite unlike any in the Western world. Japanese schools pursue two aims with great enthusiasm: preparing their charges for the society to which they will have to conform, and giving them the knowledge that will be necessary for them to be useful members of it. The job of developing their personalities and their intellectual interests, which is thought to be paramount in other countries, comes a very poor third.

Conformity is inculcated by teaching an entire class of forty to fifty pupils together, and making sure that the clever and dull ones alike move forward at the same speed. Teachers expect either to lecture the members of their classes or to interrogate them, but not, in general, to invite their opinions.[24] In primary school, the classes are divided into *han*, groups of five or six pupils chosen at random, who will then work together as a group when asked to perform duties like serving lunch to their schoolmates or cleaning the classroom. Although there has been pressure to change, most schools have long and detailed rule books, which govern everything from what the children may do on Sundays to the length of their hair and the color of their underwear. Games are usually compulsory, and there is little choice. At more than half the Japanese schools, pupils wear uniforms: high-collar Prussian tunics with brass buttons for boys, sailor suits for girls.

As for equipping the students with the skills they will need to function in society, the syllabuses of Japanese schools are laid down centrally by the Ministry of Education, which even publishes a list of "approved" textbooks that have passed a process of screening by its committees.[25] They emphasize mathematics, which is extremely well taught in Japan, and English, which is rather less well taught. But a feature common to all subjects is that knowledge is much more important than analysis: tests, even for entry to Tokyo University, are largely factual and multiple choice; plenty of students can spend more than a decade in school without being forced into the risky business of expressing their own opinions freely in an essay.

Schools are more determined to ensure that the average pupil does well than that the best does very well — and they succeed in this endeavor. Official figures suggest that only I percent of Japan's population is functionally illiterate, compared with almost 20 percent in the United States; this is helped by the fact that 94 percent of students finish high school at eighteen or nineteen; in Britain, less than 40 percent of the population at that age is still in school. As well as staying on longer, Japanese schoolchildren also spend more time learning while they are in school: they learn on Saturdays too, summer holidays are shorter, and the eerie silence in class means that more gets done. One expert estimates that by the time they finish, Japanese students have spent the equivalent of a full extra year in school.

The result is that Japanese schools produce ideal factory fodder: clean, thorough, obedient, hard-working people, used to hardship and to being forced to get along with neighbors they did not choose, and convinced by having been told so often that continuous application will eventually win out over brilliance. This is hardly an educational recipe that many Western politicians would approve of; it is, however, the nearest thing that Japan has to an industrial secret weapon.

Over the past five years, a growing chorus of specialists has begun to complain that the very regimentation of Japanese schools is suppressing the original thinkers that the country will need over the coming decades if it is to come up with its fair share of Nobel prizes and scientific discoveries. In response, the Ministry of Education has announced a thoroughgoing curriculum reform, which is due to produce a new national curriculum in 1994. Various proposals have already been made. But the civil servants in Tokyo, with their extensive powers over local education committees, know just how much hangs on their decisions. They are unlikely to do anything hasty that will reduce the quality of the Japanese work force. Change will come very slowly in Japanese schools.

Many other things in Japan are changing rather quickly,

however. People are taking more vacations abroad than they used to: since 1989, when the number of outbound travelers from Japan topped 10 million, it has become increasingly difficult to get a seat on just about any flight out of Tokyo. Sales of luxury goods were dented by the slowdown in the economy in 1991, but the public has acquired an irreversible taste for German cars, Italian wine, French handbags, and British china. And borrowing — something the traditional Japanese family shunned, preferring to squirrel away its savings for a rainy day however low the interest rates offered by the banks — is growing with a vengeance. In 1985 the average household had nonmortgage debts of ¥2.9 million; by 1990 it was up by two-thirds to ¥4.9 million ($39,380).

Companies are already beginning to respond to this. Noting that workers in Japanese manufacturing companies spend 171 more hours a year on the job than their counterparts in Britain, and 526 hours more than German workers, some are trying to give their employees more free time. Matsushita, for instance, was planning in 1992 to cut its workers' annual hours to 1,800 within a year — giving them more free time than either British or American workers. In an attempt to combat the problem of pressure from colleagues making workers take less than their vacation entitlement, Nissan has already set up a system to make sure that its employees have at least five consecutive weekdays' vacation a year. And more and more young people are shunning the institution of lifetime employment. In 1991 Toyota bowed to this trend by making the fateful decision to hire for the first time some outsiders in their thirties or forties. This may not sound like much, but it will cause far-reaching changes in the way the company works over the coming decade, as these new employees find their places in the corporate ranks.

Under a wide-ranging agreement between Japan and the United States in 1990, more fundamental economic changes still are being made. The old rules that restricted the spread of large stores — and hence of imports — are being eased. One of the first beneficiaries has been the U.S. firm Toys "R" Us, which has begun a program of opening vast toy supermarkets in Japan, and seems set to circumvent the distribution system altogether by dealing directly with Japanese toymakers. A program of ¥430 trillion ($3.204 trillion) of public works has been promised during the course of the 1990s; if it materializes, this should solve many of the problems of Japan's creaking infrastructure by providing new roads, new sewers, and underground electricity cables. And the Fair Trade Commission, whose efforts to prevent collusion among businesses have not been notably successful so far, seems imbued with a new spirit: in 1991 it began for the first time to impose serious penalties on those who break Japan's competition laws.

Changes are taking place in the financial markets too. The growing ability of companies to raise money themselves by issuing corporate bonds is likely to reduce their dependence on the old *keiretsu* links that have been the hallmark of the postwar Japanese economy. And as banks are increasingly forced to offer free-market rates to depositors, they are coming under pressure to earn more from their investments in order to pay those rates. Big Japanese companies are therefore under more pressure to pay higher dividends, and thus to increase the profitability rather than simply the size of their operations.

Combined with the structural changes already taking place, these decisions are likely to reduce Japan's trade surpluses over the 1990s.[26] Will they make Japanese companies less competitive, however? In one sense they will: the old complaint that Japanese firms can tolerate a much lower rate of return on new businesses is likely to prove outdated. And the structural changes in the distribution system at home in Japan will increase imports and force Japanese companies to cut prices in their domestic market, thus making it harder to tolerate razor-thin export margins with fatter margins at home.

But in other ways, the liberalization and market opening in progress in Japan are likely to make the economy as a whole more, not less, efficient. Farming and distribution will absorb less of the labor force, freeing more people for work in the more competitive sectors of the economy; more women will work after marriage, thus forcing Japanese firms to recognize the skills of the half of the population that they have so far largely rejected. And better infrastructure will cut costs at home and make manufacturing more efficient.

This chapter has argued that Japanese companies owe their competitiveness partly to the highly skilled and highly motivated work force that comes out of the country's schools, and partly to a competitive domestic market that builds up the manufacturing muscles of firms that want to sell abroad while at the same time providing low-cost financing and reliable components supply. But the overwhelming reason for their success in world markets — and increasingly their presence abroad — is that the best Japanese firms are well managed and highly efficient.

Perhaps the best way to illustrate this argument is to start by looking at a Japanese export industry that is neither well managed nor efficient. In recent years, a great deal of fuss has been made about the expansion abroad of Japanese banks and stockbrokerage firms. Closer inspection, however, reveals that they are not nearly so threatening as they seem.

THREE

The Long March of
the Japanese Bank

AT FIRST SIGHT, the two buildings have little in common. One is a Gothic *palazzo* begun in 1473, which looks out onto an elegant square in the Tuscan town of Siena. Decorated with early Renaissance paintings and furniture, it is part of the headquarters of Monte dei Paschi di Siena, a bank founded in 1624, which claims to be the oldest in the world and has a roomful of old account books written on vellum to prove it. The other building is a nondescript piece of British industrial architecture that used to house the administration of the post office for the City of London. Its cavernous interior, masked by false floors and ceilings and equipped with the latest wiring for computer and telecommunications equipment, looks like many other offices in the city. Ancient and modern, the two buildings symbolize two poles of the European financial system.

But they have something more specific in common. Both of them are examples of the rising influence of Japan in the European financial system. Although Monte dei Paschi remains, as a charitable trust under the wing of the Italian public sector, fiercely independent of outside interests, it sold in 1989 a 5 percent slice of its Milanese subsidiary Credito

Commerciale to the Taiyo Kobe Bank of Japan — a firm now merged with Mitsui Bank and known as the Sakura (or cherry blossom) Bank. The old post office building, on the other hand, now houses the European headquarters of Nomura Securities, the world's largest stockbrokerage firm. Nomura and its various subsidiaries and affiliates have 950 employees at work there.

These are not by any means the only two examples of a Japanese financial presence in Europe. Sumitomo, another Japanese commercial bank, spent $144 million in 1984 on a majority stake in Banca del Gottardo, one of the most respectable private banks in the Swiss town of Lugano. Five years later, the Bank of Yokohama acquired 65 percent of Guinness Mahon, in a deal that valued the London merchant bank at £95 million ($155.8 million). Japanese firms make markets in French shares. They arrange acquisitions in Britain and loans in Italy. They underwrite bonds in Switzerland. They sell warrants in London and arrange interest rate swaps in Frankfurt. In early 1992, Nomura Securities won the prestigious job of managing a $1 billion international public offering of shares in GPA, the Irish aircraft-leasing company. (Unfortunately for Nomura, the deal was abandoned at the last minute.)

These activities are in addition to the far more extensive business that Japanese financial firms already do in the United States. Banks and brokerages have sent personnel from Tokyo to many of the best-known houses on Wall Street. They have sent promising young graduates to Wharton and to the Harvard Business School. They have set up joint ventures with mergers and acquisitions specialists in New York, and have acquired the biggest banks in California. They dominate the financing of hotels in Nevada and resorts in Hawaii. At one stage, they were responsible for placing a third of the bonds issued by the federal government of the United States.

Some say that simply allowing Japanese financial institutions to make large portfolio investments in the U.S. or European economies raises dangers. Michael Lewis, a former Wall Street banker who revealed the excesses that were taking place at Salomon Brothers at the end of the 1980s, predicted recently in a long magazine article that Japanese insurance companies, securities firms, and banks control so many American assets that one of the first results of an earthquake in Tokyo would be that Japanese insurance firms would dump their extensive holdings of U.S. government bonds to raise money to meet claims on buildings in the Japanese capital.[1] The result, he warned, could be to drive down the price of those bonds — which by definition would push interest rates in the United States up by no fewer than five percentage points, thus causing an instant and profound depression.

Earthquake or no, Europeans have become nervous for another reason. Finance, specialists say, is a qualitatively different business from manufacturing. It is one thing for a Japanese firm to make money by supplying televisions or cars to overseas customers. But control of a big banking or brokerage business, giving firm access as it does to the very blood of a modern economy, is something else. Governments depend on the financial sector to help set economic policy, to raise funds for public services, to influence exchange rates. In 1987 a Belgian management consultant and an American business school professor published a worrying set of predictions about the move abroad of Japanese financial institutions. They called it the "Second Wave," in contrast to the first wave of manufacturing exports.

> Ten years ago, the Japanese took the world by surprise with a frontal assault on world consumer electronics, automobile, motorcycle and photographic markets. The techniques that they used in that attack seem almost more appropriate in a military context than in an international business setting: they have even been compared, by the more vocal of the many disgruntled western businessmen, to the techniques used by the Japanese in the attack on Pearl Harbor: stealth, surprise, an unprepared adversary, a specific target, and an overwhelming attack force . . .
>
> The Japanese are once again on the move, and a Second Wave of Japanese exports is about to flood the markets of the

western world. This time they have targeted the financial services sector as their area of conquest, and once again it appears that the West will be taken completely by surprise. And yet, the signs are all unmistakably there: a massive cash war chest flush with funds from a trade surplus which dwarfs even OPEC in its heyday, a government committed to expanding Japan's international financial clout while staunchly protecting the domestic market, and a disciplined, educated population devoted to hard work and self-sacrifice to an extent unrivalled in the West . . .

Today, through the use of joint ventures or outright purchases of foreign firms, and an intense devotion to studying and mastering the most modern techniques and skills, the Japanese are positioning themselves to become *the* dominant force in international financial services. Already, Japanese banks and securities houses dominate the ranks of the largest of their international peers, with the trend likely to continue in the future, while becoming increasingly adept at mastering the intricacies of the latest financial product innovations. If anything, the conquest of financial services may be even easier than that of automobiles or electronics, because of the worldwide trend towards financial market liberalization and the lack of extensive technological research and capital expenditure required to play the financial services game. If the prospect of a Toyota in every garage frightened you, what about a Nomura Securities office in every city and a Dai-Ichi Kangyo Bank on every corner?

In 1987 such an argument might possibly have looked plausible. By 1992, however, it had become laughable. This chapter will argue that while it is true that Japanese bankers and brokers have expanded very quickly overseas in the course of the 1980s, the so-called Second Wave is a myth and many of the fears mentioned above are unfounded. Specifically, Japan's financial sector, far from posing a competitive threat to Europe or the United States, is actually far behind both of them. Far from reinforcing the competitive challenge posed by the success of Japanese manufacturing, finance is proving a salutary reminder of the fact, pointed out in chapter 2, that Japan does not by any means do everything well.

In a single year between autumn 1990 and autumn 1991, Japanese banks and stockbrokerage firms were struck by a lethal cocktail of crashing share prices, rising interest rates, and spreading financial deregulation at home, and heavy losses on their investments abroad. To make things worse, almost all the leading firms in Japan's financial sector were discredited in the same year by their involvement in a series of financial scandals that ranged from helping gangsters to manipulate share prices and property sharks to evade government credit controls to widespread flouting of the country's Securities and Exchange Law. The events of that single year will set back the overseas expansion of the Japanese financial sector by at least a decade, and possibly two.

Drastic as the effects were of a downturn in the economic cycle, the parlous situation in which Japan's financial houses found themselves in 1992 was far from cyclical. On the contrary, their problems were more structural. As the two preceding chapters have shown, firms do not become dominant in world markets just by a simple process of slashing profit margins to zero and waiting for customers to come along. To be competitive, a firm has to have some advantage to begin with: more flexible management than other businesses, more efficient production methods, more skill in introducing new products at the right price and the right time. And as it progresses, it must hone its skills still further. Yet as even a cursory look at Japanese financial institutions reveals, not one of these sources of possible advantage is in evidence.

Underlying this is a crucial difference between finance and manufacturing, which makes it nonsense to talk of a "Second Wave" that uses the same methods as the first. Under the right conditions, a company that makes widgets can cut prices and expand production; then, with a factory running at full tilt, it can learn how to make widgets more cheaply and thus sell the same widgets that were previously loss-makers at a healthy profit. This has come to be seen as a classic Japanese strategy for gaining a competitive position in the world. As the firm grows, it can safely ignore the widgets it has already

made, provided only they are not of such bad quality that customers start bringing them back. In banking, by contrast, the
situation is somewhat different. Both in straight moneylend-
ing and in the sort of mergers and acquisitions (M&As) in
which a bank has a direct financial stake in the deal, business
already done cannot be so safely ignored. Customers who
have borrowed money may stop paying it; buildings that have
been built on borrowed money may not bring in enough rent
to cover the interest payments of the loan; companies that
have been taken over using leveraged buyouts (LBOs) may not
trade profitably enough to pay the coupon on the bonds that
were issued to finance the deal.

It is in the nature of the banking business that nobody
knows what or where tomorrow's bad loans will be. Third
World debt, LBOs, and property companies have each in turn
been the darling and then later the nemesis of the world's
bankers. One thing, however, is clear: a bank that tries to increase its market share quickly in any loan-related business
is likely to find that the customers who come most readily
are those who have been refused financing elsewhere. The
quicker the expansion, the greater the danger. And the more
ambitious the bank, the more likely it is to find itself saddled
five or ten years later with a lot of bad debts. That is precisely what has happened to Japan's banks in their overseas
business.

The problem of the brokering industry is a slightly different one. What allowed Japan's securities industry to expand
abroad was the wave of deregulation in the United States and
Britain in the 1980s: as brokering commissions were liberal-
ized, old dealing cartels were broken up and new entrants allowed into the market. The trouble was that greater competition meant lower profits; and as Johnny-come-latelies with
only modest customer bases, Japanese securities firms started
out with higher costs. They lacked expertise in the parts of
the securities business, such as arbitrage and the creation of
innovative financial instruments, that have proved most profitable at the beginning of the 1990s. And in the bread-and-

butter business of dealing in shares, they have lacked the solid research skills that bring in customers. As a result, they have been forced to fall back on the old-fashioned technique of competing for big-name underwriting and bond business by the simple device of tolerating only razor-thin margins. So far, only one minor Japanese financial institution has swallowed its pride and closed its London operations. Others are in pain, however. "Most of us are losing money," said the manager of a leading Japanese brokerage firm's London branch, "and wish we could just pack up and go home. It is only the fear of losing face that keeps us here."

What went wrong? A good place to start is in the basement of the Urbannet building, one of the smartest and newest of the smart new office blocks in Otemachi, Tokyo's financial district. It is the hot summer of 1991. Twenty or so stories upstairs, firms like Nomura Securities and Salomon Brothers are paying rent of some $20,000 *per desk* — higher than in any other building in the world, some say — and fighting for supremacy in the Tokyo stock market. But this is a surprisingly modest Italian restaurant, and over bowls of steaming fresh pasta with basil and tomato sauce cooked to perfection by a Japanese chef, an American investment banker is telling the story of the roller coaster ride that Japan's banks have taken in the 1980s.

With his year-round tan, short fair hair, and athletic build, Christopher Roberts[2] looks like the sort of investment banker who exists only in the movies. He jogs every morning, slobs around the house barefoot in shorts and T-shirts every weekend, and appears at the office every weekday morning with a ready smile, a well-tailored suit, and a characteristically American red or yellow tie. He would need only a pair of brightly colored suspenders to walk straight onto the set of Oliver Stone's film *Wall Street.*

This is probably no coincidence. The Japanese bank that hired him had little experience of dealing with foreigners, and was probably reassured to find an American banker who looked the way American bankers are supposed to look. True to standard Japanese methods, his present employers were more keen to know that he had worked for a leading New York investment bank than to ask how well he had done there, and they were pleased to know that he had attended a respectable East Coast university without feeling it necessary to go too closely into his grades. An added bonus was that Roberts came to them through a connection: he was introduced to them by an American employee who had known him in New York. A senior Japanese executive of the firm interviewed him in New York at 3:00 P.M. one day on a stopover during a business trip. At 5:00 P.M. the same day, he made Roberts a job offer. By 5:15 P.M., the two were drinking cocktails and discussing when he would move to Tokyo.

Two things must have come across clearly, however: Roberts's easy sense of humor and his straightforward approach to business. Proof of the latter was that soon after he arrived in Tokyo, the fledgling banker found a quick way to make money outside his job. He would book a Tokyo restaurant for a private party on a Friday evening, paying a deposit to guarantee that at least a certain fixed number of guests (perhaps a hundred or so) would come, and then agreeing to a sliding cost per head that fell as the number of guests rose. Then he would contact a dozen friends and offer them the chance to be "host" at the party, which would give them the right to a free ticket and to have their names printed on the invitation. He would typeset the invitations on an Apple Macintosh at work and run off a few hundred on the office photocopiers. The "hosts" would then offer the invitations to their friends, who would go to the party and pay at the door ¥5,000 ($35) a time. In the early days, before restaurants realized how easily he was able to find "guests" using this system, Roberts could easily make a couple of thousand dollars each time. Later on, however, things became more difficult: the restaurants demanded more exacting terms, and his friends bridled at the idea of making money for him by going to parties. Roberts never quite understood their hostility; after all, he used to say, they would have been quite happy to spend the same amount of money if the restaurant made all the profits. Why should they resent his enterprise?

Even if his friends did, his employers did not. Within weeks of starting work in Japan, Roberts was on a plane bound for the United States for his first major assignment. It was 1990, the American property boom was on its last hurrah, and the bank was intent on making as much money as it could until the last possible moment. Roberts and his new colleagues crisscrossed the United States, flying everywhere first class and staying in the best hotels. The job was straightforward. American banks would come to Roberts's firm, suggesting that it might like to try to find a client for such-and-such a hotel, golf course, or holiday resort complex. Roberts's colleagues would take a look at the figures presented by the American bankers. If they were satisfied that it seemed a good bet, the bank's M&A department would then find a client in Japan. Meanwhile, the bank's lending department would set to work to come up with the funding. It was an elegant and convenient package, from the customer's point of view.

Work back in the bank's head office in Tokyo was less glamorous. Used to the private offices and plentiful computers of American banking, Roberts was shocked to find himself in a cavernous room full of army-issue gray desks in orderly lines, with several employees sharing a single computer and no direct-dial incoming phone lines. He would arrive every morning at 8:30 A.M. for a breakfast of cold eggs, coffee, and toast in the company cafeteria. Like every other employee, he was expected to be at his desk at 8:50 A.M., when a bell chimed to open the working day. At 11:30 A.M., the department's general manager, or *bucho*, would get up from his desk and the rest of the department would know that that was the signal for them, too, to go and have lunch. All the banking work was done by men, but the office was also full of uniformed office ladies, trilling out phone conversations in their high voices and bringing the bitter green brew of Japanese tea that every office worker drinks to keep up his energy during the day.

No funds could be spared for Roberts to learn Japanese, although the bank was apparently happy for its best M&A merchants to spend their afternoons watching "Sesame Street" to learn English — so he worked entirely in his native tongue, even in meetings with Japanese clients. Every decision, no matter how small, had to be brought to the *bucho* so that he could stamp the documents with his ivory *hanko* to signify approval. Rules were strict: one day, Roberts came to the office in a natty Brooks Brothers bow tie. His colleagues eyed it anxiously all morning. When the boss appeared just before lunch after a morning of meetings outside the office, he summoned Roberts to his desk.

"What's that?" he asked.

"It's a bow tie," said Roberts, astonished that this piece of sanctioned corporate eccentricity, quite tolerable in New York, should provoke raised eyebrows in Tokyo.

"Save it for parties," said the boss bluntly, and sent him immediately down to the subterranean shopping arcade beneath the bank's head office to buy a black nylon tie of the kind bought by office workers summoned to a company funeral at short notice.

Although he was forced to obey the small rules, Roberts had privileges not extended to his Japanese colleagues. Most important was his salary: although Roberts did not benefit from the low interest loans that helped Japanese bankers to raise the $1 million or so necessary for a modest four-room house in the suburbs, he was paid twice as much as people older than he. (Even that salary was probably only half what an American investment banker working in Tokyo for an American firm would have earned, not to mention the allowance of $5,000 or so a month that an American firm would expect to have to pay to house its expatriates in Western-style apartments in the center of town.) Altogether, in fact, Roberts was outside the corporate hierarchy. The most important symbol of this was that every other male employee of the bank wore a lapel pin with the bank's logo on it. This pin is the ultimate symbol of belonging: new graduate employees usually receive it on their first day at work, and are given blood-curdling warnings of what will happen if it is lost. But Roberts, although he was given a set of business cards that identified him as a full-time employee of the bank, clearly was in a different class. He was never offered a lapel pin, and he never asked for one.[3]

At the time, interest rates in Japan were at a ten-year low. Property companies of doubtful creditworthiness were able to raise vast sums in Japan to buy assets in the continental United States or in Hawaii. Because it was so cheap to borrow, the income from the hotel or golf course in question bought did not have to cover very high interest bills, so the Japanese customer was usually willing to pay more than an American who had to pay 10 percent to get his money from Citibank and therefore demanded more than a 10 percent return from the asset in which he invested the money. For some big Japanese companies, money was not cheap, but free: they were able to issue "convertible bonds" denominated in foreign currency, which gave the holder a stream of interest payments like any other bond, but conferred an extra right to convert the bond into a share in the company at a certain specified price at a certain time. Because Japanese share prices were rising so fast in the late 1980s, buyers of these convertibles expected to make money so easily by converting them into shares that they were sometimes willing to accept even a zero rate of interest — so the Japanese firm had to pay nothing at all for its money, except the cost of hedging the currency risk.[4]

As the 1980s drew to their close, however, the huge amounts of money swilling around in Japan's financial system had begun to bid up the prices of all sorts of assets, from impressionist paintings to Californian hotels. Combined with fast-rising share prices in Tokyo, this made it easy for almost anyone to make money. For borrowers, the trick seemed just to be to get their hands on as much money as possible, and to be as ambitious as they dared: if they had second thoughts about a purchase, there would always be someone else — a "bigger fool," as the theory goes — to buy the hotel or golf course in question at a handsome premium above what they had paid for it. Decisions to buy began to be based increasingly more on guesses about the psychology of other buyers than on a sober estimate of the value of the asset.

The most extravagant example of these deals, argued Anthony Downs, a fellow of the Brookings Institution, in an analysis for Salomon Brothers that was reported in *The Economist,*

> is the Grand Hyatt Wailea Resort and Spa on Maui [in Hawaii]. Billed as the most luxurious hotel ever built, it sports a 2,000 ft-long network of pools, grottos and rapids, as well as what *Hospitality* magazine calls a "water elevator" that "raises and lowers swimmers using a system of canal-like locks." The hotel, which opened in September 1991, cost $600m to build, or more than $700,000 per room. Mr Downs recks its managers need to charge $700 per room and achieve a 75% occupancy rate for the hotel to break even. Since this is, he says, "impossible in any hotel on earth," the owners face a huge loss.[5]

Roberts found that his new colleagues at the bank were no exception to the herd, even when they were giving a big client supposedly expert advice on what to buy and what prices to pay. Too often, they would accept without question the financial projections made by the American bank representing the seller — projections that were usually cast so as to be as optimistic as possible while just on the right side of the line dividing truth from falsehood. Bankers used to refer to the charts they would present as "hockey sticks": even if there had been a slight dip in business in the past year or two, the predictions for the future would show handsome growth and profit in a straight line as far as the eye could see. Most American buyers would take such charts with a grain of salt; in Japan, by contrast, an intermediary acting for a seller would consider it compromising to his own good name to present a more optimistic picture than he really believed to be the case.

Roberts found to his surprise that his new colleagues at the bank actually appeared to believe the numbers they had been given by their American counterparts.

That was all very well when the market was going up. But as the year 1990 drew on, something began to change. The speed with which prices of U.S. properties were rising began to slow down. Then prices stopped rising. Then they began to fall. From then on, the game was to be played by different rules. The bank began to take a second look at many of its biggest clients, wondering whether it could be sure of getting back the money it had lent them. Roberts suddenly found that the valuation techniques he had learned in New York but found unnecessary during his first few months in Tokyo were back in demand. He was asked to build up a financial model for calculating the worth of real estate assets, and to run through it many of the properties bought by the bank's clients. The results were frightening. Many of the bank's clients, huge property empires though they were, turned out to be insolvent. It was quite clear that they would be unable to continue paying even the interest on their debts, let alone the capital.

Had the banks' own business been continuing satisfactorily, all might have been well. But the Tokyo stock market, too, had begun to fall. The Nikkei share index reached a peak in 1990 of 38,713 points. By December it had fallen back to under 22,000. And as the next decade began to unfold, the drop continued. In 1991 share prices were over 40 percent less than they had been at the peak; in April 1992 the index was below 16,600, which meant that the average share on the first section of the world's biggest stock exchange was worth 57 percent less than it had been worth little over two years before. The value wiped off the paper value of Japan's stock exchange was nearly five times 1991 estimates of the cost of bailing out the United States' savings and loans, and almost three times the total value of outstanding Third World debt.[6] The irony was that only five years earlier, the Japanese had shrugged off the "Black Monday" of October 1987 that hit stock markets elsewhere in the world. As Tokyo share prices continued to chug steadily skyward, investors and analysts had begun to believe all the old nostrums about Japan being unique and Japanese shares being unsusceptible to Western methods of analysis. By 1992 Tokyo's fall had been twice as great as that of the Western markets that had suffered in 1987.

In the past, investors had always believed that the bureaucrats at the Ministry of Finance could prevent the market from falling too far. More than two thirds of all Japanese shares were off the market in the safe hands of institutions, people believed. The government and the Big Four stockbrokers were able to produce dramatic rises in share prices almost at will. Yet although the ministry pulled out all the stops to save the market — driving share prices up by over 7 percent on a single day in autumn 1990, relaxing the "margin requirements" in 1991,[7] forcing brokers to publish their arbitrage positions in 1992, and many other administrative changes designed to ease share prices back to their former levels — it proved unable to defy the gravity pulling Japanese shares back to earth. To make things worse, a conservative governor at the Bank of Japan, Yasushi Mieno, was cranking up interest rates. At a dramatic speech at the Foreign Correspondents' Club in Tokyo in autumn 1990, he declared himself willing to see a fall of 20 percent in property prices — thus puncturing with a few words the myth that had been almost universal before, that land prices in Japan could only go upward.

In any industrial country, banks suffer when share prices fall. But in Japan, the position was rather special. Whereas banks in the United States and Europe had been forced by their regulators in the 1980s to make large write-offs in their accounts to cover the cost of bad debts, Japanese banks had not. This was not because they had avoided lending money to unreliable people; on the contrary, many Japanese banks had been as carefree as the next bank in lending to Third World debtors and to American managers organizing LBOs. Rather, it was because the Japanese authorities knew that Japanese banks had massive portfolios of shares that had been bought decades earlier and were still marked in their accounts at what had been paid for them — far, far less than what they were really worth. This, Japanese bankers had always argued, was their equivalent of the provisions for loan losses that Western banks had been forced to make. There was a crucial difference, of course: in Japan, there was no need to admit the embarrassment of bad debts. While Western banks were cutting dividends and declaring losses, Japanese banks could continue to declare profits, quietly confident that money lost to bad debtors could never submerge the huge pile of cash they had in the form of unrealized share profits.

Until the end of the 1980s, this strategy seemed to be proof that Japanese banks had a long-term view to put competitors to shame. The very reason that they had such huge share portfolios was because of the tradition that a bank in Japan takes a substantial stake in its biggest customers (and sometimes vice versa). In return, the customer agrees to treat the bank as its "main" bank, giving it not only the accounts of its employees,[8] but also first refusal on most financial transactions the firm does. Together, the banks and their customers had benefited from the growth of the Japanese economy; and sitting comfortably on the cushion of those hidden shares, the banks seemed smugly immune to the problems that had beset competitors abroad.

As the stock market fell, however, things started to unravel. When there were few bad debtors, the unrealized share profits were merely a bonus. But in 1990, the banks needed badly to point to those hidden profits kept in reserve to fight off demands that they make provisions against bad debts. When Tokyo share prices started falling back to earth, things suddenly began to look worrying. The crucial measure of a bank's financial health is the ratio between its own capital and the "assets" that it has lent out to customers. (This is because if too many debts go bad, the only way that people who have lent their savings to the bank will get them back is from the shareholders' funds.) With those unrealized share profits melting away, the banks' underlying capital base was beginning to shrink — and their portfolio of doubtful loans to Japanese market speculators and to the owners of Hawaiian golf clubs and Manhattan skyscrapers suddenly began to look recklessly overleveraged.

To make things worse, at the very same time as the market was falling, the banks were trying to knock their balance sheets into shape so that they would meet a new set of international standards on capital adequacy set by the Bank for International Settlements in Basel. To establish rules for fair competition among banks from different countries, the BIS had ruled that by March 1993 all banks wanting to do business abroad must have capital equivalent to 8 percent of their assets. When agreement was reached on the 8 percent, the capital ratio of the big Japanese banks averaged less than 4 percent. So they agreed to a makeshift plan: an agreed proportion of their unrealized share profits would be counted as capital. As the Nikkei index fell, the banks felt themselves sinking closer and closer to the BIS line. They were in a fix: with share prices so low, it was out of the question for them to issue new shares themselves.[9] The only way to get even close to meeting the BIS requirements was to scale back their lending sharply. In other days, the banks might have been tolerant toward customers who had borrowed to invest unwisely, and given them a few years' grace for the investments to recover. Not now; the banks' priority was to get their money back intact, no matter what the price to their customers.

So began a second phase of Roberts's job. Abandoning the zeal with which it had pressed deals on customers the year before, the M&A department of the bank found itself forced to take control of the biggest of its problem clients. In the United States or Europe, the clients would simply have declared themselves unable to pay their debts and filed for protection from their creditors. In Japan, the system was much less open. The very last thing a bank wanted was for one of its customers to go publicly and humiliatingly bankrupt. That would damage the bank's reputation and its credit standing, by making it clear to the entire world that it was unlikely to get back all the money it had lent. So the bank would send over a couple of its crack M&A people to the troubled client. After a cup of tea and the ritual exchanging of business cards with the client's employees, the Japanese M&A man would turn to Roberts so that the real business could begin. In the blunt way that seemed to him natural, Roberts would ask for all the paperwork concerning the transaction: title deeds, contracts, legal opinions, accountants' reports, everything. The property firm's flabbergasted managers would hesitate but in the end know that they had no choice. Within ten minutes, a pile of papers was on the coffee table, and the bankers were ready to leave. A week later, they would be back. This time, however, there would be a team of a dozen bankers, and they would come equipped with specially printed business cards identifying them as employees of the client firm rather than their own. Their job would be to take over the running of the business — and to supervise, if necessary, an orderly liquidation of its assets. To make the best of a bad job, the bank's staff could always telephone their opposite numbers in the client company and blame everything on the troublesome American.

What they asked of Roberts was clear: to do a cool-headed valuation of the assets of the most problematic client, and to identify those abroad that could be sold off as near as possible to their purchase price. (Not one deal could be sold at a profit; in one case, however, the bank forced the firm to offload an asset bought ten years earlier for a price a few percentage points above the purchase price. Bizarrely, the Japanese press dutifully reported the sale as a good deal without stopping to realize that when interest payments were added in, the firm had in fact made a hefty loss.) When he delved into the paperwork, Roberts found that hundreds of millions of dollars' worth of property had been bought in the United States on the strength only of the analysis done by the buyers' advisers. Only when he did his own study was he able to get an idea of what they were worth.

One thing was unmistakable: the bank was faced with an

unpleasant conflict of interest. It had an obligation to its client as the firm's "main" bank. It was the bank that had suggested a program of wild overseas expansion, the bank that had come up with the specific deals that had been done, the bank that had lent the money to finance them. Yet in a typical transaction, the bank would have supplied only 60 percent of the money needed to buy the resort hotel or golf club in question, the rest coming from the firm's own reserves or from elsewhere. When the crunch came, and the bank lost faith in its client's ability to continue to pay interest on the debt, the bank had only one objective: to make sure that it got its 60 percent back, whatever the consequences. If that meant forcing the firm to sell off its best assets at fire sale prices, so be it: the bank must come first. The bank would force its customer to sell off an asset it had bought only a year or two earlier for a price 20 percent or 30 percent lower. The bank would get its money back with interest, but the customer would lose three-quarters of the 40 percent of the price that it had put up itself. The long-term vision that Japanese banks were wont to boast of now seemed like a cruel joke. "How long is long term?" asked an advertisement put out in 1991 by the Long-Term Credit Bank, one of the firm's competitors. How long indeed?

Inside the M&A department, chaos reigned. Every few weeks, it seemed, the seating arrangement was changed and the department reorganized. One general manager left quietly and was replaced by another. The staff in the lending department who had agreed to provide the funds for all those disastrous acquisitions were moved into different jobs in the bank. The M&A department was told that a travel moratorium had been imposed from on high, limiting all trips abroad to a week — but with an elegant ability to obey the rules in defiance of all logic or real attention to the firm's interests, Roberts and his colleagues continued to take the two-week trips to the United States they had planned by the simple device of splitting them into two, and flying back across the Pacific for a day or two in the office in Tokyo in between.

In early 1991 Japanese banks succeeded in keeping the extent of the disaster secret. But as the year wore on, the losses became just too big to hide. In the course of the 1980s, Japanese banks had increased the sums they lent abroad by an average of 25 percent a year. In an attempt to win market share among foreign customers, they had accepted lending spreads (the difference between the interest rate paid out to depositors and that received from borrowers) only a fraction of their spreads at home. They had lent anything up to $40 billion to finance LBOs in the United States. They had made more than 12 percent of all the outstanding property loans in Britain. They were among the leading lenders to Olympia and York, the doomed Canadian builder of London's massive Canary Wharf development. And they had financed the wildest excesses of the Tokyo, Kyoto, and Osaka property booms, only to see prices slip by a third and so few deals being done that it was actually impossible to know exactly where prices stood. According to the *Nihon Keizai* newspaper, some 70 percent of all the country's property companies had stopped paying interest on their debts. No wonder foreign banking analysts in Tokyo estimated that at the end of 1991, fully 10 percent of all the outstanding loans of Japanese banks — some ¥60 trillion, or $473 billion — had gone bad. Nor that the Japanese industry itself began, with macabre humor, to talk of the problem as a case of AIDS, an acronym for Azabu Building, Itoman, Dai-Ichi, and Shuwa, the names of four of the most prominent billion-dollar real estate empires to collapse as property prices fell. The only mitigating factor was that the mandarins of the Ministry of Finance had managed to prevent a wholesale collapse of the financial system. One small bank, an Osaka credit union called Toyo Shinkin, had to be rescued by the Industrial Bank of Japan with the help of the Deposit Insurance Corporation. And two small regional banks, Iyo Bank and Toho Sogo Bank, were merged.

In the course of the collapse, a surprising thing had happened: the country that had appeared poised to buy up the rest of the world suddenly became an importer of capital. For the first time in eleven years, Japan had a net capital inflow, of almost $37 billion. But the banks were too preoccupied with their own problems to see such wider issues. Ten years earlier, they had been small and conservative. As the 1990s dawned, Japanese banks occupied nine of the ten slots in the rankings of the world's biggest. But what good had it done them? Their foreign business was making little money. They had been badly stung at home in Japan. And their balance sheets were in tatters. In 1992 Christopher Roberts went back to the United States to go to business school, a wiser and slightly sadder banker than when he had arrived.

Puneet Chadha was at his desk in the Tokyo head office of Nomura Securities on June 24, 1991, when he heard the news — or rather, when he *saw* the news.[10] For the world's biggest securities company did not think it necessary to warn its employees beforehand of the resignation of its president, Yoshihisa Tabuchi. Most of them found out about it from the Quick machines on their desks — the computer terminals that deliver up-to-date share prices and snippets of financial news. "Luckily, it was 8:15 A.M. on a Monday morning," said Chadha, "and because most of my clients are in a different time zone, they hadn't started to call. So I had a little time to think about it." But for some of the firm's salesmen, the news came while they were on the telephone, trying to push shares to their customers.

To many people in the stockbrokerage business in Japan, the day Yoshihisa Tabuchi resigned as Nomura's president is a day they will remember all their lives — just as their parents remember the day President Kennedy was assassinated. Nomura was the world's most powerful securities firm, they believed: the firm whose influence rivals that of the Japanese Ministry of Finance; the firm that grew from a small money-changing shop in the back streets of Osaka in 1872 to a business that made more money in the boom year of 1987 than Nissan and Toyota, the country's two biggest car makers, put together. To have the head of that firm brought down by scandal was a profound shock to the entire Japanese financial establishment. Inside the firm, however, the shock was all the greater. So great was the blow to the company's prestige that it would be no exaggeration to say that the events of that week brought about the fall of the House of Nomura.

Tabuchi was unseated by the unhappy coincidence of two different scandals. One was that his firm was shown to have done business with organized crime. The other was that it was shown to have made huge under-the-table paybacks to compensate some of its biggest clients for losses they took in the stock market — and to have tried to disguise some of those payments as entertainment expenses.

Nominally illegal, organized crime is more open in Japan than in any other of the world's industrial countries. Every year, the Japanese police publish solemn statistics showing the number of members they think the Japanese crime syndicates have (more than 100,000), and giving a ludicrously precise breakdown, down to tenths of a percentage point, of where they think organized crime makes its billions of dollars of income every year: prostitution, illegal gambling, drug sales, and so on. Organized crime *à la japonaise* has a few curious peculiarities. One is that it is extraordinarily open. There are entire magazines devoted to the doings of the *yakuza*, or gangsters. Television stations broadcast long and serious interviews with the heads of crime syndicates, in which the criminals profess with perfectly straight faces to be performing a useful function in Japanese society by keeping undesirables off the streets and by keeping the country a peaceful place. (Swords are preferred to guns for most business; protection rackets are so commonplace and patches sewn up so thoroughly that only on the rarest occasions does gang violence erupt onto the streets.) Another is that the syndicates like to see themselves as the inheritors of the samurai tradition: they are rigidly hierarchical organizations, and they install new leaders in elaborate Shinto ceremonies with sake, sacred fish, rice, and the rest of the religious trappings. Finally, they perform a useful but ruthless function in the business world: they help the rich and powerful to overcome the weak without having to do so in public. Hence big companies pay heavy bribes to *sokaiya*, or "AGM-men," in return for the useful service of refraining from asking embarrassing questions in front of the shareholders at the firm's annual general meeting, and promising to drown out any bona fide shareholder who dares to stand up with a hostile question.[11] *Jiyageya* are a slightly different breed: they are gangsters who facilitate the consolidation of large plots of urban land for redevelopment, by terrorizing little old ladies who exercise their legal right to stay in their homes rather than accept a developer's offer to rehouse them elsewhere.

Although few Japanese are unaware of how far the tentacles of organized crime extend, and even fewer think that big business has nothing to do with big crime, Japanese firms had until 1991 been completely successful in preserving the façade that they had nothing to do with gangsters. What was so shocking about the Nomura case was that it tore this façade away, exposing to the eyes of the world the degree to which the two were linked. For in 1989, Nomura had lent ¥36 billion ($254.2 million) to Susumu Ishii, the head of the 8,000-strong Inagawa-kai syndicate, in a series of thinly disguised paper transactions. It had bankrolled the gangster, helping him to acquire on margin 2 percent of all the outstanding shares of the Tokyu railway company, one of Japan's leading private railway operators. In the space of a few weeks, between late October and early November 1989, Tokyu's share price rose from ¥2,000 to ¥3,060. Using the strong-arm tactics of his trade, Ishii tried to get the management of Tokyu to buy back the shares from him at a heavy premium to the market price. While he was doing that, Nomura itself was speculating heavily in Tokyu stock. In the period during which Tokyu's share price ran up so fast, Nomura accounted for almost 30 percent of all the deals done in its shares. To see how shocking this was, one would have to imagine Merrill Lynch in the United States conspiring with the Mafia to greenmail American Airlines, or in Britain James Capel participating in a similar conspiracy against the Virgin group.

Shocking though it was, that scandal was actually a mere canapé, a morsel to whet the appetite, that had been discovered by inspectors from the national tax administration of the Japanese Ministry of Finance while they were in search of a far more serious story. Late in 1990, the tax inspectors had become embroiled in a bitter dispute with several brokerage firms about the tax treatment of certain entertainment expenses. In his previous job, the head of the national tax administration had been in charge of the ministry's Securities bureau and therefore in charge of supervising the brokers. So he knew the industry well; and either information he had picked up in his previous job, or simply a feel for the way brokerage firms work, made him suspicious about what the brokers were up to.

What eventually emerged was greater than any of the investigators had imagined — and also far more serious than the gangster connection. For bad though it was for a securities firm to have had dealings with a crime organization, such an incident could be excused as an aberration. In any case, it was not clear that any laws had been broken. Nomura had certainly breached ministry guidelines by being responsible for such a large proportion of dealings in the Tokyu shares in late 1989, but that could be explained away as a minor transgression of a relatively obscure securities law. On delving into what looked like entertainment expenses, however, the tax inspectors discovered that they were dummy bills to fill a space in the company accounts left by secret payoffs from the broker to some of its biggest customers. Those payoffs, executed from late 1990 onward, had been made in order to compensate some of Japan's biggest institutional investors for the money they lost as the Tokyo stock market dived from its peak.

Perhaps surprisingly, there is nothing in the country's securities and exchange law that makes it specifically illegal to compensate a client who loses money in the market. In most of the stock markets in the world's developed countries, mere prudence, rather than government legislation, is enough to prevent such guarantees from being made. Everyone knows that share prices can go up as well as down. It is clearly impossible for a broker to guarantee every one of his clients that he will make good any losses, while allowing the client to keep the profits. So no sensible broker would do it. He is an intermediary, perhaps an adviser, but he is not in the business of making gravity-defying promises that things will go only one way.

Yet this, astonishingly, is exactly what Nomura was promising some of its biggest clients. By necessity, it could only make such promises to a few highly favored clients, and the promises had to be kept secret. This policy was based on two assumptions. One was that if a few of the shares that the brokerage recommended fell unexpectedly in value, the brokerage could always use its powers as a discretionary manager of many of its clients' investments to transfer the shares retrospectively into the account of a less popular customer, who would then take the losses. The other assumption made by Nomura was that the market overall would continue to rise. The less-favored clients would still make a tolerable return, even after having dud shares dumped into their portfolios at above-market prices.

The first of these assumptions was right: so lax were many investors that Nomura was able with impunity to get away with this manipulation. The second, however, proved to be disastrously wrong. Not only did the market fail to rise, it actually fell, and fell so far that the losses could no longer be switched discreetly from one account to another. The brokerage had made its promises; it had to stick to them. Hence its attempts to pass off some 70 percent of the compensation paid as either entertainment expenses or its own trading losses.

As Japanese newspapers and weekly magazines uncovered further revelations, it became increasingly clear that Nomura Securities and Nikko Securities — Japan's third-biggest stockbroker, whose president also resigned — were not the only houses involved. At least one Japanese bank lent money to finance the gangsters' share shenanigans. And the other two of the so-called Big Four brokers, Daiwa, and Yamaichi Securities, were as deeply implicated in the loss compensations as Nomura.

In the early days of the scandal, the spotlight was focused on the securities firms themselves, the ¥67 billion ($517 million) that they were thought to have spent to cheer up their clients, and the all-important question of whether they had paid the compensation voluntarily, which would be unwise but legal, or whether they had actually given key customers formal written undertakings in advance that they would only profit from their investments. As market leader, Nomura had to take the most pressure. Even after announcing that they would resign, Tabuchi and his counterpart at Nikko were hauled before Ryutaro Hashimoto, the finance minister, for a ritual dressing-down. And the Nomura chairman, who had passed on the executive duties of the company's presidency five years earlier, was forced to give up the job of chairman of the Japan Securities Dealers' Association that was to be his due the following month. He also had to resign his vice chairmanship of Keidanren, the country's most powerful business organization. Nomura, and the other companies involved, made a public show of "disciplining" those of their employees who had been involved.

But soon, more searching questions began to be asked. The public began to wonder just how carefully the Finance Ministry was supervising the securities industry, if it was only a surprise tax audit that had unearthed the massive payments and the brokers' earlier attempts to push the losses onto other clients by switching falling shares from account to account. Why had the regulators directly responsible for the brokers failed to notice? And why, if it was illegal to make formal written promises to compensate clients for losses, had the brokers been operating managed stock market funds in which they promised minimum rates of return, rain or shine? Such guaranteed rates of return may not have been explicit undertakings to cover losses, but that was exactly what they were.

And so attention began to move toward the Finance Ministry itself, whose securities regulators seemed to be far less keen than the tax inspectors to investigate the ever widening scandals. Its first response was to impose only token penalties on the errant brokers: they were told to close down their head offices to corporate business for four days — a measure described by analysts as "nothing more than a slap on the hand" — and fined a total of ¥16 million, or $122,000. Later, however, it emerged that one of the institutional investors to have received compensation from Nomura was the Pension Welfare Service Public Corporation, a public pension fund affiliated with the Ministry of Health. And brokers began to whisper that the Finance Ministry had actually known all along about loss compensation.

Hashimoto, whose matinee-idol looks and ability to raise money for the Liberal Democratic Party had made him popular both with the public and with political insiders, tried to defuse the crisis by announcing that he would "take responsibility" for the crisis by returning a tenth of his salary for three months to the government's coffers. As the summer wore on, however, it became clear that window-dressing would not be enough. In the autumn, the government was forced to introduce changes to the securities and exchange law that made it illegal to pay, rather than merely to promise, loss compensation. And on October 14, Hashimoto flew back to Tokyo from Bangkok, where he had attended his last meeting of the Group of Seven industrial nations, and resigned.

At the time the scandals were breaking, the financial community was obsessed by a single question: how much would the age-old practices of the Tokyo market be forced to change? "This is a clear signal," argued Al Alletzhauser, author of a best-selling book on Nomura Securities which earned him a libel suit from the company at the High Court in London. "It's the end of the stranglehold of the Big Four. It's the end of their domination of markets in stocks, bonds, and underwriting." The revelations, Alletzhauser insisted, were merely evidence of a trend that had already begun. Tokyo insiders were more cynical. "Just wait," a Nomura broker told me as he sipped a predinner glass of tomato juice in the bar of the marble-clad new building that houses Nomura's head office in Tokyo. "The brokers will lie low for six months, but then we'll be back. I took some clients out last night, and they didn't even mention the scandal."

The question at issue here, however, is a rather different one. Whatever long-term effects the scandals will have for the future of the Japanese stock market — and a year later, it remains hard to predict — they show something important about the way Japanese securities firms operate. They are, at least in part, prisoners of their own histories.

Nomura Securities was started in 1925 by Tokushichi Nomura, the son of an Osaka moneychanger who in later life became a drunkard. From an early age, the younger Nomura was fascinated by the fledgling stock market that had sprung up as if from nowhere in Japan's second-biggest city. But his first attempts at speculation were disastrous. On one occasion, according to Alletzhauser's book *The House of Nomura*,[12] he bought shares with ¥500 (equivalent to thousands of dollars in those days) borrowed without permission from his father's safe — and lost it all. On another, he persuaded one of his father's customers to invest in shares whose price began to fall almost as soon as they had been bought. Once again, his father was forced to cover the losses.

In 1904, however, Nomura's luck began to turn. In a triumph of hope over experience, his father lent him the astronomical sum of ¥20,000 to start up his own brokerage, and the twenty-six-year-old financier made his first fortune the following year, using a method that was similar to what the great Wall Street manipulators were doing thousands of miles away in New York at the same time. Nomura started looking at a firm called Fukushima Boseki, and came to the conclusion that its business prospects were better than everyone else thought. He started discreetly buying shares. As he bought more and more, it began to dawn on Nomura that because the market was almost unregulated, many of the people who had contracted to sell him shares were selling shares they did not actually own and were hoping to buy the necessary shares at a much lower price before they were forced to deliver the certificates.

What Nomura executed was a classic stock market maneuver that has become known as a "corner." Quietly, he bought up so many of the shares that there were not enough shares left on the open market for the "short sellers" (those who were promising to sell shares they did not yet own) to cover their positions. Nomura drove the price of Fukushima shares higher and higher, in the full knowledge that when the time for settlement came, the short sellers would have to buy back from him in the marketplace the shares they had already sold. In the end, Fukushima's share price quadrupled, and Nomura doubled his father's money.

He went on to do the same again barely two years later, Alletzhauser records, making money from the 1906 bull market that followed Japan's war victory over Russia, and then making money again by selling short just before the crash of 1907 that drove many of his competitors into bankruptcy. That made him one of the richest men in Japan. By the time World War II came, Nomura had begun to build his own industrial conglomerate, with rubber plantations in Borneo, a bank, and Nomura Securities itself, which had expanded to Tokyo in 1930, five years after its establishment. He had also acquired political respectability, as a member of the House of Peers (the upper house of the Japanese parliament). The occupying American forces who came to Japan after the war saw Nomura as a prime target. His empire was dismantled; yet even though the securities firm that was left had only a fraction of the group's prewar glory, it was still the seed of a business that is now the world's biggest brokerage.

Nomura himself and those who led his firm after his death had one thing in common: not merely skill, but also ruthlessness. Early on in the war, he had known from the information coming from his researchers that Japan would lose; accordingly, he continued to mouth patriotic sentiments but sold shares very discreetly. Later, he prepared to buy for the recovery afterward. During the occupation, one of the firm's employees was arrested on suspicion of carrying out an elaborate scam involving buying and selling shares to take advantage of the new currency that had been issued during the months of collapse immediately after Japan's defeat. But the scheme was too complicated for the investigators to understand — and the loyal Nomura employee, by refusing to cooperate even under police pressure, kept the firm in the clear.

It is Nomura's phenomenal skill at handling the small investor, however, that has been the foundation of its great success since the war. In 1953 the firm hit on the brilliant marketing device of lending wooden savings boxes to housewives. It asked them to put ten-yen coins into the box. As soon as the box was half full, the customer would call a Nomura employee, who would open it up and deposit the total in one of the company's investment trusts.

This was no soft sell, either. From the 1960s to the present, Nomura salesmen have been expected to sweat for the salaries that make them the highest-paid stockbrokers in Japan. They visit customers from door to door and spend hours on the telephone every day trying to meet the firm's demanding sales targets. Stories are rife of salesmen being told to spend their entire day in the office standing up, or being dressed down in public by their bosses if they fail to meet their targets.

Many of Nomura's most skillful sales experts are in fact women. Since it is women who control the family finances in Japan — men usually hand over their entire salary, and receive pocket money in return, while their wives are responsible for investing the money, paying for the education of their children, and keeping something in reserve for a rainy day — it makes sense to use women to gain their trust. Go into any of the Nomura share shops in Japan today, and you are more likely to see a woman behind the desk than a man. Such thinking is rather advanced for an industrial country where sex discrimination is the rule rather than the exception.

It was only in 1965, however, that the firm rose to the top of its field. The occasion was a slump in the second section of the Tokyo stock market, which had only a few years earlier been an ill-regulated group of shares traded over the counter. Old traditions died hard: in 1965 little reliable information was available on the firms, and the brokers who dealt in them were able to move prices with worrying speed by the simple device of spreading rumors.

Yamaichi Securities, Nomura's great rival since the war, had dominated the market. When prices began to decline, however, the firm ran into financial difficulties. In 1965 a regulator at the Bank of Japan worked out that Nomura's net worth was ¥17.1 billion, compared with ¥9 billion for Nikko, ¥2.6 billion for Daiwa, and minus ¥18.2 billion for Yamaichi. The government was later forced to mount a rescue operation, in which the presidents of the three other firms were forced out of office. Only Nomura's president survived. "Before the crisis," writes Alletzhauser, "it was common for Tsunao Okumura and Minoru Segawa to pay courtesy calls to Yamaichi's office during the course of the year. From 1965 onwards, it became customary for the Yamaichi president to call on Nomura."

With hundreds of branches, thousands of salesmen, and millions of customers, Nomura was able to move the market regularly by the 1980s. More of its income came from brokering — simply from buying and selling stocks for a commission — than from the other more complex operations that British and American houses had learned, such as underwriting, program trading, or arbitrage between the market index and the shares that underlie it.

Yet with the firm's tremendous market power came a temptation. If it was clear that a share Nomura recommended to its retail customers was likely to go up when they piled into it, an astute investor could make money by buying the share before it was recommended and selling it soon afterward. In 1991 the firm had two "shares of the week" that it recommended to its small investors. Which they were to be was decided at a Tuesday meeting on the sixth or seventh floor of the Nomura offices in the Urbannet building in Otemachi. Sitting around a table in what must be some of the world's most expensive office space, twenty or so dealers from inside Nomura would listen to presentations on the stock market while they ate a *bento* box lunch. After lunch they would carry the gospel out to the branches. "Without fail, these stocks open in the afternoon session much higher than they closed in the morning," recalled one Nomura employee. "I've often been able to pinpoint the stocks beforehand. Once in a while, sell orders come in during the course of the afternoon from people who have bought them a couple of days beforehand."

In the great bull market of the 1980s, none of this mattered. Small investors were doing so well themselves in the rising market that only envy or greed could make them complain if a few big institutions and other privileged people were getting tips a few hours before they were. And the Ministry of Finance, which under Japanese law has wide discretionary powers over brokerage firms, turned a blind eye to some of the abuses. In a sense, the ministry had made a pact with the devil. In return for the right to call in brokers in times of crisis and order them to buy shares to keep the market on an even keel, the ministry had left the brokerage industry largely to regulate itself.

It was not only the brokers who had been caught misbehaving. While some banks simply swallowed their losses as share and land prices plunged, others resorted to covert illegality in an attempt to save their reputations. In October 1990 the country's most aggressively expansionist city bank, Sumitomo, lost three of its top executives after the $6.79 billion collapse of the Itoman property empire. They resigned to take responsibility not only for the monumentally bad decision to back Itoman, but also for a tax evasion scandal that hit the firm at the same time. In July 1991 employees at three more banks were found to have helped property companies stave off bankruptcy by issuing false certificates showing that they had handsome sums on deposit — which the firms then promptly used to raise still more money from other lenders. In August

1991 a sixty-one-year-old Osaka restaurateur was found to have played a similar game with certificates falsely suggesting that she had ¥342 billion ($2.52 billion) on deposit with the Toyo Shinkin credit cooperative, which were used as collateral for more loans elsewhere. (It did not seem to have occurred to many of the blue-chip bankers to whom she went for money that if the certificates were genuine, she would be single-handedly the holder of 90 percent of the bank's entire deposit base.) The restaurateur, named Nui Onoue, had the most bizarre story of all. She had borrowed ¥300 million ($2.3 billion) from the Industrial Bank of Japan, one of the country's most respectable financial institutions, and used it to play the stock markets. She told the consortium of investors whom she advised that she chose shares by reflecting on the curriculum vitae of the company's president and by receiving midnight advice from a spirit. (In later testimony, she admitted that the spirit had in fact been a middle manager at the local branch of Yamaichi Securities.)

One of the many presidents forced to resign that summer made an elaborate public apology in which he said that his bank, and perhaps the entire financial community, had been too mercenary in its pursuit of profit. They had failed in their social duty, he suggested.

Sadly, the truth was more prosaic. Had the banks and brokerages truly been profit-seeking, they would never have done half of the dishonest and reckless things they did. They would never have lent money to people who appeared unlikely to be able to pay it back. They would never have given absurd promises to investors that their portfolios would only go up, not go down. They would never have forged documents, told lies, and attempted to mislead the investigators who were trying to find out what they had been up to. On the contrary, it became increasingly clear that what had happened in Japan's financial sector in the second half of the 1980s was a sort of collective madness in which investors forgot the most basic rules of prudence, and banks and brokers fought blindly for market share without thinking about profits. In the end, they got their reward: both banks and securities firms declared heavy losses in the financial year that ended in March 1992, and prepared for a long period of restructuring and retrenchment before they could even begin to think again about expansion.

Brokers and pundits in Tokyo can safely be left to argue whether the Japanese financial system will now really change, or whether things will simply carry on after a discreet pause as they always have. The signs are mixed. On the one hand, the country's Fair Trade Commission has made the first serious attack on the *keiretsu* system of cross-shareholdings by demanding that Nomura Securities dismantle an elaborate series of contracts by which it managed to park most of the shares of one of its former subsidiaries in safe hands. This has led to speculation that the combined weight of falling share prices, outside pressure, and closer bureaucratic supervision may bring an end to the *keiretsu*. On the other, there was the unforgettable scene when Setsuya Tabuchi, the disgraced former chairman of Nomura, came up before a parliamentary committee investigating the scandals. He appeared with all due contrition — bowing low, speaking in a subdued voice, addressing his questioners as *Sensei*, or teacher. But his confidence began to grow as he told the story of his firm's contacts with organized crime. And when he was asked to name the man who had introduced him to the gangster Ishii, he looked up with a faint smile on his face.

"I knew the name yesterday," he said to his questioners, "but I'm afraid I've forgotten it today." The statement produced howls of laughter from the reporters watching the hearing. For it was an echo of a statement made a decade earlier by Kakuei Tanaka, the great manipulator of 1970s Japanese politics, when accused of receiving hundreds of thousands of dollars in bribes from the Lockheed Corporation while serving as prime minister. With an exquisite politeness that made it clear that he knew very well the answer to an embarrassing question but had no intention of giving the answer, he replied, *"Kiyoku ni gozaimasen"* ("I'm afraid I've forgotten").

To the pessimists, Tabuchi's confident quotation from Tanaka summed up the danger that nothing in Japanese finance will ever change.

Whatever else they show, these tales from the banking and brokering industries make one thing clear. There is not a single respect in which the Japanese financial sector can claim to be fundamentally more efficient than its Western competitors.

The overseas expansion of the Japanese banks was fueled primarily by a single regulatory wrinkle: until the end of the 1980s, Japanese law prevented banks from fighting for depositors by offering competitive interest rates. Instead, deposit rates were fixed far below market rates. Banks were able to dip into the vast pool of the savings of some 120 million of the world's thriftiest people, to pay measly interest rates on deposits, and then to lend out those same deposits abroad at rates that could easily undercut the Western competition. According to one analyst, this system of regulation gave Japanese banks a massive subsidy over its life: $382 billion more in profits than they would have gained under the American or British systems.

Starting in 1986, however, the Japanese authorities began to deregulate interest rates. Starting with very large deposits fixed for long periods of time, they began to allow the market to set interest rates for depositors. Little by little, the deposit necessary to attract a market rate shrank, and the period of time for which it had to be left in the bank shortened. By 1992 the process was almost complete; more than two-thirds of all the deposits of Japanese city banks were receiving market rates. Thus disappeared the single trump card held by Japanese finance.

What is left? The answer is, not a great deal: banks whose overseas profitability was dependent on a closed domestic market, and whose internal controls have been demonstrated to be lax to the point of incompetence; brokers who make their money by market manipulation and by control of a large distribution system in their home base. At the moment, neither the banks nor the brokers can compete with their Western counterparts in any of the brainier corners of the business. Those years of regulation, in which the government assiduously excluded foreign competition from the market in order to build up the strength of the Japanese financial sector, appear to have had depressingly little reward.

Over the coming five years, both sectors face tremendous uncertainty. The artificial wall between banking and brokering which the occupying Americans built — known as Article 68 in Japan, and as Glass-Steagall, or the 1933 Banking Act, in the United States — is thought to be on its way down. The fixed commissions that make Tokyo the only large market where brokers can make money just from brokering, without having to do anything else, are unlikely to remain intact past the end of the century. Meanwhile, both groups of firms will have to rebuild their balance sheets and work out how they can catch up with their Western counterparts.

In the long run, of course, they may still succeed. Thorsten Düsser, a German investment banker who has written his doctoral dissertation on the Japanese banks' strategy in Europe, believes that even after the events of 1991, Japan's financial sector may still pose a competitive threat to Europe. They have size on their side, he argues, which cannot hurt. They have a loyal Japanese work force, willing to work abroad for half the salaries or less of comparably qualified Europeans or Americans. And they have an uncanny ability to pick themselves up after being knocked down. They have a determination to succeed.

The way in which Christopher Roberts's employers used him — hiring him from New York, sucking dry his knowledge of property finance, and then allowing him to leave — is paradoxically rather promising. It shows that at least one bank is flexible enough to realize its own failings and humble enough to learn from outside how to cure them.

To find a proven Japanese business success, however, the onlooker has to turn to an industry that can claim some more concrete qualities than determination or humility. It is to humdrum things like efficient management or low costs that the most famous names of Japanese business owe their global power. A case in point is the car industry — which, when car assembly and the businesses that serve it are counted together, accounts for one in ten of the jobs of many industrial economies. Automobile manufacture is seen as the backbone of modern industry. In both Europe and the United States, it is the industry that is most obviously, and most painfully, under attack from Japan. Why?

FOUR

Kill or Cure in
the Car Business

WHEN MAZDA opened a new car factory at Flat Rock, Michigan, in 1985, it took a gamble. While the competition at Honda, Toyota, and Nissan had deliberately chosen to start their American manufacturing operations outside Michigan, far away from Detroit — Toyota's factory is in Kentucky, Honda's is in Ohio, and Nissan's in Tennessee — Mazda, on the other hand, resolved to set up shop right in the middle of the U.S. automobile belt. One of the consequences of doing so was that the firm was able to draw on a large pool of potential employees who had already worked in car factories. Almost 100,000 people applied for the 3,500 jobs that were on offer at the new Flat Rock; many of them found to their surprise, however, that prior experience in the car industry was not necessarily useful.

"The Big Three [General Motors, Ford, and Chrysler] had been interested only in hiring workers to build automobiles," discovered a pair of local researchers who spent two years on a comprehensively detailed sociological study of the new plant.[1] "Mazda wanted people who could become part of a team." During the ten or twelve weeks of training new Mazda workers received, a great deal of the emphasis was on team-work. In discussion groups, they were asked what they would do if a neighbor's Mazda car broke down — and were told the ideal answer: help to fix it, and apologize on the company's behalf. In a week-long session on "interpersonal" exercises, they were invited to discuss how to manage the delicate job of telling a close colleague to shower more often without causing offense. And in one exercise, which seemed at first bizarre but was in fact enormously significant, the teams were given boxes of components and diagrams, and were set to work learning how to assemble flashlights.

Their new employers were not satisfied when the teams had puzzled out the procedure and managed to produce a tolerable imitation of a flashlight assembly line. On the contrary: they asked the workers to go straight back to work, and try to find ways for their team to assemble more flashlights per minute. When the bemused workers returned with evidence that they had succeeded, the managers added another twist: they removed one person from each assembly team, and told the teams to find a way of covering for the missing worker so as to keep production going at the same rate as before. The teams were also asked to look at videotapes of themselves at work on this experimental assembly line — and to try to find further inefficiencies that could be taken out.

Several of the workers who participated in this process — the Japanese called it *kaizen,* which means continuous, incremental improvement — were suspicious. It seemed to them an alarming reminder of the work of Frederick Winslow Taylor, one of the earliest management gurus of the twentieth century, whose ideas prompted Henry Ford to introduce the world's first industrial assembly line in January 1914[2] and whose descendants were the time-and-motion men walking up and down the aisles of factories in Europe and the United States as late as the 1970s. Yet there was an important difference between these homegrown techniques and what Mazda was doing. At the Flat Rock factory, the workers were their *own* time-and-motion men. It was up to them — not to advisers from outside, brought in by the management but resented by the workers — to look for ways to squeeze waste out of the system and to make the factory produce more cars per day.

That flashlight-building exercise provided Mazda's new American workers their first glimpse of a much bigger system, which was as different from the traditional mass production of cars as Henry Ford's 1914 assembly line was from the old craft system that preceded it, in which the automobile was in effect built by skilled specialists, entirely by hand. The system Mazda was to use at Flat Rock had in fact been pioneered by Toyota, Japan's biggest car maker, in the 1950s. The company's engineers call it the Toyota Production System; increasingly, however, it is coming to be known as *lean production* — a term made popular by James P. Womack, Daniel T. Jones, and Daniel Roos of the Massachusetts Institute of Technology in their book *The Machine That Changed the World.*[3]

Over the past twenty years, Japanese firms have been using the methods of lean production to compete with spectacular success in the American market. Yet the rise of the Japanese car in the United States has had devastating effects on the American auto industry. It has halted and reversed the growth of General Motors, Ford, and Chrysler (so much so that the "Big Three," as they used to be called, is no longer an accurate name: Honda has succeeded in selling more passenger cars in a single year in the United States than Chrysler). This change has forced the American makers to look at their own businesses and try to remake them in the Japanese image.

The same cannot be said of Europe, however. Although there has been a public and acrimonious debate about Japan among European automobile makers, Japanese competition has not yet produced in Europe anything like the dramatic effects it has had across the Atlantic. This is not because European car manufacturers do their job any better than their counterparts in the United States. Far from it: despite appearances to the contrary, cars are made less well by European firms than by American ones. That will become increasingly apparent as Japanese competition is brought more fully to bear.

Over the coming decade, two specific questions will have to be faced: Can Europe continue to support six different independent car companies, each of which sells a broad range of products? And for how long can Europe hold on to its cherished tradition as the supplier of the world's luxury cars? Before looking for answers inside a European company, though, it is worth examining a little more closely where lean production came from, and what it is all about.

Losing the Second World War was devastating for many of the businesses that had helped Japan's war effort, and the Toyota Motor Company, based near Nagoya, was no exception. One of its factories was forced to build a flour mill and bakery in order to provide food for its workers; others, unable to sell any cars, had to diversify into pots and pans. Five years later, as the firm continued to lose money, its banks told it to renege on a deal it had struck with its workers and to fire a fifth of its 5,000 employees. Understandably, they went on strike — and only came back some months later after receiving a promise that Kiichiro Toyoda, the company president, would resign. Thereafter, the firm managed to achieve an informal compromise that has later come to seem characteristically Japanese: 1,760 workers — more than the number of redundancies originally demanded — would retire "voluntarily," and in return, the company would undertake to guarantee lifetime employment to those who remained.

Yet as the 1950s continued, Toyota was still far behind its competitors abroad. How was it to succeed in selling its products abroad, wondered Taiichi Ohno, the man in charge of final assembly, if the firm had to compete with the vast, integrated factories of the United States? Unlike Ford and General Motors, Toyota could not hope to benefit from huge economies of scale by making millions of nearly identical cars; not only did the Americans have equipment that it lacked, but also the Japanese market was just too small and too fragmented for Toyota to be able to sell a single model in such numbers, even if the firm could make it. To make things harder still, while the American builders had been able to hire and fire temporary workers as the demand for cars dictated, Toyota had to treat labor as a fixed cost — or else risk another strike that might finish the firm off for good.[4]

Ohno made virtues of these necessities, and in doing so was to revolutionize the world's car industry. First, he gave to the employees themselves the jobs that in other mass-production car plants had been assigned to specialists. Instead of having supervisors watching them from the factory aisles, the workers were arranged in self-supporting teams. Instead of having technicians to fix small problems, the line workers were expected to help themselves and each other. They were to act as their own cleaning staff by keeping their own work areas tidy. And most crucial of all, they were also to act as their own quality controllers. Instead of letting a car continue down the production line with a part missing or wrongly installed, they were told to stop the line so that the mistake could be corrected. (In the traditional factory, the power to pull the cord that halts production had always been a jealously guarded supervisor's privilege.)

Second, Ohno decided that Toyota would have to make parts for its cars in much smaller batches if it were to meet customers' demand for many different kinds of product. Rather than use the same die-presses to stamp out from sheet metal the same body panel of the same car for months on end, the firm got its workers used to changing the heavy dies in minutes rather than hours so that production could switch from one model to another.

Third, Ohno intensified and streamlined a system that Kiichiro Toyoda had dreamed up in the 1930s. While Western car makers used to keep piles of spare parts at every stage in the production process in order to make sure that the line would not be held up by a problem with a single machine, Toyoda simply could not afford to tie up so much money in stocks of spare parts. So he told his workers that they should turn out parts for the next stage of the process "just in time" for when they were needed — no later, and no earlier. Ohno went further, and extended the principle all the way down to the final assembly of the car.

These changes seemed suicidal. They flew in the face of everything that had made Ford and General Motors so successful. Henry Ford had thought that the key to making good cars cheaply was to simplify the manufacturing process by making the cars as standard as possible. "Any color you like," he famously told a group of disgruntled dealers who had come to beg him to offer his Model-T in different colors so that Ford would not fall behind its competitors, "as long as it's black." He had split the manufacturing job into as many simple steps as possible, so that it could be done by unskilled, hastily trained workers while supervisors controlled the speed of the production line and thus the rate of production. And he had thought that high inventories all through the process were necessary to keep the line going at all times.

Sure enough, Toyota found that the first result of Ohno's new approach was chaos. The line kept stopping whenever a worker found himself without the parts he needed to do his job. But within a very few months, things began to change. The people on the assembly line began to do their jobs better, because they knew they could not rely on someone else farther down to correct their mistakes. Without the buffer of a pile of spare parts, every stage of the process had to work properly: any problem in delivering them, and someone would have to pull the cord to halt production until some new parts could be found. And every time the line stopped, a fault was immediately exposed in the manufacturing process which could then be corrected. When everything was taken together, the result was apparently miraculous: lower costs *and* higher quality.

But Toyota was not content with overturning the conventional wisdom only in final assembly. The firm was already turning its attention to design, component manufacture, and the rest of the nonassembly jobs that make up five-sixths of the final cost of a car. There too it evolved methods that are strikingly different from those of the average Western maker. In many American and European firms, the job of bringing a car into production is made slower and more expensive by rivalry between departments, and by the fact that it has to be done step by step. In Toyota's design process today, a project leader is made responsible for each new model, and is given enough power to make sure that the people from different departments in the company who have to work together on it do so without duplication of effort or waste of time. Because they are part of a much tighter team, they can do concurrently many of the jobs that traditionally are done consecutively — and because less work is duplicated or wasted, the entire job of designing a new car takes on average just over half the engineering hours. As for components, all but the most crucial parts of Toyota's cars are provided by outside suppliers, who are told the criteria that their component must meet — price, size, and performance — but not how to meet those criteria. They do not win business by being the lowest bidder for a specific component, as General Motors' suppliers are; instead, the firm allows them a profit margin but then expects them to cut prices year by year as they get more efficient at making the component. Like the workers on the assembly line, they are asked to use their imagination to find ways of increasing quality and cutting costs.

In the fiercely competitive Japanese market, it could not be long before some of the firm's competitors — such as Nissan, Honda, Mazda, and Mitsubishi — began to imitate the Toyota system. Not all of them did so, but enough did for the Japanese car industry as a whole to become far more efficient than either the United States' or Europe's. A few statistics show how sharp the differences are.[5] Taking the volume car makers in each of the three main regions and making compensating adjustments for the differences in complexity between the models being assembled, the MIT researchers found that assembling a car took 16.8 hours of work in the average Japanese-owned assembly plant in Japan. In the average American-owned plant in North America, it took 25.1 hours; and in the average European plant, it took 36.2. The average Japanese plant kept only 0.2 days' production of inventories; American and European plants had to pay for 2.9 and 2.0 days respectively. There were 60 defects on average per 100 cars produced in a Japanese plant; there were 82.3 in a plant in North America, and 97.0 in a plant in Europe. As if that were not enough, the Japanese factories also required 27 percent less factory space than both European and American factories to make the same number of cars. They needed to devote only a third as much of that space to the repair area at the end of the line where mistakes are corrected. They spent more than twice as many hours training new workers. And their workers were coming forward with 100 times as many suggestions for ways to make an already better system work even better still.

Puzzlingly, given the tendency of their own leaders to say tactless things about other countries, Japanese newspaper and television pundits have always been inordinately sensitive about the things foreigners say about their country. One of the jibes they found most hurtful was President de Gaulle's curt dismissal in 1962 of visiting Japanese prime minister Ikeda as a "little transistor salesman." By 1992, however, the Japanese were able to savor the irony of seeing the situation reversed. George Bush might have been expected to use his first visit to Japan since the end of the Persian Gulf war to talk with the Japanese about the problems of reform in the former Soviet Union or about the stalled Uruguay round of international trade negotiations. In fact, he did neither of these. Instead, with an eye clearly on his coming re-election campaign later in the same year, the president used the opportunity of his visit to press Japan to buy more American cars and more auto components. As if to emphasize that he had come as car salesman rather than as president, he brought with him the heads of General Motors, Ford, and Chrysler — who had lobbied him jointly face to face in Washington the previous year. "President Bush's visit has produced much confusion and distress among the Japanese people," observed the Japanese management consultant Kenichi Ohmae dryly in the *Wall Street Journal.* "Most of us don't understand why the president of the United States has taken up issues usually handled by assistants to Carla Hills [the U.S. special trade representative]."[6]

It was already evident that the visit was not going well when the president collapsed at a state banquet in his honor, in full view of the world's television cameras. But it was not until afterward that it became clear what a turning point the visit had been in the history of the U.S. car industry. Since before the First World War, U.S. automotive firms — believing themselves the best in the world — had been unhesitating supporters of free trade. Although the first signs that Japanese makers were turning out products of higher quality had come much earlier, Americans' faith in their own ability to beat all comers was not dented until after two successive oil shocks. As the recession of 1990 began to bite, a second round of shrill calls for protection began to be heard. First, the Big Three accused Japanese firms of dumping minivans — one of the last segments in which American firms were still able to make high profits — in the U.S. market. Then a political row blew up over Honda's American credentials, in which the Japanese firm was accused of avoiding $20 million in customs duties by manipulating the U.S.-Canada free trade pact to make it seem as though its cars had a higher "local content" ratio than they really did.[7] By 1992 the firms were willing to support even such economically dyslexic ideas as Representative Richard Gephardt's proposal that Japanese companies' cars sales in the United States, whether imported or not, should be linked directly by tariffs or quantitative limits to an acceptable fall in the bilateral trade deficit between Japan and the United States.

The car industries of both Japan and the United States professed themselves disgruntled with the results of the Tokyo visit. Top executives of the big Japanese firms felt they had been pressed into giving guarantees to buy fixed dollar values of American-made components — $19 billion a year by 1995, of which $4 billion were to be imported into Japan and the rest used in their factories in the United States — no matter what their quality, and without any promises that the American firms would do more to provide them with the parts they wanted. The Americans, on the other hand, considered pitiful the promises they had received from five Japanese makers to sell up to fifty thousand more American cars a year through their own distribution channels in Japan. Lee Iacocca, Chrysler's outspoken chairman, made it clear what he thought the new relationship was as soon as he returned home. "We ship them food and chemicals and raw materials, just like a colony," he said. "And they ship us value-added cars and machine tools and electronics, just like a mother country." For Yutaka Kume, president of Nissan and chairman of the Japan Automobile Manufacturers' Association, that was the last straw. "Mr. Iacocca's behavior and remarks were outrageous and insulting to us," he said — and swore not to meet the American trio again.

To be fair, some of the American industry's complaints against Japan were justified. It is true that Japan's car industry has a history of protection against foreign competition. The American firms that dominated the Japanese market in the early days were subjected to restrictions in 1936 and expelled outright by the military government in 1939. They returned at the end of the war, and then found themselves squeezed back out only a few years later by tariffs and bans on foreign investment. They were encouraged to invest in Japan once again only in 1970, and it was not until 1983 that the Japanese government stopped trying to restrict imports by insisting on inspecting carefully all imported cars one by one.

All the same, car firms that have tried hard to get into the Japanese market have not only succeeded, but have also begun to make handsome profits there. A case in point is Rover, the former publicly owned car maker now under the wing of British Aerospace, which found suddenly that its Mini — a design classic more than thirty years old, which was only remaining in production in its home market — was becoming the object of a retro craze in Japan. With the help of Honda, the firm was able to take advantage of this: Rover had almost 120 dealerships in Japan by 1990. More seriously still, the German makers BMW and Mercedes-Benz, whose cars were at first most notable for being the favorites of the *yakuza*, Japan's organized crime bosses, managed to turn Japan into their second most important export market after the United States.

At the turn of the 1980s, BMW and Mercedes-Benz had found themselves in a difficult position in Japan. They were unable to get their cars into the dealerships that sold Toyotas or Nissans; like European car makers, the Japanese firms had kept tight control of their distribution networks by forbidding dealers to stock the cars of other makers. So imported cars were tied to a handful of specialist firms. Unable or unwilling to invest the money necessary for a national network of dealers, these specialists would offer imported cars at astronomical prices — often four or five times the going rate abroad — and make a tidy living for themselves by making up in margins what they lost in volume.

By the time the yen began to rise in 1985, the German car makers were the first to see an opportunity. After years of being uncompetitive with the efficient domestic makers, their products now had at least a fighting chance. Mercedes-Benz and BMW therefore made a momentous decision: to take distribution out of the hands of their old importing partners, and to find better ways to get into the market. Mercedes-Benz ended up eventually with the Mitsubishi group, as a result of the wide-ranging strategic alliance between the two sets of firms signed in 1990. But between 1986 and 1989, its sales in Japan rose from under 14,000 units to almost 32,000. BMW has invested tens of millions of dollars in sales and service centers of its own. A report in the *Financial Times* in 1990 concluded:

> While the West's importers might still have a hefty thicket of Japanese customer preferences, prejudices and other subjective aspects to hack through before being assured of long-term market success, they can no longer claim that any serious legislative or regulatory barriers stand in their way. Since 1986, there has been a steady dismantling of the last of the discriminatory practices hindering imports. The streamlining of motor vehicle certification systems, adoption of international standards and taxation reforms coupled to a government programme for the acceleration of imports in 1985 have had a cumulative effect.
>
> A particularly important development came in April last year, when prices of new cars of over 2 litres — which accounted for 46 per cent of last year's imports — fell sharply as a result of the replacement of commodity tax on luxury and high-priced goods by a new consumption tax, plus a restructuring of Japan's annual automobile tax. The changes in effect reduced the prices of such cars by around 10 per cent.
>
> Finally, changes to vehicle insurance regimes by the Automobile Insurance Calculation Association of Japan in 1988 brought to an end one of the last blatant discriminatory practices. Before the revisions, insurers were demanding up to three times as much in premiums for imported cars as their domestic equivalents, on the grounds that parts and repairs for imported cars cost more. Mounting protests from abroad led to all premium distinctions between imported and domestic cars being removed.
>
> "In short," says Mr Bassermann [president of Mercedes's importing subsidiary], "we consider the Japanese car market completely free."[8]

Yet American firms had no more than a handful of dealers in Japan in 1990. Might their low sales have had something to do with the fact that General Motors and Chrysler offered no cars there with the steering wheel on the right-hand side, ignoring the fact that the Japanese drive on the left, like the British?[9] (Ford did so only because Mazda dealers in Japan were selling a car made in Hiroshima but with the Ford Probe nameplate.) Or might it, perhaps, have been because the often-heard Japanese complaint that American cars are of lamentable quality had some truth to it? Chrysler's Jeep Cherokee, now distributed by Honda, had to be recalled four times during its first year of sale in Japan because of problems with its accelerator and brakes.

Under the spotlights of Washington and Tokyo, the leaders of the American car industry may attack Japan with rhetorical fury. In their own offices, however, they know that their problems are mostly of their own making: the problems are precisely the result of the gaps in quality and productivity identified by the MIT survey. The biggest obstacle to closing these gaps, though, is their industry's spectacular history: as Othello loved, they succeeded "not wisely, but too well." For a generation before the war and fifteen years after, the Big Three had an oligopoly in their own market — a market that was at the time still the biggest single market in the world. They were not merely the inventors of mass production but also the only car firms that had managed to establish a secure presence abroad. Their position — already dominant before the Second World War — was exaggerated afterward by the United States' disproportionate share of world output as the economies of Japan and Europe struggled to recover from the ruins of 1945. And by the time it became clear in the 1970s how much more efficient Japanese automotive manufacturing had become, the Big Three were organizations just too big and too slow-moving to respond promptly. "Revitalizing General Motors," said Ross Perot, when he left the company's board in 1986, "is like teaching an elephant to tap dance. You find the sensitive spots, and start poking."

One sign of this elephantism was the isolation from the real world that allowed people like Iacocca to draw vast salaries and to write self-congratulatory books about management even as their firms went to the dogs — and that prompted the making in 1989 of *Roger and Me,* a film about the inaccessibility of the president of General Motors and the forbidding shadow that the company cast over its local community. Another, at the other end of the ladder, was the myopia that encouraged the UAW, the country's leading auto workers' union, successfully to demand pay increases during the course of the 1970s which increased the premium of auto workers' wages over average manufacturing wages from 30 percent to 60 percent — in a decade when the American car business was losing ground to foreign competition faster than any other part of manufacturing industry save semiconductors.

Ford, Chrysler, and GM probably reached the peak of their creative and manufacturing prowess in 1955; the slow decline that many students of the industry think began in that year continued for a quarter century until 1981, when the quadrupling of gasoline prices after the second oil shock finally made it impossible for them to continue to sell the gas-guzzling chromed monsters of the past.[10] Ford lost more than $1 billion for each of two years running; Chrysler had to be bailed out by the government — which forced Iacocca to give up his executive jet, albeit only temporarily; and even GM came perilously near to the red. The shock of the early 1980s had a salutary effect on both Ford and Chrysler; they began to make sharp economies as the decade wore on, improving the efficiency of their operations. Although its profits slumped in 1981, General Motors never faced the same crisis and thus found itself unable to make such drastic changes. Protected by a "voluntary" agreement with its Japanese competitors that kept the growth of exports down, it chose to take big profits in the seven fat years between 1983 and 1989 rather than to use the respite for a thoroughgoing shake-up. When the next recession came in 1990–91, it was GM that found itself least prepared. In its North American car business, the firm lost over $6 billion in 1991 — more than $1,000 *per car sold*. Barely half a year later, Robert Stempel, the chairman of General Motors, found himself the victim of a boardroom coup. His plan to close twenty-one factories and get rid of 74,000 workers, almost a fifth of the firm's automobile work force, did not satisfy the company's outside directors that enough was being done to respond to the crisis. Accordingly, Stempel was replaced.

What had gone wrong? According to an account written by Ben Hamper, an assembly line worker in one of GM's factories, the company was just hopelessly managed.[11] It demoralized workers by laying them off for months at a time, and then brought them back with a curt order over the telephone: "Mr. Hamper? You are to report back to work at the GM Truck and Bus plant tomorrow morning at 6:00 A.M. for rehiring . . . CLICK!!!" Its managers allowed supervisors to stop the production line for trivial reasons, but insisted on restarting it after an aging woman worker had collapsed dangerously close to the machinery. They imposed scores of bureaucratic rules, but were unable to stop workers from smoking joints, drinking whiskey, popping acid, and sniffing cocaine while on the job. And because the factory was so inefficiently run, workers were driven to kill time by kicking cardboard boxes around the production line. In a feeble attempt to encourage them to pay more attention to quality, GM even sent a worker around the plant dressed up as a giant cat, and put up a huge noticeboard on which exhortative messages were displayed electronically. SQUEEZING RIVETS IS FUN! said one. "We had no idea whether this was some kind of big bro Orwellian braindunk or just some lowly office puke's idea of a nimble-witted gibe," says Hamper wryly. "Whatever it was, we were not especially amused." The workers tried to destroy the display by shooting rivets at it.

Hamper's most damning revelation about General Motors, however, is that the firm was utterly incapable of finding a way to harness the enthusiasm or the talents of its workers in order to make cars better or more cheaply. Workers who had their own ideas could benefit from them only by breaking the rules. In one of his first jobs at GM, Hamper teamed up with a colleague and found enough slack in the two jobs for one of them to do the work of both. After some practice, they got a system working so smoothly that each would work only half a shift — while the other downed beers at a bar 130 miles away, secure in the knowledge that his friend would punch his card into the time clock at the end of the shift. This was so blatant, records Hamper, that the time-and-motion men made some changes in the procedures, not to take advantage of their higher productivity but in order to prevent the two workers from "doubling up." The pair were put off. But with a taste for *kaizen* that would have made them stars at Mazda, they were not to be discouraged:

> After a couple of days of this new arrangement, I was ready to surrender. Just when I thought I'd drilled in all five clamps securely, one of them would go clanking off and land on the ramp track. I'd start cussin' my brains out and stompin' around like a madman.
>
> Thankfully, Dale was there to calm me down. Mechanical plights and misbehaving gizmos were hobbies for him. He began teaching me a new stance that would give me much better accuracy with the air gun. I practiced and practiced. Dale wouldn't allow me to give up, assuring me that we'd be right back in business within a week.
>
> And that unconcerned, soothsayin' pig farmer was right. Through determination, perspiration, acceleration and pure spite, we swallowed up the air-conditioning clamps into our routine and were back doubling-up within a week. We made for a helluva team.
>
> As exasperated as they probably felt, [our supervisors] knew there was nothing they could really do to stop us. We showed up for work each and every day. We ran nothing but 100 percent defect-free quality. We kept our workplace spotless, provided you overlooked Dale's ugly slick of chewing tobacco juice. GM was very big on bottom lines and the bottom line as it pertained to Dale and me was that we were exemplary shoprats.

Yet GM's faults should not obscure the fact that the revival of the U.S. car business has already begun. True, it is happening slowly: it may take twenty-five years for the managerial malaise of the U.S. car firms to be cured, just as it did to develop. But the signs are there all the same. The most important force for recovery is change from within. Ford has been most successful, but Chrysler and GM, too, are beginning to look more critically at how they do business — from the way they develop new models to the organization of their factories, even to the way their head offices work. The world assembly plant survey in the MIT study mentioned above found that in 1989, the highest production quality came not from Japan but actually from a Ford factory built on a greenfield site in Mexico. In 1990 General Motors began production at a new factory in Tennessee — barely an hour's drive from the Nissan plant at Smyrna — in which it has begun to build the Saturn, under the management of a completely new organization. Early signs are that the plant is working well, but there are reservations about its first model; in years to come, however, the plant will be a telling test of how far managerial thinking has changed inside GM.

The job of changing from within has been made a great deal easier by the joint ventures that the American firms have begun with their Japanese competitors. In 1984 General Motors reopened an unused car factory at Fremont, just at the end of the San Francisco commuter train line. The name above the factory gate was New United Motor Manufacturing, Inc. (NUMMI), a joint venture between Toyota and GM. The American firm has been rotating some of its best managers through the plant ever since in order to expose them to the methods of lean production. GM also makes cars in Canada in cooperation with Suzuki. Chrysler's managers, too, had a chance to learn from Mitsubishi at the Diamond-Star Motors joint venture company (but Chrysler's increasing financial fragility forced it to sell its stake in the venture to Mitsubishi in 1991, and left in doubt how long it could hope to hold on to its 10.3 percent shareholding in the parent firm in Tokyo). Ford, with links to Mazda, was able to benefit most of all. Able to demand full access to the firm's factories in Japan by virtue of a 23 percent shareholding in Mazda which it bought in 1979, the U.S. firm sent a group of managers in 1980 to see the Hiroshima plant at which Mazda was doing Toyota-style production.

And the Japanese manufacturing presence in the United States, pioneered by Honda at its plant in Marysville, Ohio, in 1982, has been a powerful incentive. In one way, the growing Japanese manufacturing presence inside the United States is having a direct effect: under pressure to increase the proportion of components they buy locally, Japanese firms are in turn pressing American suppliers to accept the disciplines of quality, productivity, and declining cost over the cycle of the product which are such key features of the supply system in Japan. Indirectly, however, the presence of the "transplants" has forced the U.S. car industry as a whole to recognize that nothing in the success of the Japanese could not be imitated. With American management and American workers, the lean transplants show average quality almost as good as in Japan, and average productivity that lies halfway between the American-owned plants in the United States and the average Japanese factory. Given the time to improve, and to develop reliable local suppliers — a process that could take another decade, since the improvements in efficiency needed in the U.S. components industry are greater still than those in assembly — there is no reason why those factories should not close the rest of the gap.

When they do so, all eyes will be on the three American makers to follow suit. At first sight, the job ought not to be too difficult: quite apart from the joint ventures and the transplants, the American manufacturers already have some efficient factories of their own with which to encourage the elephants that are still far behind. The difficulty, however, is with just how far behind their worst factories are. Although the worst North American plant in the MIT survey was only 20 percent less productive than the average, its quality record was lamentable: 169 assembly defects per 100 vehicles, compared with an average of 78 in North America and an average of 52 in Japan. Even after these problems have been corrected, there will still remain an image problem. Just as they benefited for years in the 1960s and 1970s from Japanese cars' reputation as unreliable rustbuckets long after that reputation was no longer deserved, so in the 1990s the U.S. firms find themselves victims of the same phenomenon: with a purchase as large as a car, many American consumers who have bought Japanese cars will be reluctant to believe quality statistics that give good scores to Ford, Chrysler, or General Motors. It will take years before the buyers come back with confidence.

A more serious challenge still will be what to do about their employees. The transplants, sited, with the exception of Mazda's plant in Flat Rock, in areas of high unemployment far from the sphere of UAW influence, have been able to pick and choose the best among huge numbers of job applicants. Unless the American firms are forced to the pessimistic conclusion that they must in effect close themselves down and start up elsewhere — that is, do a Saturn on a far grander scale — they will have to make do with the workers and unions they have. Adapting to lean production is far easier for novices than for those who have experience of the old car-making techniques. At the Mazda factory, for instance, those who had worked for American car makers before complained that their jobs were far more tiring. While in the old plants they had worked for forty to fifty seconds of each one-minute cycle, with time to straighten up and stretch before the next car came down the line, in the new one they found themselves practically constantly moving. This is not surprising: it is merely a reminder of the fact that although lean production conjures some improvements in productivity apparently from thin air, simply by eliminating waste and evolving more efficient ways of organizing the factory, it also demands more effort from the people on the production line.

Patrick le Quément was headhunted from a job at Volkswagen's design center in Wolfsburg, Germany, by the French state-controlled car maker Renault in 1987. After a couple of informal meetings at the home of Raymond Lévy, then Renault's chairman, he agreed to join the company as its new head of design in October, with carte blanche powers to restructure its entire approach to designing and developing new cars. "I haven't said this in public until now," he admitted more than three years later in his office at the company's renamed Industrial Design Center on the banks of the Seine in eastern Paris. "But my aim was clear: to make Renault the design leader in Europe."

At first sight, le Quément's quest may seem to have little to do with the wider competitiveness of Europe's car industry. The design of their cars is one of the very few areas in which European companies believe they are *not* threatened by Japan. In the second half of the 1980s, the American firms paid tribute to it by buying into European names like Maserati, Lamborghini, Aston Martin, and Lotus. The Japanese had gone a step further: often with the help of design studios abroad, they had borrowed the spirit of European cars of the 1950s and 1960s, and had reincarnated them in new models for the Japanese domestic market of the 1990s. The only one that made it abroad was Mazda's Miata (known in Europe as the MX-5 and in Japan as the Eunos Roadster), an exciting little two-seater car that paid unmistakable tribute to the spirit of the old MG and was even sold in British racing green.

Meanwhile, something was going wrong in Europe: good designs were somehow watered down before they could make it to market. Walter Gropius described the designer's job as that of introducing soul into a product made by machine, but it is more than that; design is one of the last true polymath jobs in industrial society, combining art and science in equal measure, and demanding a keen awareness of what will be both attractive and easily manufactured. On that score, European designers were beginning to lose their edge. The reason Renault sought out le Quément, who had worked at Ford before he joined Volkswagen and had been exposed to the discipline of its links with Mazda, was that the firm had come to realize it needed to find a better way of putting inspired designs into practice in real cars.

In 1992 the European car industry found itself in a puzzling position. In some ways, it had resisted the challenge from

Toyota more successfully than the United States had. Simply because of its history, it had always been better at making small cars than the Big Three had; it was therefore less damaged by the sharp switch toward fuel economy that followed the oil shocks of the 1970s. And because Europe was made up of more than a dozen fragmented markets, the European assembly firms could never approach the economies of scale necessary even to think about making most of their own components, as the Americans had. As a result, there was a strong European components industry able to do its own research, development, and design.

That was the only good news, however. Measured by the proportion of their output that was faulty, the European components makers' quality was eight times worse than that of the average Japanese firm;[12] and in terms of both quality and productivity, the assembly firms themselves were almost as far behind the Americans as the Americans were behind the Japanese. This was because Europe's craftsmen had strongly resisted the imported methods of hourly paid vehicle assembly in which the job was broken down into as many parts as possible so that it could be done by unskilled hourly paid workers. Rover, the successor in turn to the publicly owned British Leyland, BMC, Austin, and Morris companies, was still trying to introduce employees at its factory near Oxford to mass production when Honda was setting up its first lean production plant in the United States. Even in 1991, Ford was still saddled at its Dagenham plant in east London with the vestiges of working practices that required more than twice as many work hours to make a car as Nissan needed in its factory an afternoon's drive north in Sunderland.

One reason for this was that the European makers had never had the international ambitions of their American competitors. Not merely did they not aspire to be global car makers, with a manufacturing presence in every major market;[13] worse, not a single European firm had managed to get a grip on the different European markets much closer to home. Even today, the most European of the car makers in Europe — measured by how evenly their sales are spread across the different markets — are General Motors and Ford.[14] Lacking adequate exposure to what is going on in the other big markets of the world, how could the European firms fail to bury their heads in the sand? Years after both managers and workers in the U.S. car industry had recognized how much better their competitors in Japan were at making cars and were beginning to do something to close the gap, companies in Europe continued to accuse the Japanese of using unfair advantages: low labor costs, bad working conditions, undervalued currency, robotization — each with a grain of truth,[15] but far from the most important reasons for Japan's success. And as if to prove that they believed sincerely in what they were saying, some firms — notably Fiat, with its glittering Cassino plant near Naples — invested monstrous sums in factory automation. This was a desperate response and was doomed to failure: unable to find a way to get its workers to produce cars efficiently and accurately, Fiat was in effect trying to get rid of them altogether. Whatever their other advantages, however, robots are a great deal less flexible than humans when the time comes to reprogram them to make a different product.

Although the reasons for the competitive gap between European and Japanese production were little understood, that gap was already visible in the import statistics in the mid-1970s. One by one, European car makers began to press their governments for protection. But the political difficulties of imposing formal barriers against Japanese imports — tariffs would make it clear to consumers just how much more they were spending on their cars in order to keep domestic firms in business, and might also invite complaints from Japan that the measures were contrary to the international rules of the General Agreement on Tariffs and Trade — made it necessary to choose another route. Just as was to come later in the United States, the Japanese were to restrict their exports "voluntarily," with the Ministry of International Trade and Industry monitoring how many cars each firm was exporting. There were just two problems. First, this restriction of supply meant that the Japanese firms were able to charge more for their cars than they otherwise would, and could use the profits to improve their production techniques still further.[16] Second, the agreements made it all too tempting for automobile makers to postpone the uncomfortable restructuring that they so badly needed. The result was that by 1990, a two-tier Europe had emerged. In the more open EC markets, such as the Netherlands, Denmark, and Ireland, the Japanese market share averaged more than 30 percent. In the countries protected by the strictest agreements — Spain, France, and Italy[17] — Japanese brands accounted for only 6 percent, 3.5 percent, and 2.3 percent of the market. Fifteen years after the Europeans had asked for temporary measures so they could catch up, the competitive gap remained as wide as ever.

That was why the prospect of a single market in Europe, in which Japanese firms would be equally free to sell cars anywhere in the Community, posed such problems in Brussels. On the one hand, it was out of the question to force consumers in Holland or Denmark to pay more for their cars; on the other, the governments of France and Italy made it clear that they would not countenance the cutting of the string that kept tens of thousands of people employed at Renault and Fiat. In July 1991 the European Commission made a vain attempt to solve the problem.

A five-page document called *Elements of Consensus* was issued under the names of Eiichi Nakao and Frans Andriessen, Japan's trade minister and the European Commission's vice president, in which the two sides agreed that the various national bilateral limits would go at the end of 1992, and that the market would be fully opened at the end of 1999. In return, Japan would hold car and light commercial vehicle exports to Europe constant until the end of the decade at just under their 1989 level of 1.23 million; and the two sides would monitor car trade twice a year. Unfortunately, this left all the important questions unanswered. "There are enough loopholes in the deal," wrote *The Economist*, "to drive a fleet of Euro-hatchbacks through."[18] For although the two sides had predicted total sales in 1999 of 15.1 million, nothing had been agreed about what would happen if this prediction turned out to be wrong. Nor was there the slightest element of consensus on how to treat cars made by Japanese companies at factories in Europe. This was particularly puzzling given that a flood of new manufacturing capacity at such factories was just about to come on stream.

In the end, there seemed only one plausible explanation for the document: it was a signal to the region's six big car makers — Volkswagen, Fiat, General Motors, Ford, Peugeot, and Renault, each with between 10 percent and 17 percent of the market — that they should start preparing to cut capacity just as the American industry was doing. With the exception of Germany, which saw a short-lived car boom as former East Germans traded in their Wartburgs and Trabants for Western cars, the 1990 recession bit painfully in Europe. Ford lost money in Britain for the first time in almost twenty years, and all the other makers but General Motors saw a sharp decline in profits as a result of falling sales. Because they make cars so inefficiently, the European firms desperately need to keep their factories running at full tilt; for many, losing two percentage points of market share would mean the difference between profit and loss.

The trouble is, that is exactly the prospect that faces them later in the 1990s. The year 1992 saw a huge increase in Japanese capacity in Europe, with Nissan raising output from its already successful operation in the north of England from 120,000 cars a year to 200,000, with Toyota opening a new plant in Derbyshire, and with Honda doing the same in Swindon. That was just the beginning; assuming the Japanese car makers manage the daunting organizational burden of setting up such large projects as well as they did in the United States, some experts predicted that the three firms could be making by 1996 or 1997 more than 1 million cars a year in those plants alone.[19] On top of that, there are eight other Japanese car manufacturing projects either planned or under way inside the Community, and three engine plants. That increase in the industry's capacity — even if exports from Japan stay fixed, as provided for in *Elements of Consensus* — is all the European industry as presently constituted can bear. Any more, and they will have to start closing factories as the American firms did.

Paradoxically, however, new Japanese capacity is crucial for the future competitiveness of the European car industry. "Every mass-producer needs a lean competitor located right across the road," argued the MIT specialists.[20] "We have found again and again that middle management and rank-and-file workers in a mass-production company begin to change only when they see a concrete, nearby example of lean production that can strip away all the cultural and economic explanations of why the other manufacturer is succeeding. US, Canadian and English mass-production plants now all have a lean-producer right across the road, but the continental European countries have lagged badly. Their relative performance on our productivity survey shows the result." Sadly, that conclusion continues to hold: the German, French, and Italian car industries — the former because of high wage costs, the latter two because their governments have seemed inhospitable to Japanese investors — have no prospect of gaining a next-door lean competitor.

An alternative approach is to learn through joint ventures. So far, there have not been nearly so many or so extensive lean-manufacturing joint ventures in Europe as in the United States. From 1995 onward, Mitsubishi will be making cars in a three-way venture in the Netherlands shared with the Dutch government and Volvo. But Honda's link with Rover, in which the British firm and the British subsidiary of the Japanese firm not merely pool designs and manufacturing but also have a 20 percent cross-shareholding, is with a firm that is too small to influence the fate of the European car industry. And the rest of the joint ventures, either planned or in operation, are either in the countries of Eastern Europe, and therefore outside the main EC manufacturing centers; or they are with smaller Japanese makers like Daihatsu whose domestic operations are hardly more efficient than their Western competitors; or, as with a European joint venture under discussion between Mazda and Ford, they are partnerships between companies that have already worked together for some years.

Experience in their own domestic market has made Ford and General Motors more circumspect in Europe than local firms. They need Europe almost as much as the European firms do. In 1991, at the height of the recession in its home market, the $2 billion in profits that GM derived from its Adam Opel unit in Germany and Vauxhall Motors in Britain were essential in subsidizing its limping North American operations. No wonder, then, that they have been more responsive. Ford has already made plans to manufacture cars in Spain in a joint venture with Nissan. In 1990 General Motors did something far more daring by beginning assembly of Opels at a new factory in Eisenach, a town just on the eastern side of what used to be the border between East and West Germany. Eisenach has a strong tradition of car making: it was used by BMW between 1933 and the Second World War, but it renamed its cars Eisenacher Motoren Werke after 1945 and began making Wartburgs. At first, the plant concentrated only on assembling cars from complete knockdown kits (CKD), but the man in charge, a Canadian named Tom LaSorda who was exposed to Japanese methods in the GM joint venture with Suzuki, is determined to leapfrog Western-style manufacturing and bring the former communist plant directly into lean production. The beginnings of a Japanese-style distribution system are already in place too: Opel dealers in eastern Germany are linked by a computer system with the factory so that customers can find out how far the car they have ordered has progressed.

The atmosphere at Fiat's headquarters in Turin, by contrast, is alarmingly complacent. The firm is manufacturing its updated Cinquecento in Poland; it is busily investing in new factories in the depressed Mezzogiorno of southern Italy and in Algeria; early in 1992 it was even considering trying to make cars in Russia; but despite the fact that it is losing market share in its all-important home market — to other European car makers, even before it is opened up to Japanese firms — Fiat appears to have no plans to acquire any Japanese manufacturing know-how. One strategist from the company blamed the government for the firm's problems. "It's not the fault of Fiat, it's the fault of the country," he said. "And forget those studies, please," he continued, refusing to recognize the existence of a gap in quality or productivity between Fiat and its Japanese competitors. "In some things the Japanese are more efficient; but on average, they're not so good as us. If our competitors think we're almost broken, we'd love to keep them thinking that way."

European optimists like to talk of two things that will keep them ahead of Japanese competition. One is the striking train of events on the European Community's eastern flank since 1989: the breakaway of the former Soviet satellite states from Moscow's control, and the disintegration of the Soviet Union itself. As a result, a number of countries — notably Poland, Hungary, and Czechoslovakia — are likely to be promising new car markets in the 1990s. What is more, the combination of low wages, economic deregulation, and their desire to join the Community are likely to make them promising places for European firms to make cars. The other is more temporary but exercises powerful control over the attention of European auto executives: the arrangement by which an assembly firm is allowed to force its dealers to handle only its own cars. In any other industry, this would be seen as self-evidently an anticompetitive practice, but the car industry has succeeded in holding on to this vertical integration as a kind of unspoken favor in return for the opening of the car market to Japanese imports after 1999. The exclusive dealership network means that firms that have a large market share now can drastically slow down the entry of new Japanese competition by forcing the Japanese firms to build their networks of dealers from scratch. This is likely to provide some residual protection for the French, Spanish, and Italian car markets as the 1999 deadline draws near.

Yet closer inspection suggests that these are less powerful weapons than they seem at first sight. First, the former East European satellites will certainly be a growing market for West European cars (if everything goes well with their economic reforms), but it is far from clear how helpful that will be. The Asian car markets — particularly Korea, Taiwan, and those of ASEAN (the Association of South-East Asian Nations) — are likely to grow much faster still, and Japanese companies will be able to reap even greater economies of scale from them. And when Japanese firms see their European competitors making a success of business in the east, they will not be long in coming in, either. As for the exclusive dealerships, they are nothing more than a barrier to entry — an expensive one, but one that can be surmounted nevertheless. Mercedes-Benz and BMW, of all the automobile manufacturers in the world, know that a decade of effort and investment is enough to build one's own dealer network; they learned that, ironically, from selling cars in Japan. Given the oblivion of Turin and the fact that Britain may no longer have a domestically owned car industry by 1999, are the best hopes for an indigenous European car industry therefore by default in Germany — at Wolfsburg, Stuttgart, and Munich, the homes respectively of Volkswagen, Mercedes-Benz, and BMW? Not necessarily. Let us return to Patrick le Quément's work at Renault.

Renault recognizes that it faces a crisis. As the smallest of the six "generalists," it has long been seen as the European mass producer most at risk from Japanese competition, most likely to lose those fatal few points of market share that keep it in profit. Its problems probably began in the 1960s, when it began to lose the fighting spirit that had helped it to spread car ownership among average French people in the first generation of owners after the war. "That was our David and Goliath period," says le Quément. "But David became a little older, and put on some weight. We also became attracted to the golden myth of the global car. Our design aim became to make cars that did not displease. Pleasing our customers became secondary: we began a long series of products that were incredibly boring." The firm, unable to motivate the new employees who came to its plants from North Africa, also faced sharp declines in quality and productivity.

The turnaround began after the firm had a brush with disaster in 1984, dipping briefly into the red and prompting a reorganization that left the French state still as its majority shareholder but forced the company to behave more like a real business. "Japanese competition is at our doorstep," Raymond Lévy was to write in one of the firm's annual reports. "We are going to have to confront it, because Europe cannot perpetually resort to protectionism and closed borders. The real problem is to see that the gates are opened gradually and to minimize the dangers . . . Renault, which has no reservations about the technology or quality of its products, will be able to learn valuable lessons from the organisation and operation methods of the Japanese, *which have proved successful not only in Japan but also in the western firms controlled by the Japanese.*"[21]

The claim that Renault had nothing to learn about quality from Japan was clearly for public consumption. In 1989 Renault set up a Renault Quality Institute, which brought in consultants to teach the company — starting with Lévy himself and his board of directors — an entirely different approach. By 1991 the new institute had gone through the management and moved on to spreading its slogan *Vive la qualité* to supervisors on the shopfloor and (for a fee) to the company's suppliers. The company resolved to learn all it could from the coming joint venture in the Netherlands between its affiliate Volvo and Mitsubishi.[22] It also abandoned some of its previous grandiose ideas. "If I were enormously rich and had unlimited resources, I would strive to be global," Louis Schweitzer, the company's new chief, explains. "But we have set a goal of Europeanizing Renault, of expanding our domain that far."

With its narrower horizons, the firm has been able to focus on getting its factories in order. There is still far to go. But Renault management seem to understand that the job is a two-stage one: they must first identify a few promising plants and try to make them good enough to serve as an example. Then comes the more mundane exercise of bringing the rest up to scratch. "Our plants were not discussing enough between them," observes Schweitzer. "There was a Not Invented Here syndrome — even between one factory and another. Plant managers had their own ways of doing things."

Patrick le Quément was given the job of radically overhauling the way Renault develops new products. He came up with a ten-point action plan for cutting the lead time for new products by 30 percent. Some of its points addressed the specific details of how cars are designed. One, for instance, laid down that work be done simultaneously on the product and on the manufacturing tools it would require, in order to save time; another urged the development teams to prepare as much as possible of a project before the firm has to commit large sums of money — and then to try to make it proceed like a line of falling dominoes, perfectly aligned. A third demanded that they choose external and internal suppliers as early as possible, and to make a conscious effort to increase the amount of design and development work they do. Other points in the manifesto, however, amounted to a recipe for the broadest changes in the way the company worked. One sought to remove the French class consciousness that places product above process, that insists that it is better to conceive than to design. Another called for *débabélisation:* demolishing the towers of Babel — the communications problems, the lack of dialogue, the petty rivalries that slow the company down. And the last exhorted Renault people never to forget CQT: cost, quality, time. "You won't believe the number of times in my career that we've talked about cost problems at one meeting on Monday, and project time problems at another meeting on Tuesday. They can't be separated: we should think of all of them together."

With a desperately weak financial structure, with continuing industrial unrest in its factories in 1991, with too great a reliance on the protected markets that will be forced open at the end of the decade, and with the problem of being not quite big enough to offer the broad product range of its competitors at Volkswagen and Fiat — with all these problems and more, Renault will be for years to come one of the weaker automobile assemblers in Europe. But something has changed. A new spirit seems to be infusing the company: a willingness, perhaps born of desperation, to learn from outside and to bring the company closer to its customers. With that on its side, it has at least a hope of survival.

Home of Volkswagen, Europe's biggest automobile manufacturer, and of Opel,[23] its most profitable, Germany nevertheless draws most of its motoring prestige from BMW and Mercedes-Benz, the world's leading luxury cars. Those who are most optimistic about Europe's car-making future often look to the formidable reputation these two companies have built up for customer service, technical excellence, and manufacturing quality. It may seem surprising, therefore, that to find the key to their future one has to travel an hour by bullet train from Tokyo to a Nissan factory tucked away in the rice fields of Tochigi. There are no secrets here: every year, some 100,000 people — many of them Japanese schoolchildren — are given a free tour of the plant, led by a smiling office lady in a neat company uniform who carries a little flag to make sure they do not get lost.

Inside, workers in immaculate polo shirts and safety spectacles weld and polish on the production line. Others sit in a glassed-off room in the middle of the assembly plant, having one of their famous quality meetings. Spare parts are delivered hour by hour, and few stocks are kept. On one line, to the right, are a dozen or so Nissan Cimas — full-sized sedans built only for the Japanese market. Yet something seems wrong. The line on the left, in most respects identical, is turning out a car called the Infiniti. With leather seats, air conditioning, and doors that make a satisfying clunk, Infiniti is aimed squarely at the buyers of Jaguar, BMW, and Mercedes-Benz. And yet it is being made by a system essentially the same as the one by which Nissan used to turn out Bluebird cars in their tens of thousands in the north of England.

The Infiniti was launched in the United States in 1989, a few months after Toyota brought out its Lexus LS400. Since then, the history of the two cars has been both breathtaking and terrifying. Breathtaking, because a survey earlier in 1991 by J. D. Powers, an American car-quality consultancy, showed that Infiniti and Lexus are now the two most reliable cars on sale in the United States. Terrifying, because in the American market, Lexus and Infiniti were each selling more every month than the BMW 7-series and the Mercedes-Benz S-class *put together.* Recession in the United States hit European makers badly but hardly touched the two new Japanese models.

Lucrative though it is, the United States is an overseas market for the European luxury car specialists. Yet since the first Lexus went on sale in Europe in 1991, the game has changed: Toyota is now challenging Europe's most respected brands in their own back yards. If these American figures show what the Japanese can do with their first stab at a luxury car, how will things look in ten years' time, when they will have had the experience of bringing out two new models?

In one sense, the Japanese move upmarket toward cars of higher quality with more gadgets has been a continuous process since the 1960s. It was an inevitable response to the higher wages Toyota, Nissan, and Honda were paying their Japanese employees — and also to the profits that they had year after year plowed back into R&D. That trend accelerated sharply in the second half of the 1980s, when the value of the yen rose by almost 80 percent against the dollar and Japanese companies were forced dramatically to cut costs and improve productivity in order to stay in business. But at least partly, it is the fault of the European car industry itself. The voluntary export restraints explained earlier that they agreed on with Japanese makers in the 1970s put limits on the absolute number of cars the firms were to sell in the European market; that gave the Japanese the clearest possible incentive to increase the profit per car by moving upmarket — an incentive that has been perpetuated for another decade by the 1991 agreement between the European Commission and the Japanese government.

The background to the two new cars was like this. In the mid-1980s, Nissan and Toyota engineers began to ask themselves a crucial question: What does a Mercedes-Benz or a BMW have that our cars lack? One difference could be easily dealt with. Luxury cars were built better than the average Japanese effort, but that was simply because more time and work was lavished on them. As the owners of the world's most efficient factories, the Japanese could, if they chose, put more labor into each car — they could do more by hand and perform still more thorough checks at the end of the line. They would then be able to produce as well-built a car as anything in Stuttgart or Munich, but more cheaply. Another gap was almost as simple to close. Many of the components in a luxury car — from the bumpers to the stereo — are simply better, heavier, and more expensive than those used in mass-market cars. Leather seats, air conditioning, cruise control, fuel injection, anti-lock braking — those things that had been left out of mass-market cars to save money could now be put back in.

Nissan and Toyota were not the first in the new game. Honda had already led the way with its Acura, and a surprise entrant then appeared — Mazda. Just before it started work in late 1987 on the MX-5, or Miata, sports car that has been such a hit in Europe and the United States, Mazda also launched a luxury car project of its own that culminated in the summer 1991 launch of 929, a new sedan priced at $30,000 in the United States. The man charged with seeing the project through from the first sketches to the showroom was Naritaka Yasuda. "I specified three things for the new car," he explains. "One was a heavy radiator grille. The second was to do with the C-pillar [the piece of metal between the back door and the rear window]: this had to be arranged so that the face of the passenger would be framed elegantly when seen from the side. And finally, I insisted on a 'side garnish' — a strip along the lower half of the sides that prevents the bodywork from being damaged by chippings from the road."

No doubt Mazda had its reasons for identifying these as the key ingredients. But all the Japanese makers knew they were up against something that was daunting but intangible: the mystique of the luxury car, carefully nurtured by years of good quality and millions of dollars spent in advertising. "It's not easy to dismantle a myth," says Takashi Oka, the project manager for Nissan's Infiniti. "Take Mercedes, for instance. Our engineering and our quality may already be superior. But we won't be able to beat them until we can make a car that is twice as good for the same price." Undeterred, however, the companies put these fears aside and concentrated on what they knew best: turning a good design into a good product.

In doing so, both of the two leading firms were true to their traditions. Toyota, as the industry leader in Japan, is above all a superb marketing machine. At home, it leaves fancy designs to its smaller competitors and concentrates on turning out the right products at the right prices. Until the mid-1980s, more than two thirds of the cars it sold were white: that was the color of choice for the middle-class Japanese office worker and his wife. Accordingly, Toyota chose a conservative design. From the front, Lexus looks like an imitation of a Mercedes; from the back, like an imitation of a BMW. And from its high-waisted side, the car looks like nothing in particular. Its most prominent aesthetic feature is a big, shiny radiator grille at the front. Interestingly, the grille is wholly redundant; modern cars can direct air into the engine through less obtrusive holes under the front of the car. But if that was what Toyota's customers thought a luxury car needed, so be it. Rather than take aesthetic risks, therefore, the company concentrated on making its design easy to manufacture. It succeeded brilliantly. "If you compare our car with those of the competition, one thing stands out: theirs are much harder to make. Other firms seem to think that the Lexus is very cheap; I'd like to ask them why their cars are so expensive," argues Kazuo Okamoto, the chief engineer at Toyota in charge of the Lexus project.

In January 1992 the British magazine *Car* discovered one tiny but revealing detail of how Okamoto's team had done their job. Given access to the teardown laboratory of a competing car maker — teardown is the process by which automotive firms painstakingly dismantle their competitors' cars to look for money-saving secrets or technical ideas to be plundered for their own use — the magazine was shown the innards of the driver's seat from a Lexus. What it revealed was partly predictable and partly surprising. As one might expect for a luxury car, the seat was very heavy, because it was made of high-quality leather sprung like a double bed, and full of electric motors to adjust its height, angle, and lumbar support. But puzzlingly the metal frame that made up the seat had been left unpainted, while a comparable frame from a cheap French hatchback had been given a lick of neat black gloss. What was more, the Lexus frame was just beginning to rust. Far from being horrified at this corner-cutting, the magazine's host was full of admiration. Think, he insisted: no customer will ever know or care whether the seat frame is painted. Even if the seat continues to rust as the car ages, that corrosion is unlikely ever to cause a problem.

Nissan's Infiniti started from a different tack. The firm introduced its car into the U.S. market with a deliberately bizarre set of advertisements. Winning praise and scorn in equal measure, its first television commercials attracted attention by showing trees, rocks, landscapes — but no cars. It took risks on the design too. The Infiniti has a softly curving shape that marks a sharp departure from the consensus view of what an expensive car should look like. Inside, the car has Connolly leather seats, but not even the thinnest slice of walnut on the dashboard. Its stiffer suspension and tauter feel make it much more of a driver's car than the Lexus. And as its logo at the front, the car has a small metal medallion bearing a delicate arabesque leaf design called *karakusa* that is traditionally used on Japanese wrapping-cloths.

In contrast to their competitors at Toyota, Nissan's designers did not hesitate to ask a lot from the factory. For instance, the rear quarter panels of the Infiniti contain a smooth 25-cm curve. "We knew that it would be easier to build if we just stuck two pieces together as Mercedes-Benz does," explains Masayoshi Horike, the man who was in charge of putting the new car into production. "But a curve works better — both aesthetically and aerodynamically." The same is true of the shape of the Infiniti door panels, which have a hard-to-paint concave section just below the windows; at the designers' insistence, the factory came up with special tools to polish it beforehand. Another innovation in the car is an unprecedentedly strong metal frame, reinforced by injecting a strengthening foam into the pillars. Volvo used to advertise the safety of its cars by piling nine on top of each other; thanks to its foam, Nissan can manage twelve.

From the point of view of Nissan's management, the Infiniti takes an extraordinary amount of labor to make. Some 813 of the company's most experienced workers produce 300 Infinitis a day; on the other line in the same factory, 738 more junior workers turn out twice as many of the mass-market cars. But the real comparison is not with mass-market models, but with the car's competitors. "Before we started production, I visited most of the luxury car factories in Europe," explains Horike as he strolls down the line. "Jaguar's productivity is about a third of ours. Mercedes-Benz is about two-thirds."

That higher productivity was true not only of the manufacturing process. Using similar principles in the design and engineering departments, Nissan and Toyota brought their new models from first sketch to production in roughly half the time it takes for European competitors to do the same. When the Infiniti came to be introduced in the factory, there was no need to close it down for the traditional few weeks of retooling. By reprogramming the factory robots, Nissan was able to slip a few of the new cars into the system alongside other models so that the assembly workers could learn how to make them. Then, little by little, it raised the proportion. When the number of Infinitis made every day had grown to the point where it squeezed out the last few standard models, the factory managers strung up a notice. It said: THIS FACTORY MAKES ONLY LUXURY CARS.

Nissan does not yet sell the Infiniti in Europe. "We don't sell it in Europe," the firm explains, "because the surveys show that we are not yet number one in customer handling in Europe. Of course, we could send over cars any time that would be ready to be driven on European roads. But that's not what we want to do in luxury cars. Until we can raise our prestige and improve our customer handling, we're not going to take the Infiniti to Europe."

Toyota, on the other hand, has been selling the Lexus all over the EC since March 1990 but keeping very quiet about it. Even now, its sales target in the EC is two thousand cars a year — barely 5 percent of its current rate of sales in the smaller market of the United States. When asked to explain this bizarre difference, Okamoto delivers a characteristically Japanese platitude. "We prefer cooperation to competition," he says blandly. If that were true, Toyota would not be the company it is today. In fact, the firm probably has two reasons for its hesitation. First, setting up a network of special dealers is an expensive and time-consuming business — and one that is much harder to do in Europe than in the United States, thanks to the tradition of exclusive dealerships that European markets share with Japan. So far, Toyota has sold Lexus through its standard dealers, depriving European customers of many of the frills that came with the Lexus brand in the United States. Nissan is more frank.

But there is another reason, which neither firm is comfortable talking about. The rise of the Japanese car industry has already provoked a furious backlash from the European mass-producers. Why make enemies of BMW, Jaguar, and Mercedes-Benz as well? Perhaps it is thinking along these lines that explains a curious wrinkle in the pricing of the Lexus. In the United States in late 1991, a Toyota spokesman explains, the Lexus LS400 cost roughly the same as a BMW 525i. In Britain, it cost 38 percent more than the equivalent BMW. In Germany, it cost DM 92,000 ($55,578) — a massive 74 percent more than the BMW. Though it is not saying so, Toyota is clearly trying to keep its prestige high and its sales low by pricing the car at an enormous premium.

This will be welcome news to those European competitors. But it is very worrying in the long run. Experience in the United States has already shown that both Nissan's and Toyota's cars can outsell them hands down; as soon as the two Japanese firms start to put serious effort into the European market, BMW, Mercedes-Benz, and Jaguar will have to streamline fast to catch up. That may not be for another five years; it might not even be for another ten. But by then, Mazda, Honda, and Mitsubishi will surely follow where Nissan and Toyota have led.

FIVE

Toshiba, Olivetti, and
the European Computer

N HOUR'S DRIVE south of San Francisco, in a sheltered valley that used to be full of fruit orchards, lies the biggest concentration of high technology businesses in the world. It is known as Silicon Valley, and its founder — if such a disparate colony of individualistic start-ups can be said to have a founder — is a firm called Fairchild Semiconductor. Fairchild was formed at the end of the 1950s by a handful of talented engineers, including one who had helped to find the first practical use for the semiconductor. More than a score of other successful companies in the area were set up by former Fairchild employees, and although the company was overtaken in the commercial chip business by more nimble competitors like Intel, Motorola, and Texas Instruments, it was still by the mid-1980s an important supplier of electronics to the U.S. weapons industry.

On October 24, 1986, Japan's biggest maker of mainframe computers, Fujitsu Corporation, announced an offer to buy Fairchild. The proposal provoked uproar. Editorial writers from New York to Los Angeles deplored the handing over of such a prize to such a threatening foreign buyer; leading figures from the computer industry warned that the loss of Fairchild would

be the beginning of the end of U.S. dominance of high technology; and Caspar Weinberger, the secretary of defense, said
in public that the deal threatened the United States with a
dangerous dependence on Japan. Faced with this storm of
criticism, the bruised Fujitsu withdrew.

Just over four years later, the Japanese company tried again.
This time, its target was on the other side of the Atlantic:
International Computers Limited (ICL), Britain's only maker
of office mainframe computers. ICL was important to the British government, which bought more hardware from it in 1987
than from any other firm. But it also had an honored place in
the wider European computer industry. A member of five different European cooperative research projects, ICL was a re-
cipient of technology subsidies from Brussels, and the only
profitable big computer company in Europe. If anything, ICL
meant more to the British and the European computer establishment than Fairchild did to that of the United States. Yet
there was remarkably little fuss when Fujitsu's offer of $1.3
billion for 80 percent of ICL was duly reported the next day on
the front page of most of the British daily newspapers; and
four weeks later, when the details of the transaction were
wrapped up, the Japanese company had bought itself a foothold in the European computer market, the world's biggest,
without attracting either public controversy or a veto from
the government.

The simplest explanation for the sharp difference in reac-
tions between London and Washington is timing. The Fairchild offer came at the end of six years in which the United
States had lost its dominant place in the world semiconductor market. Japan's success in the electronics business had
prompted Americans to question for the first time their unthinking assumption that the U.S. share of world output,
anomalously high since the Second World War, would stay at
the same level indefinitely. Europeans, on the other hand,
were much less sensitive. Although Europe had been prominent in the early development of the computer (pioneering
work was done by code breakers in Britain during the war, and

the German company Siemens could claim to have been the first firm to put a transistorized computer on the market), the region no longer aspired to lead the world in the computer industry. Nor did the Fujitsu offer come as a surprise: by the late 1980s, Fujitsu had for some years been doing business with ICL, providing many of the biggest mainframes that the British firm sold in Europe. ICL's European competitors — led by Groupe Bull, the French state-owned computer company — indicated that with its new owners, the firm would no longer be welcome in joint research projects; they also moved to exclude it from their informal club of computer companies. But there the matter was allowed to drop.

That phlegmatic response was probably wise. For until now, the story of the world computer industry has been one of struggle between the United States and Japan, with Europeans looking on from afar. Over the coming decade, though, things will be different. With the emergence of Europe as a bigger single market for computers than either the United States or Japan, this chapter will argue, it will be on European turf that the giants of the industry will fight their battles. European governments will be able to make the rules that decide which side is favored, and dramatic changes will take place in the way computers are sold which could either give European computer firms a tremendous advantage or leave them languishing in the second ranks of the industry. To understand why, we must look back thirty years to the birth of the commercial computer industry, and try to see the world through the eyes of a bureaucrat at Japan's Ministry of International Trade and Industry, or MITI.

In the year 1960, many big Japanese manufacturing firms were taking advantage of low wages and the low value of the yen to export as they had never exported before. With a keen awareness of how far their own productivity lagged behind that of their competitors in Europe and the United States, however, they saw immediately the benefits of buying the new computers that were just coming onto the market. Although several American firms were making them, one stood out as offering more advanced machines and lower prices. IBM had already taken a dominant hold on the U.S. market, leaving its competitors far behind: not for nothing did American pundits talk of the industry as "IBM and the seven dwarfs."

As soon as they began to apply to MITI for licenses to import the new machines, however, the firms found that the Japanese government was far from keen that they should buy from IBM. It was resolved to make them more efficient, but the government had bigger ambitions than that Japan should just *use* computers. It wanted Japan to *make* them too. Only a few years before, the bureaucrats at MITI had decided that computing was just the sort of business — high in value-added, low in raw materials, and linked to all sorts of other industries from telecommunications to electrical goods — that the country ought to be in. They had decided, in short, that Japan must build a computer industry of its own.

Over the next decade, the ministry conceived and executed an ambitious plan to create a Japanese computer industry. It told IBM that it would be allowed to import machines or make them in Japan only if it licensed its technology to fledgling Japanese competitors. The ministry levied high tariffs on imports of finished machines, and forced IBM to procure locally many of the components it needed. Both Japanese companies and other ministries of the Japanese government found themselves under pressure to buy computers made by domestic firms — even when those computers were more expensive and less powerful than IBM's. A special marketing organization was created that would allow Japanese makers to foist on customers their first, most amateurish, efforts at prices 40 percent below those of IBM. NTT, the national telephone monopoly, was forced to give scores of important computer orders to domestic firms. And MITI channeled hundreds of millions of dollars into joint research and development projects, in which companies such as Hitachi, Fujitsu, NEC, Toshiba, Mitsubishi Electric, and Oki Electric cooperated in an attempt to reduce IBM's lead.

This was, in short, a prime example of Japan's much-vaunted industrial policies. A recent investigation of the early history of Japan's computer industry has revealed details of how the policy worked, and has established that the government in Tokyo spent a great deal more money than outsiders ever realized on building up this new business.[1] In the course of the 1960s, for instance, the government spent almost twice as much on computer R&D as the entire private sector combined. What is more, the ministry was quite separately fostering a domestic semiconductor industry, and was using every means at its disposal to allow Japanese firms to make computer chips without paying high royalties to U.S. firms like Texas Instruments to whom all the necessary patents belonged.

By 1980 MITI was ready to declare victory. Japan had built itself a computer industry and announced that it was prepared to open its market fully to imports.[2] Yet the policy was far from an unqualified success. As is so often the case, protection had helped the suppliers only at the price of harming the customers. Japan had a myriad of different and incompatible computer standards, the largest being NEC's. As late as 1988, one could see "OLS," or office ladies, in Japanese companies reading sales figures off a printout from one computer and typing them into another for further processing. In the United States, where computers were beginning to learn to talk to each other, that labor would have been unnecessary.

One consequence of this was that computers had spread much more slowly in Japan than in Western markets. That may sound astonishing to anyone who has heard of the extraordinary efficiency of Japanese factories: they have been second to none in using robots intelligently. But Japanese offices, even in the early 1990s, remain far less automated than those in Europe — let alone the United States. During the three years I lived in Tokyo, for instance, I received every week or so a press release from Sharp, one of Japan's leading technology companies, in which a tiny slip of paper with my name typed on it had been painstakingly pasted *by hand* onto a photocopied letter. And during a visit one day in 1988 or 1989 to the MITI bureau responsible for promoting the computer industry, I observed a flurry of excitement: the office, feared throughout the world as the nerve center of a conspiracy to dominate the world computer industry, was taking delivery of its very first PCs. Until then, the civil servants had written their grand plans by hand.

But there was another problem, far more serious than the straightforward fact that the buyers of computers had been given a raw deal. In their obsession with beating "Big Blue," as IBM had come to be called, the bureaucrats had missed wider changes that were taking place in the computer industry.

In the 1960s and 1970s, IBM had thrived partly because of being one of the most Japanese in spirit of American companies. The firm had an informal policy of giving its employees jobs for life. Its hallmark was outstanding service and customer support — a policy that gave rise to the slogan "Nobody ever got fired for buying IBM." It had used a technique of which Japanese firms were often accused: subsidizing one part of its business (software and services) with the profits from another (hardware sales). Its very presence in the Japanese market, despite the harassment that it had suffered at the hands of the Japanese government, was a measure of the firm's persistence in looking for long-term growth rather than short-term profits. And its unabashed policy of using its size and marketing might to drive smaller competitors to the wall had won IBM the leading position in almost all the markets of the industrial world except Japan's — so much so that the U.S. federal government spent a fruitless decade trying to fight it in the courts using antitrust measures but found itself outmaneuvered by the larger and better-briefed teams of lawyers that IBM was able to deploy. IBM seemed an admirable model to imitate.

But while the bureaucrats in Tokyo were doing all they

could to mold Japanese computer companies in IBM's image, the world outside was changing. In 1979 a fledgling California firm founded by two university dropouts had developed a machine called the Apple II, which was to turn the industry on its head. Until then, computers had been mysterious beasts that lived in air-conditioned rooms, tended by high-priest technicians in white coats and accessible to the ordinary mortal outside only via punched cards and messages printed in smudgy capitals on heavy piles of special paper. Their buyers had been specialists inside big companies; the programs that allowed them to process accounts or to print dividend checks often had to be written specially for each user. And once a customer had bought a computer from one firm, it made economic sense to buy another from the same company; if he did not, the customer would find himself the keeper of a Babel of machines unable to talk to each other.

Apple changed all that. In itself, the Apple II machine was not much, but it gave users a glimpse of a future in which the computer would sit on their desks and they would have control of it. With the arrival of the era of the personal computer, everything in the market changed too. As the PC moved closer to the customer, it was the user of information, rather than the specialist, who made the buying decision. Computers began to be distributed through retailers, rather than by the door-to-door salesmen of the manufacturers. A new software industry sprang up to offer standard word-processing and spreadsheet programs. Moreover, when Big Blue finally moved into the PC market in 1982, a standard was created, and soon copied,[3] that allowed customers to buy machines not just from the single company that had sold them hardware in the past, but from any one of hundreds of competing firms. By 1987 even IBM was finding that half its global profits came from the personal computer, rather than from the minis and mainframes in which it had specialized in the past. Four years later, it became clear that the firm had fallen badly behind: it was too wedded to the old days to keep abreast in the fast-moving new business. IBM actually found itself losing money. The firm that had once used its financial power to face down even the government was forced to begin a painful process of restructuring — shedding jobs, merging divisions, trying to get its products to market faster, and cutting costs everywhere.

The problems of IBM gave reflective people in Japan's computer industry pause for thought. Had MITI made a fearful mistake, they wondered? Had it done the equivalent of making Japan competitive in building horse-drawn carriages in 1890, just before the invention of the motorcar? It certainly seemed so. For although Japanese firms were faithfully continuing to develop big IBM-style systems, they were more interested in an entirely different problem: the Japanese typewriter.

Japanese computer firms saw clearly that the slowness with which computers had caught on in Japan was not only the fault of MITI. It was also a consequence of the nature of the Japanese language. Written in a combination of three different scripts — two syllabaries, each containing around fifty characters, and many thousand Chinese characters (or *kanji*), of which Japanese newspapers use a standard set of 1,984, called the *Toyo kanji* — Japanese had always proved a daunting obstacle to office automation. Before the arrival of the computer, there was a simple way neither of entering Japanese characters into a computer nor of getting them out again, whether on a screen or on paper. Early Japanese typewriters were huge, ungainly things with hundreds of keys; it was in response to the problem of transmitting messages in a language of so many characters that Japanese firms had turned the fax machine, invented in the United States, into a product for the mass market.

As computer technology became better and cheaper, though, Japanese firms began to see the beginnings of a Japanese typewriter taking shape. The way to solve the *kanji* problem, the companies found, was for the user to type phonetically at the keyboard.[4] Then the machine would display the different Chinese characters with that sound, often a dozen or so, and the user could specify the right one from the list. So a Japanese-language typewriter (or, to be precise, a word processor) had to have a number of things: a high-quality screen to show all the characters clearly; a high-quality printer so that the results could be output; and lots of memory and computing power to deal with the burden of manipulating such a large and complex set of symbols.

Until the 1970s, only big and hugely expensive computers could do the job. Yet Japanese firms had a useful advantage: experience in consumer electronics. While the U.S. computer industry had never had to bother much about exterior design or size (firms competed on speed, performance, and ease of use), businesses in Japan had been fighting furiously for years to bring out radios, televisions, and hi-fis just a bit smaller and sleeker than last year's. They understood the importance of miniaturization. And since their businesses were often vertically integrated — that is, making not only the final products but very often also the key components that go into them — the firms were past masters of the thousands of incremental improvements that together can add up to a product revolution. The result was that year by year, the new Japanese-language word processors became more powerful and cheaper but were still portable. As if by mistake, therefore, the Japanese computer firms found themselves selling portable computers.

In the United States, meanwhile, the PC revolution was developing machines that became more and more powerful every year but remained roughly the same size. Once the computer had become small enough to fit on a desk, most people in California believed, it was small enough. Those who wanted to go a step further and make the computer portable (among them Adam Osborne, a British entrepreneur and writer) were dismissed as eccentrics. But Japanese firms had already seen the method in their madness: professionals in Tokyo were beginning to refer to the PC not as a desktop but as a *hitotsubo* machine — that is, a machine that takes up the space of one *tatami* mat in a traditional Japanese room.[5] Since many apartments in Tokyo had rooms of eight, six, or even only four mats in size, that nickname carried a clear connotation: too big.

Toshiba, a rather traditional company better known for its heavy industry division, was never the leading computer maker in Japan. The bureaucrats at MITI had thought it more capable of developing good peripherals, such as screens and printers, than fully fledged computers; in fact, the company they chose to promote as a maker of small computers was NEC. Nor had Toshiba been conspicuously more successful in foreign markets. It had tried to introduce a desktop PC in the United States that was incompatible with the IBM standard spreading across the industry — a product that, not surprisingly, flopped ignominiously.

In 1982 the undaunted firm decided to try again — this time in Europe. Atsutoshi Nishida, now Toshiba's head of international computer marketing, was the man sent to England in 1982 and 1983 to set up a computer business. "This was what I asked myself," he remembers. "While making machines that were compatible with IBM's, how could we differentiate our product from that of other manufacturers? We had to bear in mind how to take best advantage of our technology, our skill at miniaturization. Our disadvantages were that our computers had low-quality screens, and 3½-inch floppy disk drives that were only just gaining acceptance."

Nishida knew that one thing was key to winning acceptance in the market for his new machines: software. He therefore went to the British headquarters of Lotus Development, maker of the world's most popular spreadsheet, 1-2-3. His mission was to ask them to sell their software in a form compatible with Toshiba's new machines. "We tried to explain the Toshiba strategy, the concept of a laptop computer itself," he says. "I used a very simple example: the pocket calculator. I explained how before the calculator, people thought of calculating machines only as heavy, inconvenient things that sat on their desks. Likewise with the computer: what we were trying to do was change people's view of what a computer was. Sooner or later, I said, laptops would replace the big desktop machines."

Nishida's audience was not convinced. For all his enthusiasm, they turned him down flat. He went away. Some weeks later, however, he was back — with a new set of reasons why Lotus ought to cooperate with him. After his third or fourth visit, the firm became puzzled by his persistence, and began to wonder whether they might not have been hasty. The rest, as they say, is history. A few months later, Lotus programs began to appear in a format suitable for Toshiba's new machines. Yet the Japanese firm still had a number of problems. Most of its products were bulky and greedy with electricity, and could run only off the main power supply. Its basic model, the Toshiba T1100, was smaller and could run off batteries — but it suffered from a miserably dark and narrow screen. Its small computers were also too expensive: for a given performance, they cost nearly double the price of normal desktop computers. "That didn't worry me, though. I knew that once the market share of laptop PCs began to rise, our prices could fall," insists Nishida. "I've forgotten the exact prices, even though I set them myself."

By late 1988 Toshiba felt that it was ready to make a bigger splash. If consumers were to make the psychological leap toward thinking of a computer as something truly portable, its strategists argued, the company's engineers would have to squeeze everything into a box the size of standard office paper. And they must cut no corners, such as by providing an unlit screen, or a floppy disk drive that saved space at the price of being incompatible with anyone else's.

A team of five people was set to work in early 1989 at the company's factory-cum-research complex in Ome, a small town nestled in mountains and forests an hour west of the Japanese capital by commuter train. The five were to decide the broad features of the new project, with others underneath them tidying up the details. There was no single dominant innovation in the new machine: every major component was either wholly new or a significant advance in terms of miniaturization or performance on what had come before. "Of course, there were arguments about different aspects of the project," recalls Kenji Hibi, one of the five, "such as whether we should make the battery last longer by providing a screen without a light behind it, or whether we should ditch the idea of detachable batteries altogether. Eventually we decided to make the machine *we* would want to use ourselves."

Among its features was a function that proved to be very important: the new machine incorporated a "resume" function, whereby the user could stop in the middle of a piece of work and switch the machine off, but then carry on later from exactly the same point at the touch of a button without the delay of having to "boot" the machine again and load up all the information that was there before. Because the design process was so swift — the new model went from drawing board to the shops in little over seven months — there was simply no time for the usual methods of development: weekly progress meetings were out of the question, for the decisions would have been out of date before they were put into effect. Huddled together in a single complex of buildings were the engineers, the graphic designers, the manufacturing specialists, the people who wrote the manuals — and all worked furiously on the project, day, night, and weekends.

What the project team at Toshiba did not know was that halfway across the world, Zenith Data Systems, a company that until 1987 was the world leader in the portable computer market, had quite independently set itself precisely the same target. The U.S. firm was working on a new machine to be called the Minisport, identical in size to Toshiba's within an eighth of an inch in each direction, and with almost the same specification. The two products came out within weeks of one another in the summer of 1989. Essentially, there were only three differences between them. One, the Zenith had the same traditional white case of all American computers; the Toshiba was the same matte dark gray that was popular in Japan for hi-fis and cordless telephones. Two, Zenith's engineers had not quite succeeded in fitting everything into the box: to get the floppy disk drive in, they had had to drop the standard 3½-inch model and replace it with a specially designed, unique 2½-inch drive that worked perfectly well but condemned the Minisport to isolation from the mainstream computer market.

Toshiba had unquestionably scored a marketing victory. Zenith's small disk drive, technical marvel though it was, turned out to be a marketing disaster. Since they could not buy any commercial software on the new disk drives, customers could only use the Zenith machine if they had another computer; and even then, they could only transfer data between the two by a cable, rather than simply by taking the disk out of one machine and popping it into the other. It was all the more surprising, therefore, that the third difference — the price — was in Toshiba's favor. Zenith's machine cost $2,000; Toshiba's, even with the superior full-size drive, cost only ¥198,000, which was worth $1,400 at current exchange rates. No one noticed the comparison at the time, because the two machines were at first sold only in their own home markets.[6] But that summer was the turning point in Toshiba's fortunes, and the turning point in Japan's growing dominance of the portable computer market.

It was also the beginning of a new market. Just as the Walkman had, and the camcorder was still to do, Toshiba's new computer crossed a psychological borderline with its combination of small size, low weight and price, and high power. Thousands of people who had never before believed that portable computers were serious products started to want one, and scores of companies all over the world realized at last that this would be a growing market for the 1990s. This was no accident: proof that Toshiba knew exactly what it was doing could be seen in the name it had chosen for the new machine in Japan.[7] Toshiba called it the Dynabook, borrowing a name from Alan Kay, a computer industry guru who had predicted more than a decade earlier that one day computers would become so small and so powerful that they could be used as personal, portable terminals to huge mainframe computers. Kay had drawn an analogy between computers and books. In the days when books were still written by hand by scribes, they were so valuable that it was necessary not just to protect them in a library but also often to chain them physically to the shelves. When the Venetian printer Aldus started to print books with removable type and moderate prices — the latter something that Gutenberg failed to achieve with his famous Bible — a book was now something that a gentleman could carry in his saddlebag while traveling. Likewise, Kay had said, the computer would become portable; and thanks to its ability to communicate with larger remote machines, it became a dynamic rather than a static source of information. Hence the name Dynabook.

In Japan the new Dynabook was a roaring success. The *Nihon Keizai Shimbun*, Japan's leading financial daily, asked Toshiba's competitors what they thought of it and was met with expressions of blank horror. "We don't understand how they can make it at the price," said a top executive of another computer company bitterly. Taken by surprise though they had been, the competition set to work. Within a matter of weeks, five Japanese firms announced that they, too, would be bringing out new notebook-sized computers. Toshiba had the field to itself for almost half a year but at the beginning of 1990, the tremendous effect of the fiercely competitive Japanese market began to make itself felt. One by one, the new models came out. Notebook-sized computers are now also made by NEC, Seiko-Epson, Citizen, Oki, Matsushita, Mitsubishi Electric, Sony, Sharp — and Nippon Steel, which thinks that the computer market is a good way to diversify out of its core business. But the competition spurred Toshiba itself on to greater efforts. In an extraordinary display of flexibility, the company brought out no fewer than eight new models in the next sixteen months, each time squeezing better features, a brighter screen, or more power into the same-sized box. It is now the world's leading maker of notebook and laptop computers.

The personal computer revolution that had caught the bureaucrats at MITI by surprise left a number of casualties in the United States as well. IBM was not the only firm derailed by the events of the 1980s. So too were Digital Equipment Corporation, Hewlett-Packard — and even Apple and Compaq, the start-ups that had been the darlings of the stock market only a few years earlier.

Looking back, it now seems that two different things were happening. First, the way computers were sold was undergoing a revolution. In the early days of the personal computer, chains of independent dealers had sprung up to supply, install, and service the customers' new machines. The dealers were a response to the fact that the new manufacturers of PCs could not support, as the traditional mainframe and minicomputer makers had, expensive battalions of their own sales staff. Yet in a way, independent dealers themselves were a transitional phase. Even with prices falling 30 percent a year, a customer would still spend thousands, rather than hundreds, of dollars on a single order. How could the dealers justify adding a thousand dollars or more to the factory price of the machine? Increasingly, customers were quite capable of setting up their computers by themselves; what they were willing to pay for was a high-quality technical service that would help them if their PCs started to go wrong. Yet if the dealer sold computers of a number of different brands, most of which were bringing out new models twice a year or more, the sales staff were unlikely to know any more about the problem than their customers. In any case, physical breakdown of the machine itself was not the most common difficulty; rather, users were more likely to find themselves stumped by the software, as they tried to incorporate a widening range of increasingly complex and power-hungry programs into their machines. What they wanted from the supplier was not a man in overalls — or, in

IBM's case, a blue suit and white shirt — who would come round, scratch his head, and change a fuse or two. Instead, customers wanted to be able to talk to an expert about the programs they were trying to run, and perhaps have that expert take control of the computer directly over the telephone and solve the problem immediately.

In the United States, computer makers were quick to see the significance of this trend. Some began to allow their products to be sold through computer supermarkets — huge, out-of-town warehouses with razor-thin margins that were aiming to do the same thing to the computer dealers that suburban shopping malls had done to neighborhood shops. A growing number of others (including firms like Zeos International and Dell, which achieved sales of $500 million by its founder's twenty-sixth birthday) realized that they could cut out retailers altogether by advertising in computer magazines, selling directly to the customer at low prices, and providing free technical support twenty-four hours a day over the telephone. Because there was no need to keep stocks of computers waiting in dealers' showrooms, these new upstart firms could keep near-zero inventories, make the computers only to order, and ship them out to customers by overnight courier. What was more, this method of doing business, which kept the computer company in direct contact with its customers, could also yield valuable information about what sort of products the market would want next year.

Companies that were less alert soon found themselves in trouble. A case in point was Compaq, the 1980s start-up that used to boast in its advertisements that it had grown faster than any other company in history. Compaq's strength in its early years had always been its ability to deliver high-quality, reliable products at prices well below those of IBM — and to keep the dealers who distributed its products happy. By the end of 1990, the combination of the revolution in computer retailing and the broader slowing of the U.S. economy started to make the company's future look much less promising. By the second quarter of 1991, Compaq was forced to report a slump in profits, and by autumn, it was embroiled in a painful price war at the same time that eight of its ten main dealer chains were in the throes of either merging or being taken over. The result was disaster. The company made the first quarterly loss of its entire history. It sacked an eighth of its work force, and Rod Canion, the firm's idiosyncratic founder, was moved aside to make way for Eckhard Pfeiffer, a German who had previously run the company's European operations.

Although change was sweeping through the PC business, there was still a matching market in larger machines for big corporate customers, which had proved surprisingly resistant to the trends in personal computing. When a big bank, for instance, wanted to buy a mainframe computer to handle the processing of millions of accounts, it would have to pick a computer from one maker and then stick to it. Although the manufacturer's next model might be slower in coming out and higher in price than that of a rival, it would cost too much to rebuild the system from scratch: the customer, once attracted, was a captive. By the middle of the 1980s, even the biggest corporate customers could see that fierce competition in the personal computer industry had produced astonishingly fast advances in performance and price. If only mainframe computers, some of them mused, could exchange data with each other as PCs could; it would then be easy for them to pick and choose computers according to which firm's latest model offered the best deal.

Yet although customers could see it, the big computer makers were not yet ready to put it into practice. Two decades earlier, one of IBM's own crack engineers, Gene Amdahl, pioneered a "clone" industry for mainframes by selling bargain-basement mainframe computers that could work in tandem with an existing IBM installation. And Japanese firms had joined in by the 1970s to challenge the old system, by offering "plug-compatible" machines that would replace parts of an existing IBM installation. But it was not until the popularization by the late 1980s of the UNIX operating system that mainframe and minicomputer customers could see the prospect of release from the servitude of a single firm's computer standard.[8] Invented at the renowned Bell Laboratories of AT&T, UNIX is a computer operating system that is available at a price to anyone who wants to use it. Although a single international version of it has not yet emerged, it may well in the course of the 1990s give to mainframes the competitive spurt that IBM's PC software did to personal computers in the 1980s — and if it does, it will have helped to create a market for "open systems."

Meanwhile, a technical development was threatening the traditional mainframe computer business: it was being attacked from below by a new generation of superpowerful desktop computers. The change came about as a result of reduced instruction-set computing, or RISC. To see its significance, recall that all microprocessors at the heart of computers work by translating the commands given by a program into a succession of much more basic instructions, which deal with information bit by bit and which choose exactly where in the memory to put things that the computer needs to know. Every microprocessor has a fixed menu of instructions, in terms of which complex calculations must in the end be cast. In the early 1980s, though, researchers noticed something odd: many of the available instructions in a given microprocessor were rarely, if ever, used. This was probably because the instruction sets had been designed for machine-language programmers, but most programmers now write in higher-level computer languages. Why not build a microprocessor offering a far smaller set of instructions, they wondered, and therefore able to execute each one more quickly?[9] The leading firm in the field was a California start-up called Sun Microsystems ("Sun" was an acronym, from Stanford University Network). But by 1992, at least five different U.S. companies had developed RISC microprocessors. A new industry was born, selling desktop work stations that performed like mainframes but cost only twice the price of a PC.

Taking all these three changes together — more efficient PC distribution, the trend toward open systems in mainframes, and the emergence of RISC machines — a dramatic change is now taking place in the computer industry: margins are falling fast. Whereas in the early days of computing, firms like IBM could expect to sell a new machine for 80 percent more than its gross manufacturing cost, now the business of making computers has suddenly become a great deal less profitable. With lower profitability, lower growth has come too: corporate customers in Europe and the United States have often already achieved the big jump in productivity that results from changing over from manual to automated accounting and data processing, and are now beginning to look more critically at new investment in office automation. In the PC business, the rapid spread of Microsoft's new Windows graphic interface, which brought to the users of IBM computers the ease of use that had previously been available on the Apple Macintosh, gave a temporary fillip to the market. But the trend was downward all the same. After three decades of astounding growth, computing had become a mature industry.

It is for these reasons that computer companies now face the greatest challenge of their history, and one to which no one has worked out a successful response. In July 1991 two management consultants, Andrew Rappaport and Shmuel Halevi, proposed a radical approach in a controversial article in the *Harvard Business Review*.[10] The pair argued that selling computers is becoming a "commodity" business, in which consumers no longer mind whose name is on the box they buy. Profitable computer firms, the two consultants predict, will be those that recognize their business as not selling machines, but selling "solutions" to clients' problems. The article compared Apple unfavorably with the software house Microsoft: Microsoft has grown to huge stature in the industry by getting its MS-DOS operating system inside almost 100 million personal computers around the world, they argue; while Apple, riven by successive management crises, has replaced its founder with a former Pepsi-Cola executive and has been pushed into an alliance with IBM, the firm that its early advertisements used to satirize as gray and conformist. What went wrong? Easy, the two consultants say: Apple should have licensed its Macintosh interface years ago, waited for it to become the industry standard that Windows is now in the process of becoming, and sat back and grown fat on the income, as companies from Munich to Seoul queued up to pay royalties for its use. The article provoked a storm of disagreement; the debate continues.

In Europe, the maturing of the computer industry should have been prompting even more self-examination than in the United States. European firms, too, were coming under increasing price pressure as more nimble rivals came in to undercut their own offerings in their own markets. Yet there were two key differences between the European market and that of the United States. First, fewer European firms were confident that they could continue to keep pace with the relentless innovation that kept firms like Hewlett-Packard in business.[11] And second, the European computer market was far behind that of the United States.

The reasons for this were embarrassing. In the 1960s and 1970s, European governments were determined to keep their own firms at the front of the pack, and thought the best way to do so was to send huge public sector equipment orders their way in order to allow them to build up economies of scale. The result was that the barriers between computer markets in the different countries of Europe often seemed far higher than the language differences would have suggested. Few European firms managed to sell convincingly outside their own countries; the most "European" firm of the computer industry, in the sense of having a single overall strategy for selling in Europe and a strong presence in each European market, was of course IBM. Despite its reputation for rigidity, IBM took a flexible approach that was evident from the tiniest things — such as the sensitivity to local differences that led the company to allow its employees a glass of wine with their lunch in France, where not to do so might have provoked uproar, but to encourage a more austere teetotalism in its British operations.

This market fragmentation, and the inability of European firms to vault over it, meant that prices were higher and specifications generally lower in Europe than in the United States. Although the rise of mail-order catalogues in Britain at the end of the 1980s began to change the situation rapidly, it used to be almost traditional that an American company could charge in Britain the same number of pounds as it could get dollars in its more competitive home market — and higher prices still in Germany, France, and Italy. John Sculley, the chairman of Apple, was one of the few willing to admit it. "If you want to know where the major U.S. personal computer firms are making money these days," he said in an unguarded moment, "it's not in the U.S. There really is no European computer industry, so we are doing well there."[12]

Understandably, less attractive terms to the customer meant that the European market was far less well developed than the American. In many emerging technologies, from databases on compact disc to 32-bit work stations, from computer-aided design to electronic mail, market penetration two years after the technology had been commercialized in the United States showed a similar pattern: an installed base in the United States five or ten times the size of the installed base in Europe, despite the fact that the American population and annual economic output are both less. That is one reason why attempts to set up new technology businesses in Europe, whether in new companies or whether as divisions of existing firms, have so often failed.[13]

Some cynics inside the European computer industry insist that it simply failed to attract the talented people that the industry drew in both Japan and the United States.[14] "The threat to the European computer industry from Japanese companies is great," argues a former ICL executive, "but it's less than the threat the European firms face from themselves. They respond to every problem by running to Brussels: if you see two R&D managers in a bar together, are they figuring out how to whip the Japanese? No — they're figuring out how to get more money out of the European Community. And consider the information technology professionals [the people in companies who run computing departments and are therefore responsible for buying from computer firms]. Most of them aren't professional at all; nor do they see their job as one of pioneering new technology." A vivid illustration of the broader problem can be seen also in the job market for computer industry researchers. In many cases, a specialist equipped with a Ph.D. can earn three times the starting salary in a laboratory in the United States that a European firm would be willing to offer.

By late 1991 the disastrous results of this history were all too visible. Bull, Siemens, and the Italian Olivetti Group were all drowning in red ink. Each had proved unable to deal with the powerful cocktail of changing distribution, the move to open systems, and the sharp fall in computing prices prompted by the arrival of RISC technology. Bull lost so much money that the French government felt itself obliged to inject Fr 4 billion ($752 million) of new equity in the firm, incurring furious complaints to the European Commission from competitors who rightly feared that the firm would use some of the money to undercut them in the European market. Siemens swallowed hard as only a huge diversified electrical conglomerate can, but admitted that its computer division, which had only a year before acquired the loss-making Nixdorf company, was not even within sight of returning to profitability. Carlo De Benedetti, the controlling shareholder at Olivetti, moved aside the firm's chief executive to take over the running of the business himself. And together, the three firms begged the bureaucrats in Brussels to help a strategic industry on the brink of disaster. It was not protection they were demanding, the firms insisted. Rather, they wanted only two things: first, an attempt by Brussels to open up the public sector computer markets of the United States and Japan, in both of which domestic firms got some 90 percent of the business; and second, though it was hard to see how this would be necessarily to the advantage of European firms unless it were to be protectionist by favoring them over competitors outside, more European public spending on computer equipment and services.

One thing is clear: whatever their proposed solutions to the problem, indigenous European computer companies can claim neither the advantages of the American industry nor those of the Japanese. There is no second wave of innovative European firms to mirror the successes of firms like Sun and MIPS which can be weighed against the damage done to traditional general computer makers. And Europe does not have the ability to make components cheaply, particularly semiconductors, which lies at the heart of the competitiveness of Japan's computer industry. One expert calculates that at least three Japanese semiconductor firms have a larger chip-making capacity than the whole European electronics industry combined.

The paradox is that while the indigenous firms have been wringing their hands about the prospects for the European computer industry, outsiders remain far more optimistic. Fujitsu has acquired control of ICL. Digital Equipment has picked up the German firm Kienzle from Mannesmann, and the entire minicomputer business of the Dutch electronics conglomerate Philips. And other American and Japanese firms have moved into Europe, albeit more quietly, in the expectation of rich pickings as the European market opens up.

To be precise, they were already in position by early 1992. ICL had fallen to Fujitsu — and had confounded some of its critics by not merely continuing to design computers and components independently for manufacture in Japan, but also in some cases selling its products in the Japanese market. Siemens was selling some Fujitsu machines under its own name, and had linked up with IBM in a joint venture to manufacture the next-generation 16MB DRAM memory chip,[15] and to design jointly the 64MB DRAM that will follow it in the second half of the 1990s.

Most important, however, Bull had also lost its independence. Soon after Bull plunged into loss, it became clear that the firm could not continue in business for long without help from one of the major forces in the computer industry. Its own technological resources were just too weak, and the changes taking place in the market too fast, for the firm to hope to field a competitive range of products by itself. As the French government bailout began to unravel under scrutiny from the competition regulators at the European Community in late 1991, Bull began to talk to IBM and to Hewlett-Packard about possible link-ups. (The possibility of a linkage with NEC, the biggest firm in Japan's domestic market and a powerful components maker, was never seriously discussed. Although NEC already held a 5 percent stake in Bull, the feelings toward Japan of Edith Cresson, then French prime minister, made it impossible that a Japanese company should be seen to be the senior partner in a marriage with Bull.)

The discussion ranged over many issues: Bull wanted RISC technology, and it wanted a market for the portable computers produced by Zenith Data Systems, which it had bought from Zenith in 1989. In return, it could offer privileged access to the French market and use of its printed circuit board manufacturing facilities. In the end, the lucky winner was IBM. The firm and Bull's management agreed hastily that IBM would take a shareholding in the firm, would buy portable computers from it and sell them under its own label, and would sell its own small disk drives to Bull. While the details were being worked out (even the size of IBM's new shareholding in the state-controlled firm was at first undecided), Bull engineers were already off to the IBM design center in Texas to learn all about RISC.[16]

From a business point of view, many of these acquisitions and alliances made good sense. Although the computer industry was becoming more competitive year by year, it was also becoming an industry with extraordinarily high entry costs. Highest of all was the price of the memory game: Japanese firms were having to invest $1 billion apiece to buy their place in the market for 16MB and 64MB DRAMS. But designing even a new microprocessor, something that could be done for

a few million dollars in the 1970s, was a $100 million under-
taking by the 1990s. It was not only European firms that were
trying to secure their future: the entire industry was increasingly enmeshed in a web of strategic alliances. The irony was,
of course, that only twenty years earlier IBM had epitomized
the threat from across the Atlantic which drove European policymakers into a frenzy: an alliance between Bull and Big
Blue would have been politically unthinkable in 1972. Yet in-
comprehensibly, the French government was able to pass off
its 1992 surrender to IBM as a preemptive victory in the coming war with Japan.

January 1992 was not the best time to choose to visit Ivrea,
the "technology city" an hour's drive from Turin where the
Olivetti Group has its headquarters. With the exception of
Siemens, which had paired up with IBM in the memory market, Olivetti was by then the last remaining wholly independent European computer company. It was a cold and lonely
position to be in.

Only a month or so earlier, the firm's chairman and controlling shareholder, Carlo De Benedetti, had taken direct
control of the business himself, moving aside Vittorio Cas-
soni, its former chief executive, and announcing the sacking
of 2,500 staff, on top of the 7,000 of the firm's 42,000 workers
who had already departed that year. He moved to close two
of the company's most unprofitable factories in Italy and began the job of slimming its operations abroad. Depending on
how the Olivetti board would decide to account for the restructuring costs, De Benedetti made it clear that the firm
would have to declare 1991 losses above 290 billion lire ($241
million), more than 4 percent of its total sales that year. Olivetti's problem was that it had been too slow to respond to the
changes in the market described earlier. Its proprietary system sales were dull, and in the open systems and PC markets,
it had to discount its products deeply in order to keep them
selling. "We work very hard to make Bill Gates rich," said one
of the company's top managers, in a bitter reference to the

fees Olivetti had to pay to Microsoft for the use of its MS-DOS operating system. The company had also suffered from the misguided attempts of the European Commission to promote Europe's electronics industry. In an astonishing repeat of a mistake made a few years earlier by the United States, the bureaucrats in Brussels had struck an agreement with Japanese makers of memory chips that the makers would not sell in Europe below certain minimum prices. The idea was a preemptive move to stop them from "dumping" their chips and therefore damaging European makers; its result, however, was sharply to raise semiconductor prices in Europe and to make it much harder for European computer companies, which had to buy the chips, to compete with other computer makers abroad. In an angry complaint at a private lunch in Brussels, Olivetti's top management told Jacques Delors, the president of the Commission, that the new floor prices were mad. "They are a fantastic tool for making the Japanese rich," Bruno Lamborghini, Olivetti's vice president for planning and the chairman of Eurobit, an association of European computer makers, was believed to have said. "We haven't shifted a single purchase to Siemens; we've just had to pay more to our existing suppliers."

These were problems common across the industry; but Olivetti had some special problems all its own. The rigidity of Italian labor laws and the intransigence of its unions meant that the firm had lost control over the size of its work force; not even the cuts announced in 1992 were deep enough to bring the firm down to the leanness it would need to be truly competitive. Traditionally, the company had treated labor as a fixed cost, and adjusted its prices and product lines to make best use of its manufacturing capacity. By 1992 those days had ended — capacity simply had to be cut. Olivetti had also suffered disastrously from a corporate reorganization in 1989 that created two main divisions: one intended to be responsible for office products like fax machines and photocopiers, the other for computer systems. Unfortunately, the increasing convergence of these two markets had made nonsense of the divisions, and the two had sometimes found themselves fighting each other in the same markets. Worse, the company's internal accounting was so bad that it often had no idea which of its products were making money and which not.

De Benedetti's new approach began to change this by instituting new financial disciplines. Furthermore, the firm was beginning to deploy its sales force in a more intelligent way; in the past, astonishingly, the same person had often been asked to sell everything from basic typewriters to UNIX file servers. Yet the mood in Ivrea that January was far from despondent. Despite its disastrous losses in 1991, the company had actually covered its operating costs — which was more than could be said for Bull or Siemens-Nixdorf. And there was a feeling that Olivetti now had a clear idea of what it was trying to do and how it would do it.

That strategy, the company's management explained, was to make Olivetti into a "systems integrator": a firm that might not make its own products but would offer complete computer systems to clients. This, Olivetti people argued urgently, was the best way to take advantage of what their firm was good at. For instance, in 1991 the firm had a 60 percent share of the market for computing in British building societies. It had the country's largest third-party maintenance contract at Barclays Bank; it had installed a UNIX system across the whole of the National Westminster Bank. With such skills, it hoped, the firm would not be beholden to Brussels for subsidies or protection. "The fundamental reason why we can benefit from open markets," said Francisco Caio, a management consultant who had been brought in from outside to be De Benedetti's assistant, "is this: to sell such systems, you need to be long in the market. Let the Japanese supply the raw machinery; it's us who will install it. And that is where much of the value-added lies."

Caio is not the only management consultant who advances this argument. Tim Simpson, head of the London branch of the U.S. consultancy Arthur D. Little, had made a similar point two months earlier in a presentation to European clients. Simpson argues that the wider electronics industry should be seen as a four-stage "value chain," which runs from components such as integrated circuits and screens, to modules such as disk drives and operating systems, to products like engineering work stations and video recorders, and ultimately to systems and services such as custom-built computer installations for banks or value-added networks such as airline reservation systems. What is happening, he says, is that the component and module end of the industry is becoming more concentrated: in chips, for instance, NEC and Toshiba each had a 9 percent world market share in 1990; and in disk drives, the American firms Seagate and Conner between them have over 40 percent of the world market. The building blocks of the computer industry are becoming standardized. So, faced with increased competition, firms are tempted to become "systems integrators." Such a strategy allows them to invest less; it keeps them flexible; and it takes advantage of their relations with key customers. Yet the strategy has risks. By its nature, it is irreversible; it makes the firm vulnerable to suppliers who later turn out to be competitors; and it gives others a chance to slip in and do the same thing more efficiently, as Dell and Zeos did to Compaq.

Simpson insists that it *is* possible for a company to try to be a generalist, making products in each of the four stages of the chain. That is the strategy of most Japanese firms, and also of companies like IBM, Motorola, and Siemens. But it brings with it inherently lower returns on capital — usually under 10 percent in 1990 for each of those three, while more focused companies like Conner and Apple turned in two or three times the average rate of return for their sector. And it has to be done carefully: the firm has to make sure its divisions keep themselves efficient by competing with outside suppliers, otherwise it will end up paying twice over by raising the costs of the divisions that have to buy in-house. Companies that want to work at only one stage of the chain, on the other hand, must target their customers narrowly and try to be world-class at one or two crucial things. They must also keep their eyes peeled for changes in the way the chain works, for a year's inattention can allow competitors to overwhelm them.

Christoph Selig, general manager in charge of portable computer sales at Toshiba's European subsidiary, has driven up to the company's factory in the medieval German town of Regensburg for a couple of meetings with his manufacturing colleagues before he moves on to Frankfurt to see a big client later in the afternoon. Selig thinks Olivetti's strategy is mistaken. "Europeans can't become integrators," he insists. "The whole thinking is nonsense. Customers are now so educated, and they know so much about computers and what they want, that they can be their own systems integrators. There is no need for them to go to IBM or to anyone else for advice; customers know that if they do, IBM will try to steer them toward its own products. The days when big companies like IBM and Siemens-Nixdorf sell so-called total computer solutions are gone."

Toshiba is one of the very few companies that can make such a prediction with the confidence that its own position will be secure if it comes true. Portable computers, in which it specializes, are the fastest-growing sector of the world's computer market. In Europe, particularly, Toshiba's record has been faultless. Early on, it made the astute decision to have its products distributed by dealers that also distributed IBM machines: when it first entered the market, IBM had no portable machines and Toshiba had no desktops. Especially after the Bull deal, IBM is now in the portable market with a vengeance; but Toshiba has grown to become the biggest supplier not only of notebook-sized machines but also of the larger laptops. Some of the company's managers back in Tokyo think that by 1995, portable computers will account for four out of every five PCs sold — and that the company will become the third largest computer company in the world as a result.

Like many other Japanese firms, Toshiba's proclaimed long-term strategy is to make its products as close as possible to the markets where it sells them. This is partly public relations guff, as many Toshiba people admit in private; notebook computers are much the same the world over. Just as important a reason to manufacture near the consumer is that the local plant is an insurance policy against the day when international trade turns sour and Europe or the United States closes its markets to direct exports from Japan. Protectionism poses a bigger threat to Toshiba's success than to that of any one of its competitors — and is therefore worth paying a high price to avoid.

At first sight, the factory at Regensburg was quite evidently a "screwdriver" plant of exactly the kind that bureaucrats in Brussels complain about most vigorously. Nine-tenths of the parts in the portable computers made there come directly from the Toshiba factory in Ome in boxes of one hundred knockdown kits. The hard disks, bought by Toshiba USA, come from a Conner factory in Singapore; the only major German component, in fact, is the outer packaging. There was no question of even applying for "Made in Germany" status for these machines.

Yet closer inspection suggests that it is too easy to write the factory off as easily as that. So far, Toshiba is supplying less than one-third of its European sales from Regensburg; that proportion is likely to rise sharply over the coming five years. Furthermore, the factory has already started making locally the printed circuit boards at the heart of the computers. The main thing slowing down the process of adding more value locally is the fact that it is so hard to find local suppliers for many of the parts. In many cases, admits Eberhard Huneke, the factory's deputy general manager, European suppliers ask prices 50 percent or 100 percent higher than the cost of getting them from Japan.

More important, the fact that Toshiba is assembling computers in Germany at all testifies to its sincerity. Had its aim been simply to jump over the local-content rules of the EC, the company would have done better to go to Italy, Spain, Portugal, or Ireland; yet it has deliberately chosen the country with the highest wages in Europe, where assembly costs, according to the company's own calculations, are exactly the same as in the United States (give or take obscure accounting differences, such as faster depreciation in Germany). That points clearly to one thing: a plan, perhaps not yet a definite one, to increase the work done at Regensburg from mere assembly to repair and testing, component manufacture, and eventually perhaps even to product design.[17]

The German staff at the plant find it hard to reconcile that with the way things are run at the moment. They tell depressing tales of how the Japanese technical advisers who came over from Tokyo to supervise the setting-up of the production line had so low a view of their German colleagues' abilities that they insisted even on deciding how the chairs in the relaxation area next to the machinery would be laid out. In one case that infuriated the factory's local managers, Toshiba decided to install a new soldering machine that would eliminate the need to use environment-harming chlorofluorocarbons (CFCs) by carrying out soldering work in a new way: the soldering would be done in a sealed chamber where oxygen had been replaced by nitrogen, and thus there would be no need to clean anything with CFCs because nothing would get dirty. The German workers told their Japanese colleagues that a suitable machine had been on sale in Germany for two years and was already in use at another factory in the same town. No, they were told, the new machine will come from Japan. And because Toshiba's head office gave the contract to a Japanese company that was making the nitrogen-soldering machine for the first time, there was a delay of more than six months while the Japanese company learned — at Toshiba's expense — how to make this crucial tool.

Seen from Tokyo, however, the policy does not seem so absurd as all that. Evidently, the managers who ordered the machine from the Japanese firm were doing business with one of Toshiba's long-term suppliers. If the contractor went wrong, they knew, they would not be blamed for its failure to deliver the new machine on time. Had they taken the advice of their Regensburg colleagues and ordered from a German firm that failed to meet the deadline, however, their own necks would be on the line for taking a risk. That incident was a milestone: after that, the local German employees began to earn the trust of their Japanese counterparts. It is a process that must continue for years, though, before the firm becomes sufficiently international to give equal weight to what its foreign and its Japanese employees say.

But the company can be forgiven its conservatism. While it was debating what to do about its nitrogen-soldering machine, Olivetti was trying to bring out a new notebook computer called the "1," which was advertised aggressively as being designed by Europeans for Europeans to use.[18] This was a prestigious project for the company: one of the new machines appeared on the cover of Olivetti's 1990 annual report. But despite the company's best efforts, which included having the machine manufactured at its Triumph-Adler plant in Germany, the "1" missed its deadline. After saying that it would be in the shops by April 1991, Olivetti was forced to push back the first shipments until August. The new model was available in quantity only in November. But by then, it was a generation behind what was already on the market, and doomed to be a loss-maker.

"If I could do what I would like to," says Christoph Selig, "I would hire people not from the computer industry but from the consumer electronics industry. Eventually, we will be selling notebook computers like videocassette recorders. Computers will end up sold in supermarkets, with the makers responsible for filling the shelves and sticking on the price tags . . . In the long term, this industry will be dominated by the Japanese — just like the hi-fi industry or the photographic industry."

Olivetti believes that it is no longer economic for anybody to make money at consumer electronics in Europe: its palmtop computers are made in Singapore, and its typewriters in

Brazil. "Assembling these things is a low-skilled business," one Olivetti manager insists. "Those Asian women can do it better because they are good at handling small pieces." Yet the very same manager gives a clue to the real situation when he admits that Olivetti earns a much higher return on capital at a joint-venture factory it has set up in Ivrea with Canon, the Japanese firm that dominates the world market for photocopiers and laser printer engines, than it does on its own. The problem is not that Europe is the wrong place to make consumer electronics goods; rather, it seems that European companies are not managed in a way that allows them to do it profitably.

There is another view, of course. Looking at the computer industry as it progresses through the 1990s, it is possible to argue that the very biggest problem of computer makers is that they have failed to dream up extra uses for the personal computer as fast as they have managed to cut its cost and to improve its performance. In 1961, at the very dawn of the computer industry, a specialist programmer at a big company would be thought lucky to have a machine with four kilobytes of memory available; the largest IBM 1401 was a 16K machine. Today, a thousand dollars will just about buy a computer with over 250 times as much memory — not to mention faster processing and a tiny disk drive capable of storing one hundred novels. Yet with the honorable exception of Apple, computer firms have not managed to harness this power to make their machines easier to use. In fact, they have become harder. Just as the increase in car electronics means that home enthusiasts can no longer tinker under the hood, so also the job of managing a screen and acres of storage and of juggling half a dozen different memory-resident programs has made many personal computers equally impenetrable to the amateur.

Microsoft's Windows, a piece of software that asks the user to give commands by moving a mouse onto little pictures on the screen, is the first significant attempt to change this. It makes the computer much easier to use for the nonspecialist — and it does so in a way that creates a thirst for the ever increasing power and memory coming onto the market.[19] More important, it has in doing so reasserted the American firm's dominance over the world computer industry at a time when many observers expected Japanese firms to start to challenge the American lead in computer software.

More such innovations are certainly on the way. One is the idea of pen-based computing, which allows the computerphobe to dispense with the keyboard and just write instructions on the screen by hand with a light-pen. Japanese firms are furiously trying to enlist the superior skills of American firms in an attempt to find commercial uses for this technology. An example of such ventures is the alliance between Matsushita Electric of Japan and AT&T of the United States.

Still more radical is the idea of giving instructions just by talking to a computer. Contrary to the impression given by many commentators on the subject, computers are very far from being able to understand natural language of the kind that people speak every day. Natural language is far too full of subtleties — and of things that depend on understanding not just the semantic context but also something about the world — to be a realistic goal for the next fifty years, let alone the next decade. But researchers have made some limited progress in making computers respond to carefully chosen and limited vocabularies, with the words spoken unnaturally distinctly and slowly and perhaps by speakers who have had to train the computer beforehand to understand the idiosyncracies of their accents. Apple is making particularly sharp advances in this area.

Both developments have in common the fact that they are software, rather than hardware, based: they play particularly to the strengths of American computer companies rather than Japanese. If either or both of them — or some other, unconnected development — suddenly bears fruit, vast new computing markets could be opened up which do not even exist now. The industry could well be on the verge of such a dramatic breakthrough that restores the advantage to the United

States. In the meantime, however, the onward march of the Japanese continues. Competition from the east in the late 1970s and early 1980s has virtually destroyed the United States' consumer electronics industry. Are the European electronics firms doomed to go the same way? That is the question we must turn to next.

SIX

A Battle for the Future
of Digital Audio

N 1953 one of the partners of a struggling Japanese electrical company paid his first visit to Europe. He had just
concluded a business deal in the United States, and decided to cross the Atlantic and pass some time seeing this
continent that he had heard so much about but had never
seen. While he was there, the businessman thought, he might
just as well pay a visit to Philips, the world's leading electrical
company, in the Netherlands.

"I took the train from Düsseldorf to Eindhoven," writes
Akio Morita in his book *Made in Japan*, "and when I crossed
the border from Germany to Holland I found a great difference. Germany, even so soon after the war, was becoming
highly mechanized . . . But in Holland many people were riding bicycles. This was a purely agricultural country and a
small one at that. You could see old-fashioned windmills everywhere, just as in old Dutch landscape paintings. Everything seemed so quaint."[1] (Morita's book was written with
the help of an American ghostwriter.)

Barely able to speak English, let alone Dutch, and representing a small company with a long name that few people
outside Japan had ever heard of, Morita met none of the man-

agers of the famous conglomerate. But he took one of the standard public tours of a Philips plant. He wandered around the town. He stared at the statue of Dr. Gerard Philips, the company's founder, in front of the Eindhoven railway station. And he began to ponder the fact that a man born in such a small, out-of-the-way place in an agricultural country could build such a huge, highly technical company with a fine worldwide reputation. "Maybe, I thought, we could do the same thing in Japan. It was quite a dream . . . "

Over the next two decades, the Sony chairman's dream would become reality. Competition from Japan would reduce the once proud American consumer electronics industry to a single struggling firm: Zenith Corporation, which imported most of its televisions from Mexico or Asia. Then it moved across the Atlantic.

Europe had four major electronics names: Philips in the Netherlands, Thomson in France, and Siemens and Bosch in Germany. Even at home, the Europeans were being beaten on both cost and innovation. Their position in North America, battered by waves of better and cheaper products from Japan, had been eroded year by year. They were barely visible in the Japanese market, which is the third biggest in the world and will grow the fastest over the coming five years. And with an increasing Japanese manufacturing and marketing presence in the rest of Asia, the European companies appeared to have little foothold in the new markets of Southeast Asia that are likely to develop over the next twenty years or so. By 1991 Philips itself was in trouble. But its problems were a symptom of a wider malaise in Europe's electronics industry — a malaise that attracted the attention not only of national governments but also of the European Commission in Brussels.

The question seemed not whether Japan would overcome European dominance of the consumer electronics industry; it had already done that. More worryingly, the question was whether the European-owned electronics firms had a future at all. There were many specialists who believe they do not, saying that although it may remain profitable to develop, design, and assemble electronics products in Europe, European companies are not capable of doing it. That is probably too pessimistic. By recognizing and imitating the qualities that have made Japanese companies so strong in this business, and that spelled death to their American competitors, the European industry could still revive its fortunes. Doing so will be a slow and painful job, with no guarantee of success at the end of it. But it is possible — and at least one company is proving it. That, however, is to jump ahead of our story.

Six years before Akio Morita made his trip to Eindhoven, a group of scientists at AT&T's Bell Laboratories had made the most important technological discovery of the twentieth century: the transistor. Investigating how different materials conduct electricity, Dr. William Shockley and his colleagues at Bell observed that while most substances either conducted well or acted as insulators, a few, such as germanium, exhibited a strange phenomenon. Under the right conditions (which at the time meant a crystal of high purity attached to a metal disc and a pair of tungsten wires less than a thousandth of an inch apart), they would amplify the current. Until then, there had been only one way to make an amplifier: by means of a vacuum tube with a heating element. With neither heat nor a vacuum necessary any longer, the way was open to make all kinds of electronic devices smaller, cheaper, and able to run on only a trickle of electricity.

The news created a stir in the United States. "Harried scientists of the Bell Telephone Laboratories last week were busy answering queries from radio manufacturers the country over about their new substitute for vacuum tubes," reported *Newsweek* breathlessly in July 1948. "Both the Army and Navy are now testing it, hoping to produce miniature, rugged radio communication sets that will make the second world war walkie-talkies and handy-talkies obsolete." But that was nothing compared with the reaction in Japan. In government laboratories and private companies alike, researchers looked feverishly for every scrap of information that would help them to replicate Shockley's experiments. "Going to the library, I would feel the blood rush to my cheeks whenever I glimpsed 'semiconductor' in an American science magazine," wrote one of Japan's most famous electronic engineers later. "I knew real joy. My hands would practically shake with anticipation . . . If I could thank God for only one thing, it would be for giving me life in the year 1925. Thanks to that blessing, the start of my research career was to coincide with the birth of the transistor."[2]

The significance of the transistor can be summed up very simply: it brought in the age of miniaturization. The transistor made it possible to produce radios and gramophones that were much smaller than what had come before, much cheaper, much higher quality, or all three of these. To give one example, in 1920s America a gramophone cost almost a third of the price of a small car; its modern successor costs a twentieth as much.

More important than what the arrival of the transistor did to existing markets, though, were the entirely new markets that it created from scratch. Computers were the most important. But beginning with color television, and continuing on to compact discs and cellular telephones, almost every new consumer product since the 1950s owes its existence to the invention of the transistor. By the end of the 1960s, ways had been found to combine scores of components on printed circuit boards. Refinements in Japan later increased that to millions.

Although these developments carried with them tremendous opportunities, they also spelled risks. Many companies that had for years been doing successful and gently growing trade in the electrical business were suddenly to find that the rules had changed. Prices were able to fall sharply; new groups of customers had to be appealed to; new ways had to be found to make the new products efficiently; and above all, new thinking had to be applied to the job of dreaming up those products. In short, it was a shakeup; in the drastic remaking of an existing market and the creation of a much larger new market, the advantages of already having factories, distributors, and brand names were to count for a great deal less than usual. And outsiders who had previously had little chance of getting into the vast American market suddenly saw their opportunity.

Sony (or Tokyo Telecommunications Engineering Company, as it was then known) was one of them. Its founder, Masaru Ibuka, tried to make an appointment with the patent manager at Western Electric, which had been assigned the rights to the new technology, to talk about licensing it. But he was turned away; the man responsible said he was too busy. It was not until 1953 that the firm was able to acquire a license, for a fee of $25,000, and not for another six months that the Japanese government agreed to let the necessary dollars out of the country. Even then, the company's researchers worked for long months to find a way of increasing the transistor's frequency and thus make it more powerful. In the end, the solution was to reverse the transistor's polarity, which meant using phosphorus. In the course of learning this, a Sony physicist in Tokyo made another discovery — the diode tunneling effect — which was to earn him a Nobel Prize twenty years later.

Despite the prediction in *Newsweek* that the transistor would give rise to a new kind of radio, Morita says his firm was warned by the patent holders not to expect to make anything from the new technology except hearing aids. Undeterred, Sony went ahead — and developed a small portable radio, the TR55, named after the year of its introduction. Making the product was one thing; it was quite another to sell it. At first, the wholesalers did not see the point of having a radio that was portable. Electrical power was cheaper than batteries; people had plenty of space in their living rooms; why should they not just sit down if they wanted to listen? Morita's answer was a clever one. He sought to show that his firm's new radio was not merely portable but *pocketable:* you could listen to it anywhere, and members of the same family could tune in to different programs in different rooms in the house. (The trouble was, it was not quite pocketable: the TR55 was just a little too big to sit in the pocket of a salesman's white shirt. Undeterred, Morita ordered a set of shirts made for the company's American sales force with breast pockets slightly bigger than normal.)

Early on, Morita was aware of how important it was to preserve the value of the company's brand name. He recounts that several times he received offers from big American firms to buy huge quantities of Sony products, on the condition that their name, rather than his own firm's, appear on the box. He turned them down. Many Japanese firms resented the cheap and cheerful image that Japanese products had in the United States in the 1950s and early 1960s; but Sony was resolute in shaking it off by pricing its products higher, rather than lower, than the competition. It reinforced this policy at home and abroad by choosing very prominent sites for its showrooms. In New York, Morita insisted that Sony should be on Fifth Avenue, and was forced to wait some time before getting the property he wanted. In Paris, it had to be the Champs-Elysées. In Tokyo, the company bought a building at the corner of the Ginza 4-chome junction — one of the more prestigious addresses in Tokyo, and probably the world's most crowded crossroads.

Meanwhile, Sony researchers in Tokyo were doing what they knew best: refining existing technologies and turning expensive impracticalities into things that people would want. One example was the color television. In the RCA and CBS systems on the market in the mid-1960s, the picture was created by means of three different electron guns, one for each primary color. Sony adopted a different approach; it first licensed a technology from Paramount Pictures called Chromatron, which used a single gun and a series of lenses. Then it introduced its own refinement: rather than placing a mask or a set of wires between the electron beams and the phosphor-coated glass screen, as all existing products did, it came up with a much simpler metal grille. The result was a television, called Trinitron, that produced a brighter picture with less electricity — and could be taken outdoors.

A similar principle applied with the videotape recorder. It was invented by Ampex, an American firm. Yet although Ampex held the patents, it failed to have the breadth of vision to see that as well as revolutionizing the television industry — recording meant programs need no longer be live, which made them a great deal more professional but killed their spontaneity — videotape could also become a consumer product. Sony, on the other hand, did. First it made some models that were smaller than Ampex's unwieldy machines, but shared their use of two-inch reel-to-reel videotape. Then it managed to maintain tolerable picture quality while reducing the tape width to three-quarters of an inch. More important, it borrowed an idea that had just come out of Philips in the Netherlands: the compact audiocassette, which obviated the need to thread the tape carefully through the mechanism and onto another reel every time it was played, and which improved the quality by protecting it from dust and fingermarks in a sealed case. Sony translated the cassette idea into video and called its new system U-Matic. It was just a bit smaller than a suitcase (though a great deal heavier), and it later became a standard for broadcasters and big companies that were using videotape for promotional films.

Yet U-Matic, though commercially successful, was still too unwieldy to become a true consumer product. "Ibuka was never satisfied," writes Morita.

> He wanted a truly small unit with a very handy cassette. He returned to the office one day from a trip to the United States, and he called together the video development group. He emphasized that the home video tape recorder was the most important project at hand and that the size of the unit was crucial. He reached into his pocket, took out a paperback book he had bought at the airport in New York, and placed it on the table. "This is the size I need for the cassette," he said. "This is your target. I want one hour of program time on a cassette

that size." That was the challenge that created the original Betamax system.[3]

The story is striking for two reasons. First, it is a reminder
of how different Sony has always been from the widely held
view of Japanese companies, in which all the ideas come up
from the bottom and are put into practice by a cautious, informal process of consensus-seeking. Second, it reveals something interesting about the company's priorities. Rather than
looking at a technology that it had developed in the laboratory and wondering what to do with it, Sony's approach was
to start at the other end, with the consumer: to ask what consumers would want, and then to work back from a list speci-
fying price, size, and performance to something the engineers
could develop. And although Masaru Ibuka's sudden idea of
insisting that the cassette be the same size as an airport pot-
boiler may sound simplistic — the company's engineers no
doubt spent many sleepless nights from then on, wondering
how on earth they would meet such an arbitrary demand —
its very simplicity was exactly the sort of thing to jolt a hesitant consumer into buying.

Incidentally, this idea of the arbitrary demand has stood
Sony in good stead ever since. Its most recent example is the
Sony Handycam range of "camcorders," or video camera and
tape player combined. Video cameras were already a consumer product in the mid-1980s, when it was an increasingly
common sight to see enthusiasts lugging around on their
shoulders a box weighing 3 or 4 pounds. But it was not until
Sony managed to make a far smaller unit in 1990, weighing
just over 600 grams, or 1½ pounds, that the average family
began to consider taking one along on vacation. In a nostalgic
reference to the company's first transistor radio, the first
model in the range was called the TR55. True to form, it was
advertised in Japan with posters and television spots that used
an elegant trick to drum home the point that it was now
small enough to take abroad: the new camera was shown almost obscured behind a Japanese passport.

One of the things that gave Sony a head start was its inclination to take risks with new technology: not to commission expensive (and time-consuming) market research, but to make something and just put it on the market to see whether consumers approved. Morita has always insisted that the Walkman — which is probably the product that has changed more lives than any since television, measured by the number of people who use them and the hours every day they are in use — would never have come to market if the firm had polled people beforehand to ask whether they would buy such a thing.[4] As a Japanese company, however, Sony had an advantage. Customers in its home market love anything new; even today, the shops in Japan are full of electronic products on trial that never make it out of their own home market.[5]

On only one occasion has Sony made a mistake in introducing a new product so serious that it threatened the existence of the entire company. Ironically, the product was Betamax — the new video recorder that sprang from Ibuka's challenge to produce a cassette the size of a paperback book. Betamax brought Sony into a head-to-head conflict with its most powerful rival. Losing that conflict dented Sony's morale for several years; in fact, the fallout from the battle continues to this day.

The rival was the Matsushita group of companies, which sells its products abroad under the names National, Panasonic, Technics, and Quasar.[6] Although it is the world's biggest consumer electronics group, Matsushita has always been a much less flashy firm than Sony. While Morita's childhood was privileged (he describes himself as "the first son and fifteenth-generation heir to one of Japan's finest and oldest sake-brewing families"), its rival's founder, Konosuke Matsushita, was brought up in feudal poverty in a small village outside Wakayama and left school in 1904 at the age of nine to become apprenticed to a maker of *hibachi* charcoal grills. Sony, a Tokyo firm, prides itself on its international outlook: it has two foreigners on its main board, and in 1991 had more foreigners than Japanese on its 135,000-strong payroll. Matsu-shita, with its head office in Osaka, has always been more provincial and more conservative in outlook. The Osaka firm has often waited to see what Sony will do before committing itself. In 1974, a year after Sony had set up a factory in Wales, it did the same. In 1989, Sony bought Columbia Pictures in the United States; the following year, Matsushita bought its rival MCA.

While Sony was working on its Betamax, Matsushita was busy on a rival system known as VHS. By the time Betamax was ready, Matsushita had VHS on the shelf, waiting to be launched; yet it waited to see what Sony would do. In the event, Sony's product turned out to be superior in every way but one. Its cassette was smaller than the VHS cassette, its playback quality was better — but VHS could record for longer at a single stretch.

This proved to be decisive. Sony had thought the video would be used primarily for "time-shifting" — that is, for re-cording television broadcasts and replaying them later. It was right to the extent that a pair of American television net-works tried to sue the company when the Betamax came out, on the grounds that it was providing a tool for viewers to breach the broadcasters' copyright. But customers found a better use for the new machines: they would rent videotapes of feature films and watch them on television at home. (It was very hard to predict that this would be so. In fact, the film industry was at first against video rentals for fear that they would push the cinema into decline — which they did, but replaced the profits from cinema sales with tape rental income.)

While Sony was determined to squeeze the maximum profit from its new idea, and thus wanted to make as many of the new Betamax machines as possible by itself, Matsushita was happy to license its VHS technology to all comers. The result, within a very few years, was that far more makers were producing machines that used tapes in the VHS format than in the Betamax format. Video stores rented out ten VHS cassettes for every one Betamax. And soon the inevitability of econo-mies of scale began to assert itself: with more machines being produced and more companies competing to find ways to make them more cheaply, the cost of vhs technology began to fall against the cost of Betamax. By 1989 Sony was ready to concede defeat. Its commercial instincts reasserting them-selves above corporate pride, the company began to make vhs machines. Meanwhile, the man who had humbled Sony so mercilessly, Akio Tanii, had risen from running the video products side of Matsushita to the company's presidency.

By the time Tanii took the helm of Matsushita, the com-pany had acquired a disturbing reputation inside Japan as a copycat company — people still refer to it as *maneshita*, meaning imitated. That reputation is a little unfair, but it re-veals at least something important about how the two com-panies have overcome their foreign competitors.

Konosuke Matsushita founded his company in 1918, dur-ing the very earliest days of electricity in Japan. At the time, electric power had the same mystery as computers did in the United States in the early 1960s. Matsushita had acquired his electrical knowledge while working his way up to the job of inspector in the Osaka Electric Light Company; his first prod-uct when he set up in business at home on his own account was an adaptor plug that allowed Japanese families to connect two appliances rather than one to the single electrical socket that was being installed in most houses.

Throughout the company's history, Matsushita's great strength lay in two things: its ability to make incremental improvements in its products year after year, cutting their cost and raising their quality; and its founder's canny appre-ciation of marketing. In 1958 the firm won an award for the quality of its factory operations. But as early as 1943, Mat-sushita's reputation as a manufacturing genius was such that the government asked him, in addition to the munitions work his company was already doing, to start making wooden ships and airplanes. He complied with enthusiasm, and by the end of the war, with no prior expertise in either field and a drastic shortage of materials, he had succeeded in finding a way of making ships by mass production when hitherto everyone else in Japan had made them by hand.

(This enthusiasm almost cost Matsushita his business: the occupying American forces classified his family as one of the *zaibatsu* families like the Mitsui and Mitsubishi whom they held responsible for the war, and ordered him and all his top management to resign their posts. Only after a careful lobbying campaign — in which fifteen thousand of his employees presented a petition to General Douglas MacArthur, and Matsushita himself set up an organization called the PHP Institute, reflecting his newfound devotion to the rather different aims of Peace, Happiness, and Prosperity — was he allowed once again to take control.)

Proof of his marketing know-how had come still earlier on. To escape from the stranglehold that the traditional Japanese industrial combines had over distribution, he set up a network of his own retailers, some partly owned by the company, others linked to it by loans or bank guarantees, and yet others financially independent but contracted to stock only Matsushita products. The twenty thousand or so "national shops," or *nashiyonaru shoppu,* as they are known in Japanese, have kept the company in very close contact with its domestic customers, and made it able to achieve fast distribution of products it wants to promote and fast feedback on products that do not go down so well. With such a strong position in the domestic market, Matsushita never needed to be an innovator: he merely had to keep up with firms like Sony, letting them make the pioneer's mistakes and then weighing in later himself with a second-generation product that filled in the gaps left by the competition. Camcorders are a recent example. Although Sony won the kudos for the Handycam range, Matsushita introduced a few months afterward a model of its own that took much better pictures by reducing drastically the shake produced by wobbly wrists. This was done by means of an ingenious gyroscopic self-righting mechanism inside the camera.

But the group's key strength, perhaps uniquely for a firm of its size, has been its combination of rigid cost control and flexibility. A study of the firm by a pair of management consultants in the early 1980s discovered that, long before the introduction of computers had made it easy to do so, the group's different divisions had been giving to the head office accurate statistics on sales, inventories, profits, and costs only a few days after the end of every month.[7] What is more, Matsushita had introduced "matrix management," whereby its business units report both to managers responsible for geographical regions and to managers in charge of specific products, in 1953. Many American firms discovered the benefits of such an approach only in the 1980s; many European firms have yet to learn it still.

The cost control is immediately evident from a visit to Matsushita's offices in Osaka. Behind the steel-and-black glamour of the company's industrial museum and the plush of its corporate meeting rooms, the buildings are dowdy, the desks are regulation gray army issue, and it is evident that not a yen more than necessary has been spent. Outsiders rarely find out, but the company even has a rule that every piece of paper must be used on both sides.

The greatest test of Matsushita's flexibility came in the late 1970s, when the company judged that world markets for consumer electronics were maturing and therefore likely to become less profitable. It therefore set itself the goal of diversifying away from audio and video into other, faster-growing businesses like factory automation, office machines, semiconductors, and automotive electronics. In the space of the ten years up to 1988, the share of its total sales that came from this kind of product rose from 19 percent to 55 percent. The new businesses are not yet nearly so profitable as the old consumer core, but the change — accounting for more than $10 billion in sales — must represent one of the biggest and most successful diversifications in business history.

Producing a turnaround of that order was not, of course, something that could be done from the head office — it was the cumulative effect of hundreds of different entrepreneurial initiatives. One of the more prominent ones was in 1987, when Matsushita suddenly realized that it had no up-to-date Japanese-language word processor, while its competitors were making high profits from a boom in demand.[8] In the space of little over a year, it rushed out a new product that had all the traditional Matsushita virtues. The machine contained an important technological refinement, in the form of new software that saved time by using context analysis to predict more accurately which of the many possible identical-sounding Chinese characters the writer wanted to use. It was keenly priced and cleverly designed. And the new product helped to solve a problem that other companies had not even been aware of before: the fact that many Japanese did not understand their machines well enough to get the benefit of more than a very few of the things they could do. To overcome this, Matsushita had a series of training videos for its new model made by a popular young actress, which it then rented out and sold to tens of thousands of male customers. Not surprisingly, the new model immediately became the best-selling word processor on the market.

In 1996 or so, a new office building will dominate the skyline of Berlin. Rising from the Potsdammer Platz (the site of the wall that divided East Germany from West from 1961 until 1989), the tower will be a potent symbol of the advanced, newly unified Germany. It will contain a mixture of restaurants and shops — and also the European headquarters of Sony Corporation.

The choice of such a location shows that Sony has lost none of its traditional flair for publicity. But the building will be more than good marketing: it is a reminder of how Sony sees the changes now taking place in Europe. Sony bought the site for its new building in June 1991, well before the German government decided to move the capital from Bonn to Berlin.[9] The decision to move the company's European headquarters — made well ahead even of many European competitors — was the result of a view taken by Sony's board in Tokyo that it will be Germany that dominates the European Community over the coming decades, and that the center of gravity of Europe is moving eastward.

In January 1992, however, the only hint of what the new headquarters might look like was to be found in a neat pile of architectural books in an office in Cologne. The office was that of the chairman of Sony's European operations, and he was musing over the competing ideas of a handful of the world's most prestigious architects, including Helmut Jahn, the German architect, and Kohn, Pedersen Fox, the flamboyant U.S. practice.

Coffee table books? Bright white walls decorated with large abstract canvases? High-tech furniture, and a vast tropical flowering plant against the ceiling-to-floor window? This office did not look quite right for a Japanese businessman. Nor did its occupant. The man who runs Sony in Europe — and who sits on its main board in Tokyo too — is a Swiss national named Jack Schmuckli.

Schmuckli first came into contact with Sony between 1968 and 1975, when he was head of the Japanese operations of Polaroid, the U.S. camera company. There were good relations between Edwin Land, the company's founder and the inventor of instant photography, and Ibuka and Morita. At one stage, on instructions from the head office, Schmuckli spent some time discussing the possibility of starting up a joint venture with Sony. His opposite number was Norio Ohga, a former opera singer; now, Ohga is the Sony president. When Morita heard in 1974 that Schmuckli was planning to leave Japan for family reasons and return to Europe, he offered him the job at the top of Sony Deutschland. Schmuckli therefore became the first foreigner to head a subsidiary of a Japanese company. Further promotions followed: he was given the job of running the entire European operation in 1986 and offered a seat on the board in 1989. The title is not just an honorary one: he times his four or five visits to Japan every year to coincide with the meetings.

Board meetings at Japanese companies are largely cere-monial affairs, like stockholders' meetings in Europe and the United States, where decisions made beforehand are rubber-stamped. But the title on Schmuckli's business card is a pow-erful indication of just how far the firm has gone toward mak-ing itself a true multinational. Other Japanese companies are struggling even to begin the process of making their foreign employees feel that they are trusted as fully as their Japanese colleagues. Toyota and Honda, for instance, have just begun to send newly hired Americans off to their factories and show-rooms in Japan for six months, where they learn the hard way first how to make and then how to sell cars, just like every other management trainee. Sony is at least a decade ahead. Prompted to expand abroad early on by the impossibility of dislodging Matsushita and other Japanese electrical firms from their powerful positions in the domestic market, the firm now makes just under three-quarters of its total sales abroad. The division — 26 percent in Japan, 29 percent in the United States, 28 percent in Europe, and 16 percent else-where — is approximately in proportion with the size of the world market for consumer goods. Sony is Japan's nearest thing to a global company.

The process of becoming one has not been easy. Although the firm has been in Europe for thirty years, it always had the standard Japanese bias toward the United States. That was where the market was biggest and most open; that was the place where you only had to learn one foreign language to do business, rather than Europe's nine. Things began to change in the 1970s, when the company's national organizations all over the world began to start making money. Until then, its European business had been under the umbrella of a holding company in Switzerland. But under Japanese tax law, only "first-tier" subsidiaries could avoid paying taxes in two juris-dictions, so the company was forced to reorganize its struc-ture so as to create direct lines of ownership between head-quarters in Tokyo and the different European subsidiaries.

Wanting to be closer to its customers, but also prompted

by Morita's keen sense of political trouble ahead, the company was already beginning to manufacture a growing proportion of its products outside Japan. It had opened a factory in San Diego in 1970 and in the Welsh town of Bridgend in 1973. But by the 1980s, Sony found it had not moved fast enough. In the recession that followed the second oil shock, sales in Europe began to fall fast; but because the company's production divisions were separate business units, which sold Sony products to the overseas sales organizations at negotiated prices and volumes on half-year contracts, Sony factories in Japan just continued shipping boxes to Europe. The hapless European managers found themselves choked with unsold stocks; when the time came to renew the contracts, the factories back in Japan were suddenly hit with a much sharper fall than they would have been under a more flexible system. And by late 1985, a still more serious problem began to emerge: as a result of the Plaza Accord, a secret agreement among the leaders of the world's most important industrial nations following a meeting at a New York hotel, the yen began to rise steadily against the dollar. Sony, which had 70 percent of its business but only 20 percent of its production outside Japan, found itself hemorrhaging money.

The *endaka* (high-yen) crisis forced the company to think again about its world strategy. It decided to rationalize its operations, determined to make itself competitive even if the yen rose in value to only one hundred to the dollar (luckily, it never did). And it decided to diversify away from consumer electronics and to make itself a truly global company. This global strategy was brutally simple: Sony resolved to increase its production overseas from 20 percent of the total to 40 percent. Reaching the first target had taken two decades to achieve; for the second, Sony gave itself only five years. But the important question was where the new factories were to go. The production people wanted to tap the cheapest combination of skills and wages, and therefore insisted on Southeast Asia. "But this did not fit with our industrial or political understanding of how the world works," admits Schmuckli frankly. The Sony board made a firm decision as a matter of policy: the new investment would be divided broadly into thirds and would be sent equally to the United States, to Europe, and to Southeast Asia. And the company itself would be managed as a group of four zones: the home market in Japan, North America, Europe, and Asia. Allowing Sony staff in Singapore to make decisions about the Asian market was quite shocking enough for the conservatives in Tokyo. More shocking still was the result that Sony Europe suddenly gained an importance in the company it had never had before. Top executives of the firm now say that the 1986 decision by the European Community to try to create a single market by the end of 1992 confirmed that the strategy was right.

Sony has been working hard to procure more in Europe. Some mature lines, such as televisions and audiotapes, now rely almost entirely on local components; others, such as laser pickups for CD players, the company has had to make itself because it could not find any European company capable of supplying them at the right price. Altogether, its operations in Europe now buy locally about 45 percent of all the components and services that go into its products. "We don't have to go to 100 percent," insists Schmuckli. "We will have fulfilled the political expectations if we reach 50 percent [roughly the same local-content ratio as European-owned firms themselves] . . . There are indeed places in the world where production is more economical, and there are products which are global products that can be produced anywhere." Yet the process of bringing manufacturing to Europe (there are now a total of ten Sony factories inside the Community — in France, Britain, Italy, Germany, Spain, and Austria) is dragging other parts of Sony's business there too. One example is the design of components. "As long as our engineers sit outside Europe, they will build in technologies which they are familiar with. If I bring the same engineers over to Europe and expose them to the capabilities of European industry, they will start to build in European components. That means local development is an absolutely necessary part of increasing local content." It has begun too. Sony has full technical centers at Basingstoke and at Stuttgart, and smaller groups of technical staff working in Brussels and at some of the company's factories. Today, the job of these engineers is mainly to adapt Sony products to local markets, but they are the core of a possible research and development presence for the future.

The irony is unconscious, of course. But in the office of Dr. Ad Huijser, head of technology at Philips Consumer Electronics in Eindhoven, three pictures stare out from the walls: a pair of the brilliant mathematical graphics of M. C. Escher, the Dutch artist of the 1920s; and on the other side of the room, peeping out cunningly from behind a plant, a print of a Japanese samurai.

Huijser is a respected scientist in his own right. His doctorate was in solid-state physics, and when he joined Philips in 1970 upon finishing his graduate studies he did pioneering work on the optical storage technology that eventually led to the creation of the compact disc. In the course of that work, he produced patents of his own — which he turned over to the company in return for the one-dollar fee that is standard in high-tech industries all over the world. Now he is one of the team that oversees all of Philips's new consumer electronic goods, but his special responsibility is to turn into moneymakers the ideas that the three hundred researchers in the company's consumer electronics laboratories dream up. It is no easy job, and he came to it in 1991 at the end of a string of embarrassing company failures.

One thing should be made clear immediately: Philips cannot be accused of the Leonardo da Vinci syndrome — producing ideas that are brilliant in principle, like the Italian artist's imaginative designs for helicopters and machine guns, but whose details are simply left for others to work out. Nor can it be accused of being like Ampex, the American firm that invented the idea of recording video images on magnetic tape but was unable to make its machine small, cheap, or reliable enough to have a place in the home.

On the contrary, Philips can claim to be the leading setter of standards in the late twentieth century. Both the audiocassette (officially known as the compact cassette) and the compact disc (CD) are Philips ideas, the former exclusively its own and the latter with some patents shared by Sony. On these products, all other companies in the world still have to pay a small license fee to the Dutch electronics firm. The ability to set standards for an entire industry, something that in another field only a handful of American computer companies can claim to have done, is proof of the keenest ability to predict what kind of thing consumers want.

Yet the failures are there all the same. Philips invented Laservision, the system of recording television pictures and digital quality sound on large optical discs — but left it to Pioneer, a Japanese company, to refine the technology, keep upgrading the machines on the market, cut costs, and eventually earn a fat return from the product. The fact that Philips invented the compact cassette shows that it recognized what a leap there was to be made between the old, inconvenient reel-to-reel machines and a truly convenient and portable high-quality audiocassette player. Yet it left it to Sony to complete the revolution by shrinking the player to the size of a box only half an inch bigger than the cassette itself, and to make a world-famous brand name and a mint of money at the same time. Even with the CD, which came on the market in 1983, long after these managerial problems inside Philips were already visible, the company failed to get the full benefit of its inventiveness. Bewitched by the dramatic improvement in quality that digital sound offered over the old black vinyl disc, Philips convinced itself that the CD was a product for the very top of the audio market. It therefore put little effort into making budget-priced CD machines. Sony, on the other hand, developed models at both ends of the market — and the result is that the cheapest CD players now cost less in real terms than the old record players they replaced, and Sony not only is a leading maker of complete CD players, but also has a highly profitable business supplying key components to other makers all over the world.

These are not the only examples. One spinoff from the CD was the idea of using optical discs to store information rather than sound. In 1991 Sony introduced a Data Discman, consisting of a portable CD player for miniature discs, a keyboard, and a screen to display the dictionaries and databases that it could store. Another was a player for another kind of CD, this time a full-sized one called CD-ROM[10] that could be read directly by a computer. In 1992 Philips found itself caught by surprise when people began to buy the players in earnest, hooking them up to computers to take advantage of a growing library of reference books and newspaper databases available on CD. But it had already been beaten to the start: Sanyo, another Japanese maker, had brought out in 1991 a budget-priced CD-ROM that could be plugged into the back of the computer just like a printer, instead of through a special board that had to be installed by unscrewing the back of the machine.

More damning still, as we have seen, Philips missed the 1990 boom in combined video camera recorders, which had become one of Sony's and Matsushita's bigger moneyspinners by the turn of the 1990s. "In the early 1980s, about ten years ago, we developed quite a lot of the components necessary," explains Huijser sadly. "But our people didn't want to go for it. Now all our camcorders in Europe and the United States are OEM [that is, they have the Philips name on the box but are actually made by outside companies]." It is too late to go back, Huijser admits. Having decided not to commercialize the camcorder, Philips now has only a low level of production of the advanced charged-couple devices (CCDs) that are the key component of the new video cameras. What is more, its Japanese competitors have learned so much in the process of making the hundreds of thousands they have already sold that

Philips would be unable to re-enter the market: to offer a model competing with the Japanese offerings in price and performance, it would have to sell far below cost.

One product remains in the balance. When Japanese companies were investing heavily in liquid crystal displays — a technology they already knew well, having used it for years in electronic calculators — Philips was tangled in a territorial row. The company could not make up its mind whether LCD technology should more properly be handled by the company's components division, or whether it should count as a consumer electronics activity because of its possible future applications. As a result, Philips started work on LCD in earnest only in 1987. Five years later, in 1992, it was making three-inch and four-inch screens on a pilot basis, and planning to move up to six-inch models later in the year. But by then, Japanese companies were already hard at work on ten-inch screens — and Toshiba and IBM had teamed up to manufacture full-color flat-panel screens for portable computers at a new plant in Himeji, in western Japan, while Sharp was trying to become the dominant maker of flat-panel color screens for television. Philips saw its own strategy as rather Japanese: having arrived late, it was trying to work backward by first assembling bought-in components and then trying to learn to make the components itself. In one sense, it had no choice but to pursue a Japanese strategy. Precisely because it had arrived late, it was forced to practice "forward pricing." The company had to offer its new flat screens at a price below marginal cost, in the hope that low prices would generate enough volume for the factory to be able later on to cut its production costs and eventually make a profit.

What went wrong? Most of the simple answers seem inadequate. It cannot merely be that Philips grew inefficient as it became bigger, or that it spread out into too many different businesses. Matsushita, for example, is bigger than Philips. And some of the most profitable Japanese electronics firms have a bizarre spread of activities — Toshiba, for instance, makes nuclear power stations, elevators, and semiconductors — while others, such as Sony, remain much more firmly focused on audio-visual products.

Nor can Philips be accused of seeking short-term profits at the price of long-term growth by failing to invest in the key technologies necessary for future products. Quite the reverse: the firm bore enormous losses in its American semiconductor subsidiary for years with a good grace, and it had an introspective zeal for making everything by itself which would have made the average Japanese industry executive feel quite at home. And although Philips's shareholders have become restive in recent years, the firm has never been threatened with the sort of hostile takeover that has gutted so many American companies.

Nor did Philips make the mistake of the European car companies, concentrating too much on its home markets and failing to see the wider changes that were taking place in its industry across the world. Philips has always been a dedicated multinational company — its first language is probably English, which its Dutch employees speak with a skill that puts all other nationalities to shame — with a keen understanding of the importance of distribution. Its network of national sales companies all over the world is the envy of the industry.

What is more, the company saw the Japanese challenge coming. Although Akio Morita visited its operations in Eindhoven incognito in 1953, his company was absolutely unknown outside Japan at the time. Philips was already doing business with its rival Matsushita before the war; in 1952 it signed a technology-transfer agreement with Matsushita in which Philips received an up-front fee of $550,000, a net technical guidance fee (after deduction of a management fee exacted by its Japanese partner) of 1.5 percent — and a 30 percent shareholding in Matsushita Electronics Corporation, one of the key Matsushita subsidiaries, which Philips continues to hold to this day. Although Konosuke Matsushita professed himself very happy with the agreement,[11] no one could say that Philips undersold itself as many of its American competitors did in the 1950s.

Huijser suggests that Philips started to go wrong in the 1970s, and there were three reasons behind its decline. First, there was the arrival of new competition. It is important to remember that although there were plenty of firms in the United States, the Western electronics industry in the 1960s had settled down to an equilibrium in which few firms wanted to rock the boat. The Japanese electronics industry, led in the assault by Sony, was the first real challenge to that equilibrium; and it was not for a decade or more after they had started working on the American market that the new hungry competitors turned their attention to Europe. "When you're running fast and ahead of the pack," says Huijser, "you don't look around."

Second, the industry began to slow down in the 1970s after two decades of spectacular growth resulting from Europe's postwar recovery. When sales were growing at more than 10 percent a year, as first radios and then color televisions had still to penetrate all households in industrial countries, shortcomings of management and failures to produce good new products at high speed were not so evident. By the 1970s, the industry had begun to mature. The process is now complete: in 1991, color television sales fell 1 percent in Europe, 2 percent in the United States, and even more in Japan.

Third, consumers became more choosy as the different gadgets available proliferated. "The old weapons didn't work any more. We used to think that people would buy technology [for its own sake] . . . Someone had a good idea based on some technology, and could make a success of it — almost without limit. The managers we had created in that boom thought that everything they brought to market must automatically succeed."

Despite its strengths, Philips had become too bureaucratic a company to respond to these changes. Many of its best products were getting held up between development and marketing. Conflicts over responsibilities were occupying too much time between divisions. And, insiders now admit, a feeling had grown up among employees that they were working for a civil service rather than a profit-seeking business.

In 1990 everything changed when a new man took the helm of the company. Jan Timmer, a baker's son who had entered Philips while still in his teens and then spent more than a decade outside the Netherlands running subsidiaries as far apart as South Africa and London, brought himself to the board's attention by making drastic changes at the company's consumer electronics division: after being ruthlessly slimmed down, the division accounted for 45 percent of Philips's group sales, but for 75 percent of its operating profits. Timmer started to shake things up as soon as he became the company president. He decided straight away to make 55,000 of the company's workers redundant — which proved shocking in a firm that had previously had an informal policy of standing by its staff and sacking people only for dishonesty. He retired two people from the company's group management committee, and three from its supervisory board. He took the company out of the defense industry, and also raised over $1 billion by disposing of two substantial businesses: to the U.S. firm Whirlpool he sold Philips's 47 percent share of a joint venture the two firms had set up to make washing machines and other household appliances in Europe; and to Digital Equipment he sold the ailing Philips minicomputer business, which had lost money for years and was too small to compete in an increasingly fierce and homogeneous market. And he began to put pressure on the company's different divisions to weed loss-making products out of their catalogues.

More important than the sum of these specific measures, however, the new president launched a wide-ranging campaign, known as Operation Centurion, to change Philips's entire corporate culture. "It involves calling entrenched views and habits into question," wrote Timmer in the 1990 annual report, "simplifying methods of work and constantly improving quality awareness, customer orientation and cost consciousness. It also involves raising productivity, one of the key indicators of competitiveness and profitability. [In 1990 sales per employee at Philips were less than half those at Sony and Matsushita.] A more critical and more selective use of capital is another area on which we are focusing attention."

Timmer's strategy has brought criticism on both sides. Employees of the company wonder why they have to risk losing their jobs because of failures in the firm's management. But some outside analysts and shareholders believe that he has not been sufficiently sweeping. "What Timmer has done so far is fine," argues one consultant who has worked extensively inside Philips. "But he needs to take another 30 percent out of the ranks of the company's management." Whether or not the cuts have gone far enough, however, one thing is clear: the atmosphere in Eindhoven has changed forever. Philips will not die in its sleep.

One thing Timmer could not be praised for was his timing. His decision to restructure the Philips group — and to take an extraordinary $2.2 billion charge to the company's accounts in order to do so — hit just as the United States was preparing to drive Saddam Hussein out of Iraq, and just as the main electronics markets of the world were going into recession. No one was spared, not even the Japanese firms. To make things worse, the awakening of Philips has also coincided with the greatest period of technological innovation in consumer electronics for decades. For at the turn of the 1990s, Philips is preoccupied with three new products: high-definition television, the wide-screen, cinema-quality television that is supposed to take over from today's TV toward the end of the century; CD-I, or compact disc interactive, a kind of CD-ROM (discussed earlier) that allows a computer to retrieve sound and pictures and thus makes the first faltering steps toward a truly interactive visual medium; and the digital compact cassette, or DCC.

Of these three, it is the last that is likely to have most effect on Philips's future. The future of high-definition television is in the lap of bureaucrats in Washington, Brussels, and Tokyo, who must decide to what extent they should force television broadcasters and satellite and cable companies to use a new standard that they do not like. CD-I is one of a number of competing media that raise far broader questions about the problems of trying to bring in a new technology that is extremely clever but has no obvious use. But the story of DCC is likely to be the story of a standards battle pure and simple, just like the battle between Matsushita's VHS and Sony's Betamax. What is more, this will be a highly public battle into which some of the world's biggest electronics firms are putting their best talent. In ten years' time, it may be looked back on as the first sign of Philips's revival; if it fails, on the other hand, observers all over the world will conclude that the boys at Eindhoven, Timmer included, are ripe for retirement.

The background to the story is a revolution half finished. Over the past five years, the long-playing record has been driven out of music stores by the dramatically better sound quality of the compact disc. The CD's superiority comes from the fact that it stores music digitally, as a series of ones and zeros, instead of as a series of analogue impulses on a black vinyl disc.[12] As well as better sound quality on a prerecorded disc, digitalization has another crucial benefit: it allows users to make a perfect copy, while with old-style analogue recordings every successive copy makes the sound quality worse. Yet between 1983 and 1992, the revolution was only half finished: there was no digital tape recorder to go with the new digital record player.

To be precise, that was not strictly true. In the mid-1980s, Sony and Philips developed a machine called digital audio tape (DAT) that met the technical problem exactly. It was a smaller version of a cassette player, which could both play and record digitally. But DAT never took off. The world's music companies and record labels were suspicious of a machine that appeared to offer their customers the chance to make unlimited numbers of copies, and they feared an explosion of illegal home taping that would kill the sales of recorded music. They therefore refused to cooperate: music publishers boycotted the new technology, and some even tried to sue Sony, claiming that its new machines were encouraging others to break the copyright laws.

That knee-jerk reaction from the music industry was probably misguided. One of the key problems that publishers of all kinds of information are likely to face over the coming decade as more and more books, films, and music become available in a digital format is that the old view of business — which centered on a physical good like a videocassette or a record carrying the information — is now out of date. Music companies are selling a service; and rather than shying away from change, they must come to terms with the fact that their "software," as it is now called in the industry, can quite easily be delivered without any physical packaging at all. Few music firms have given this crucial strategic issue much thought.

Either way, the opposition of the music industry was enough to tip the balance against DAT. For the new machines had two other drawbacks. They were expensive, and they were not "backwardly compatible." All the people who bought a new DAT machine were condemning themselves to throwing away their existing collection of tapes and starting again. Many people had done that once in the past decade by replacing records with CDs; they were rather more reluctant to do it a second time by replacing cassettes with DATs.

The result was mayhem. Philips, which had helped to develop the new technology, got cold feet at the last minute. Sony, ever the pioneer, soldiered on and made both DAT decks and DAT Walkmen. By early 1991, however, it was clear that the new standard was doomed to be a mere curiosity for moneyed enthusiasts. A sign that Sony itself had lost confidence in the medium was the fact that its own music publishing arm, the CBS record company (which it bought in 1988 for $2 billion and then renamed Sony Music Entertainment), had a DAT record catalogue composed of a miserable total of nine titles. If there was to be a new digital tape technology, therefore, DAT was not it.

About 1988, after it pulled out of the DAT project, Philips started thinking hard about how to improve on it. Dr. Gerry Wirtz, the senior product manager who had been in charge of it, came up with three answers. Any son-of-DAT, he concluded, must be cheap, must be able to play existing audiocassettes, and must be supported by the music companies.

Wirtz came to this conclusion by looking at the music market. What he found was that CDs had taken over from vinyl records largely as a result of the efforts of a relatively small number of enthusiasts, who bought the machines and then proceeded to spend on lots of discs to go with them. The cassette market was very different: there were over a billion cassette machines in use all over the world, with an average of three machines per household, but cassette owners were much less keen on buying new recordings. Although many owners had thirty or more cassettes, the entire music industry sold only about one for each machine in 1990. In that same year, however, sales of cassettes started to fall — and the technology was already considered so old that customers would buy boom-box stereos without even bothering to look at the cassette player inside. It was high time to find a replacement.

Philips quickly decided that its new digital tape player would only have a chance if the concerns of the music industry were met. So it agreed to install in the new machines a gadget called the Serial Copy Management System, which allows customers to make as many perfect copies as they like from a prerecorded CD or prerecorded digital tape, but not to make digital copies of those copies. (The system works by recording inaudible codes alongside the music which can then be used to prevent the machine from copying it digitally once again.) This was less than the hawks of the copyright brigade would have wanted, but it was a compromise that satisfied most without making the machine wholly useless to customers.

The problem was how to make DCC cheaper than DAT had been. Looking back, the key reason DAT had been expensive was that it was actually very difficult to squeeze all the necessary digital data onto a tape without making the tape so thin that it would easily tear or stretch. To succeed, the engineers who designed it had been forced to borrow a trick from the video industry: instead of the stationary head that had been used to play and record music in the old compact cassette, they used a rotating head that spun at an angle, and recorded the data in elegant diagonal lines on the tape like slices in a baguette. It was a technical triumph, but a commercial disaster: DAT machines were condemned to hit the market at a thousand dollars, and cutting the price would depend on mastering a new and subtle technology. In short, it was exactly the sort of mistake that Japanese firms usually avoided.

Wirtz was determined that Philips should avoid repeating it with a replacement for DAT. "I told the engineers exactly what I wanted," he remembers. They came up with a brilliant solution. Rather than trying to squeeze too much data onto a tape, they realized that it would be better to have less data to begin with. That could be done quite simply by reducing the sound quality of the new system; but it would hardly satisfy consumers whose ears had been sharpened by the quality of the CD. So the engineers looked closely at the physics of recording and noticed that plenty of the information that is recorded on a CD is never heard by the listener — for instance, a quiet sound will often be drowned out by a louder sound of similar pitch. (A good example of that is the way in which a whisper that is audible in an otherwise quiet room cannot be heard in a noisy street.) Working backward from the listener, instead of forward from the microphone, the Philips engineers found a way of compressing the music into only a quarter as much digital data as on a CD.[13] The result was that they could drop the expensive and difficult rotating head but still record ninety minutes of music on a cassette the same size as the old audiocassette. As a bonus, there was also enough space to install a playback mechanism for standard cassettes.

By the end of 1992, with Jan Timmer taking a close interest in the project, Philips was preparing to launch DCC as a fully fledged replacement for the cassette. It had the support of the world's big music companies, and a list of hundreds of albums already on the shelves. By then, however, Sony had hit back. It announced that it was preparing its own replacement for the cassette: a tiny, recordable compact disc called Mini-Disc. Mini-Disc overcomes the unreliability that was the biggest problem of the CD Walkman by the simple device of installing a memory chip that would act as a buffer, storing a few seconds' worth of music and then forwarding them on to the player so that the flow will not be interrupted when the disc jumps.

It has one technical advantage over DCC: like CD, Mini-Disc can find a piece of music anywhere on the disc by simply rotating the disc and moving the head. DCC, by contrast, still has to wind through the entire tape to find something at the end — more quickly and accurately than a compact cassette, it is true, but far more slowly than its new disc competitor. Yet apart from that, Mini-Disc appears to have little to recommend it. Most damningly, Sony has no plans to put on the market either CD players that can play Mini-Discs or Mini-Disc players that can play CDs. It will have to work hard to persuade consumers who have invested heavily in CD collections to start all over again with Mini-Disc.

Philips's prospects for the new technology therefore look very promising. Having learned from its mistakes with CD, the company is determined to dominate the market in the key components inside the new players. It has set up a separate business unit whose job will be to sell the crucial recording heads and other bits of the mechanism on an OEM basis to other companies that want to build DCC players. Furthermore, it has already planned four generations of the product. In late 1992 six different models were on the company's shelves, ready to be released at the end of the year, one every two months for a year; and there were even plans for a DCC Walkman, using only a single chip, that would be only slightly more expensive than existing top-of-the-line Walkmans today.

Matsushita has already thrown in its lot with Philips by announcing that it will make the new machines. Sony, on the other hand, continues to hedge its bets by backing its own technology aggressively but reserving the right to come into the DCC camp if Mini-Disc does not work out. It will probably be five years before the winner is clear, but for once, the European firm seems to be the favorite. Perhaps an early sign of that came in early 1992, when Philips turned tentatively into profit, and Sony, hobbled by slow sales in its home market, suffered operating losses for the first time in living memory.

One of the features of the battle for the future of digital audio is that it is being fought entirely between companies. The same cannot be said for high-definition television, whose fate will be largely decided by governments.

As the single European market began to take shape in early 1992, the question of what governments can do to make European business more competitive was being addressed with renewed vigor. In London, a Conservative government had a firm answer: not a great deal. The job of the government is to protect the consumer and then get out of the way, John Major's ministers were saying. Only a few hundred miles away, however, a different view entirely was in the ascendant: in Paris, the dying government of Edith Cresson was busily trying to promote European mergers in order to create "European champions" that could fight the Japanese on their own terms. And in Brussels, the European Community was offering an increasingly broad range of subsidies in order to promote research and development in high-technology industries. Which was right? That is the topic we must turn to next.

SEVEN

The Pitfalls of
European Industrial Policy

ONE OF THE THINGS that struck me as most mysterious when I moved from Tokyo to Brussels in early
1992 was the number of copy shops in the neighborhood around my new home. Everywhere one looked, it
seemed, there was a small business that appeared to do nothing but make photocopies. This is not so in Tokyo. There,
making plain black-and-white photocopies is not a service
that is lucrative enough to sustain anyone in business. The
vast majority of Japanese firms — from the largest industrial
firms down to the smallest rice dealer or sushi shop — seem
to have a photocopier. The only people who cannot make copies on their own premises are private individuals — and they
go to late-night convenience stores, where they can have copies run off at the same time as they pay their electricity bills,
have their vacation photos developed, send faxes, rent videos,
and buy cans of beer and packets of dried squid to consume
while they watch them. In Tokyo, the only photocopier that
is worth hanging a special sign outside the door to advertise
is a color copier — a gadget that is now so sophisticated that
it can be used for forging banknotes.[1]

Why should the copy shop industry, which was born in the days when copying machines were expensive and unreliable, have survived longer in Europe than in Japan? The answer may well lie in the prices of machines. One of the most basic copying machines available in both Japan and Europe is a Canon model called the FC-1. In spring 1992 this machine cost ¥82,400 all in, or $626, at a standard electronics shop in Tokyo. In Brussels, on the other hand, it cost 37,000 Belgian francs, or $1,103. It requires little imagination to see why, with the cheapest available machine costing over 75 percent more in one market than in the other, far fewer small businesses in Europe than in Japan feel they can afford to invest in a photocopier.

Given that the only difference between an FC-1 sold in Brussels and one sold in Tokyo is that one works on 220-volt current and the other on 110 volts, such a large price difference may seem surprising. What makes it truly astonishing is that the price difference is the opposite of what a conventional analysis of Japanese business patterns would suggest. As countless surveys, both private and governmental, have shown, many products tend to cost more in Japan than abroad because of the high cost of distributing them and because Japanese firms are in general able to get away with more illegal price-fixing activities there than in other industrial countries;[2] changing this, and thus improving the lot of Japanese consumers, is one of the key objectives of the Structural Impediments Initiative, a long-running set of trade negotiations between the United States and Japan. In this case, however, the tables are turned: it is the European consumer who suffers and the Japanese consumer who benefits from the difference.

There may be a number of possible explanations for this startling difference. With some products, a company has a particular commercial reason for wanting to charge a very different price in one market than in another: witness the pricing of Toyota's Lexus luxury car in Europe noted in chapter 4. In this case, however, Canon has no such incentive. Perhaps the reason might be just that this machine is an anomaly —

a victim of lack of information in a market where prices are increasingly being eased together by efficient transport and cheap communications? No — in fact, the price gap for the FC-1, although larger than the gap on many other copiers, is evidence of a wider trend of enormous economic and political importance. Both the FC-1 and other copiers are more expensive in Europe because of a deliberate and conscious attempt on the part of the European Community and its member governments to make European industry more competitive.

At first sight, the idea may seem ludicrous. How, a cynic might ask, can the bureaucrats in Brussels help European firms by making it more expensive for them to make photocopies? Higher photocopier prices are a burden to business, just like higher telephone bills or bad roads, which makes it harder for a firm to do business and thus puts it at a disadvantage in relation to its competitors. Yet there is a theoretical case in favor of intervention. Although it may raise prices for customers, allowing an industry to charge higher prices will, other things being equal, make it more profitable and thus encourage more firms to enter it. And in theory at least, after a period of time under the wing of government, the protected industry can then sally forth with new confidence, its costs brought down by the artificial boost of economies of scale and its products improved by plowing profits back into research and development. At that point, whatever restrictions were in place can be removed, and the newly invigorated industry can then be allowed to fight for its corner in world markets unaided.

This is not the place for a sweeping judgment between these two views of how economies ought to work. It is enough to say this: although there are tremendous disagreements in the West about the role the government has played in Japan's economic miracle — some think the native free-market skills of the Japanese would have come to the fore even earlier and more spectacularly without the involvement of the bureaucracy, while others insist that the state is so tightly bound up in the nation's business that it makes no sense to talk of a distinct private sector in Japan at all — it is clear that there has been extensive intervention in the Japanese economy since the war. Each of the business sectors we have looked at so far bears that out.

In the United States, government intervention in the economy is already so extensive that it amounts to an industrial policy in all but name. Examples are the federal government's controls over interest rates; the way in which it is able to rescue companies in crisis, like Chrysler, or even entire sectors, like the savings and loan industry; the extensive subsidies given to exporters of farm goods, which have produced dramatic (and dizzyingly fast) changes in resource allocation in the American economy; the use, often highly selective and responsive to complaints from American business, of trade policy against imports; and, perhaps above all, the money paid out by the federal government for research and development — much of which is apparently military research but has wider benefits throughout the economy.

The champions of industrial policy in the United States argue that since such choices are routinely being made day by day, the United States ought to call them by their proper name and coordinate them into a single, coherent group of policies specifically aimed at promoting the competitiveness of U.S. industry. Since the tools of trade and investment policy that Washington already has at its disposal can have such dramatic effects on the competitive balance, the argument runs, they should be used in an organized and strategic way rather than unthinkingly by default.

In Europe, by contrast, the debate remains at a rudimentary stage. National governments inside the Community are fond of talking about industrial policy, but when they use the words they usually mean only one thing: doling out hefty subsidies to a handful of big firms in the hope of making them world-beaters. Such policies are usually little more than short-term fixes for the political problems that face a government when one of the biggest firms in its jurisdiction runs into trouble. When they are more thought out, however, they tend to be based on a view of the world that runs as follows: "Companies from that country are doing well in our market, and everywhere else in the world. They are much bigger than the firms from our country that try to compete with them. If our side is to survive, it must become more like them. So we must force our firms to amalgamate so that they can do battle with these behemoths from abroad." Such was the strategy behind the creation of the British Motor Company, later to be known as British Leyland and Rover Group; such, too, was the strategy behind Edith Cresson's ill-fated attempt to build a pan-European electronics conglomerate in 1991.

The problem with such a strategy is that it mistakes the direction of causation. Only rarely is a firm good because it is big. More often, it becomes big because it is good; and putting two bad firms together in order to beat it will more often compound their faults than their strengths. The industrial landscape of the Western world is littered with troubled big companies whose size failed to protect them from the greater agility of competitors abroad. This book has pointed to some of them: General Motors, in the car industry; Philips, in consumer electronics; IBM and Compaq in the computer business. Yet in present-day Europe, the debate over industrial policy continues to be fought in such terms.

To make things worse, there appears to be alarmingly little coordination in Brussels over different policies. The most obvious conflicts arise between those whose job is to promote competition inside the Community by outlawing cartels and price-fixing arrangements and by removing the barriers to free trade, and those who assert the need for policies that they admit are detrimental to competition in the short term but which, they argue, are actually procompetitive in the longer term. But there are other conflicts too. Given the interpenetration between the European market and that of the rest of the world, external trade policy is likely to have a dramatic effect on anything the industrial-policy doctors do for European business. Yet when I asked Filippo Maria Pandolfi, the member of the seventeen-strong European Commission in charge of promoting research and development, how the Community's policy on antidumping fitted into an ambitious plan he was proposing in early 1992 for the spending of several billion dollars of taxpayers' money on research and development, his answer was extraordinary. "That's trade policy," he said — and insisted that it was none of his business.

On the contrary: trade in general, and antidumping in particular, is the place where any look at European industrial policy must start. Sadly, the evidence is far from reassuring: although they are the single most powerful administrative tool in the Brussels armory for strengthening Europe's industrial base, antidumping actions do not appear to be helping firms inside the Community compete against Japan. The evidence on public subsidies to research and development appears to be more mixed. Despite this generally depressing picture, however, there *are* things that can be done, both in the national capitals and in Brussels, to help Europe to meet the Japanese challenge. This chapter will end by looking at some of those. First, though, the story must return to the photocopier whose price varied so sharply between Brussels and Tokyo.

If there were a single product that embodies all the virtues of Japanese technology, it would be the Canon FC-1. It is a smooth, dark gray plastic box weighing about ten pounds, about five inches high, and a little bigger in width and length than a sheet of 8½-by-11-inch paper. A handle on one side allows it to be carried like an attaché case. With the exception of a power switch at the back, it has no buttons; instead, there is a discreet slider on the front to vary the copy quality from light to dark, and a small light that glows green to show that the machine is switched on. Using it is elegantly simple: the owner simply lifts up the top, puts a document on the glass, and slides a piece of clean paper into one side of the machine. Six seconds later, the paper appears on the other side of the machine with a copy of the document printed in bold black on top of it. The quality of the copy is indistinguishable from that of copies made on the most expensive machine on the market.

To understand why the FC-1 is such a marvel, however, it is necessary to look back a generation at another copier and another company: the Xerox 914, made by the Xerox Corporation of Rochester, New York. In 1965, when sales of the 914 reached their peak, analysts declared that it was the most successful commercial product in history. But it was no fluke: Xerox had devoted years of effort and millions of dollars to developing a compact machine that could make photocopies on plain paper, and it was careful to protect its work with a string of patents. The $27,500 machine, explained an awestruck American business writer in the *New Yorker* in 1967,

> which is painted beige and weighs six hundred and fifty pounds, looks a good deal like a modern L-shaped metal desk. The thing to be copied — a flat page, two pages of an open book, or even a small three-dimensional object like a watch or a medal — is placed face down in a glass window in the flat top surface, a button is pushed, and nine seconds later the copy pops into a tray where an "out" basket might be if the 914 actually were a desk. Technologically, the 914 is so complex (more complex, some Xerox salesmen insist, than an automobile) that it has an annoying tendency to go wrong, and consequently Xerox maintains a field staff of thousands of repairmen who are presumably ready to answer a call on short notice.[3]

The most common fault of this wondrous but temperamental machine was a paper jam. Xerox specialists called this a "mispuff," because the 914 used a puff of air to lift sheets of copy paper into position. When this happened, and the paper came into contact with a hot part inside the works, the 914 was apt to emit an alarming cloud of smoke. Even without mispuffs, it required frequent replenishing with black toner powder, and its light-sensitive selenium drum had to be cleaned and waxed regularly with special materials. It was no wonder that each machine had assigned to it a full-time operator, usually a woman. "A 914," the writer continued, "has distinct animal traits: it has to be fed and curried; it is intimidating but can be tamed; it is subject to unpredictable bursts of misbehavior; and, generally speaking, it responds in kind to its treatment."

Even at the high Brussels price, the Canon FC-1 is about one five-hundredth of the price of the 914 in real terms, and less than a fiftieth of the size and weight. What makes it such a marvel, however, is its simplicity and reliability. Far from requiring a full-time operator, the FC-1 can be used by anyone, anywhere, five minutes after unpacking it from its box. Because of the extremely basic design, the copy paper follows an almost straight path through the machine; in the 914, it was bent acrobatically around a series of rollers. As a result, paper jams in the FC-1 are rare — and when they do happen, the user simply presses a button to open up the box and eases the sheet out from the works inside. Best of all, however, the Canon machine requires no maintenance. Replenishing the toner — a job for the expert repairman in the old days — is now simply a matter of replacing a sealed cartridge, which also contains a number of the sensitive machine parts whose deterioration most affects copy quality. As a result, the machine performs like new every time the cartridge is changed. The complexity of the Xerox 914 (the salesmen's comparison with a motorcar was probably based on the fact that the copier had more parts) therefore proved in the end to be not its selling-point, but its downfall. Xerox itself, which had made 62 percent of its 1965 operating revenues from the 914, was too slow to realize the mistake it had made. It was a case with striking similarities to that of IBM: the firm that had created a market found that its creation took on a life of its own. Luckily for Xerox, it survived — after a rocky few years in which it was saved from destruction only by the ingenuity of its own subsidiary in Japan.

But that is to jump forward. Until 1973 Xerox was able to use its patents to keep competitors out of the plain-paper copy market. In that year, however, the U.S. Fair Trade Commission effectively ended its monopoly by forcing the firm to license its technology to outsiders. The result was a worldwide scramble as companies in Europe and Japan rushed to enter the copier market to take advantage of the opportunity offered by the FTC ruling.

Xerox continues to this day to maintain its lead in the miracle machines at the top of the range, which can at the touch of a few buttons feed in a long report printed on both sides and make fifty perfect copies of it, each neatly sorted and stapled in its own basket. But competitors soon noticed that Xerox had long neglected the bottom end of the market. Having made fat profits for years from leasing high-specification machines with service contracts to big companies, the firm never thought it needed to turn the photocopier into a product for the small business or the household.

That was a job for which the Japanese considered themselves ideally suited. A dozen Japanese firms began to make copiers, and to work hard at finding ways to reduce the cost and complexity of Xerox's temperamental mechanism. Canon's sealed toner cartridge was probably the single most important development, but there were scores of others.

Japanese firms were not the only ones competing with Xerox, however. A number of European companies, too, saw opportunities in the fast-growing new market. But the competition was fierce, and it was not confined to the United States. From 1976 to 1980 the prices of small plain-paper copiers in Europe fell an average of 7 percent every year. By 1981 the European makers were badly lagging: they were hardly selling at all in Japan, and Japanese firms had an 81 percent market share in the Community. As the market almost doubled in size once again between 1981 and 1984, the Japanese firms increased their exports to Europe from 272,000 units to 492,000, and edged up their market share to 85 percent by 1985. Not merely did prices fall, but Japanese firms also brought out a welter of new models, adding new features and making improvements to basic models year after year.

European consumers were delighted. As the new plain-paper copiers became more affordable, companies flocked in droves to buy them. As elsewhere in the world, the result was to change the way copiers were perceived. This machine, which had at first been a high-technology product for a few rich companies, now became a tool for anyone. It prompted a publishing revolution: individuals and pressure groups now have it within their power to produce and distribute high-quality copies of a poster or document in quantities that used to be too small to be economic. The greatest tribute of all to the photocopier is the fact that the repressive regime of the former Soviet Union considered it, along with the typewriter, a dangerous and possibly counterrevolutionary device to be kept out of the hands of its citizens. A few hundred miles to the west, the European Community in Brussels depends for its very existence on the photocopier: without the ability to turn out in nine different languages billions of pages a year of draft directives, minutes, proposals, memoranda, and press releases, the Community would seize up in a matter of days.

But the European producers were not so happy. Although their sales were growing rapidly, they were not growing as fast as the market as a whole, and the business of making copiers, which had been rather profitable in the early days, quickly became a trade that demanded high investment but promised only thin profit margins. Meanwhile, a shakeout was taking place back in Japan: companies were installing new manufacturing plants and cutting prices sharply to the levels necessary to win enough sales to keep their factories running at full tilt.

Looking back at the broader changes that were taking place in the industry, it is hard to see that the Japanese were doing anything unfair. It may be bad luck for a company to find itself overwhelmed by competitors who are willing to work harder at developing new products and to take slimmer profit margins, but it is certainly not reprehensible. The European copier makers disagreed with this view, however. The Japanese firms, they alleged, were selling copiers in Europe at artificially low prices in order to drive the competition out of business — and they were subsidizing losses in Europe by selling in their home market at high prices. Once they had succeeded in eliminating the European makers, the Japanese would thus be free to use their monopoly power to raise prices. Such behavior, known as "dumping," is condemned under the internationally agreed rules of the General Agreement on Tariffs and Trade: the agreement gives importing countries the right to impose special duties on dumped imports in order to prevent damage to their indigenous industries. It was in an attempt to persuade Brussels to do just this that four European copier companies made a formal complaint to the European Commission in 1985. The case was to become a cause célèbre — not just because the twelve Japanese exporters were among Japan's most respected industrial companies (they included such names as Canon, Matsushita, Minolta, Ricoh, Sanyo, Sharp, Toshiba, and Fuji Xerox), but also because the case was later to be seen as one of the most aggressive uses of antidumping legislation as a tool of industrial policy.

For an organization that has the most sweeping powers over companies and their customers, that has (at least in theory) the ability to raise hundreds of millions of dollars of duties, that is quite consciously setting out to shape the future of European industry, the antidumping unit of the European Commission is a curiously unimpressive place. When I visited it at the beginning of 1992, the unit was at work in a small Brussels office block just like many others.

There was also an unmistakably defensive feeling in the air. One top official of the unit told me that I was the first researcher to visit for a long time, and complained bitterly about hostile journalists and economists who criticize the Community's antidumping strategy without troubling to find out how it looks from the inside. Another handed me a set of notes he had written for a presentation, in which he complained of a public campaign against the unit orchestrated by the *Financial Times* — a newspaper that has rarely in the past been accused of being a tool of interests antagonistic to European industry. A third official referred throughout our discussion to "the Japs," and made it clear by gestures and by throwaway lines that his practice was to treat any information he received from Japanese companies under investigation with the utmost suspicion.

To be fair, the unit does its work under difficult circumstances. Its full-time staff was only twenty-six in 1986, compared with a corresponding number involved in antidumping investigations for the U.S. government of about five hundred. In 1987, after repeated pleas, the twelve member states of the European Community allowed the unit to raise its numbers to forty — but insisted that, for budgetary reasons, the new arrivals should be sent on a temporary basis from the national governments. Since antidumping is a highly complex and specialized field, almost none of the temporary staff are any use when they arrive at the beginning of a three-year assignment. The workload of the full-timers is increased considerably by the job of training this constantly rotating band of amateurs. Astonishingly, given the amount of financial accounting that has to be done, only twelve of the officials and two of the "experts," as the amateurs from the national capitals are paradoxically known, have access to a personal computer.

In many ways, the unit has a much harder job than its counterparts across the Atlantic at the offices of the U.S. Trade Representative and the Department of Commerce. Unlike them, European antidumping officials have to show not merely that dumping has taken place and that it has injured domestic industry, but also that it is in the broader interests of the European Community to impose a duty. The unit's work is also slowed down by the fact that all the official documents that it produces have to be translated into the Community's nine official languages — which often takes a month for a ten-page report, and a week even for a single-page document. The unit also has to consult the different services of the Commission in the course of its investigations: the legal service, the customs, and those responsible for the internal market, for industry, and for the enforcement of competition law. To make things worse, it must also keep the twelve member states informed before it opens an investigation, while it is carrying one out, and after it has finished. All these things combined help to explain why European antidumping investigations can take up to two years, while the U.S. machinery takes less than six months.

But the fundamental problem that the investigators face is that it is often very hard to find out whether a foreign company is selling a product at a higher price in its home market than in Europe. The investigators are mandated to compare the prices charged by the maker to the "first independent buyer" — usually a wholesaler or distributor. The trouble is, differences between markets mean that simple comparisons are impossible. The first independent buyer in France might be a large office equipment wholesaler. In Japan, it might be a discount warehouse that has bought the product from a distributor in which the maker has a small shareholding. As a result, the antidumping experts usually find themselves trying to construct a "normal value" for what the product *would* have cost in Japan had it been distributed through European-style channels.[4] Even then, there are great uncertainties.

The result is that the investigators from Brussels end up doing almost a full-scale audit of the exporters' business, asking them to give them a degree of detail about their manufacturing costs, their sales methods, and the nature of their clients far greater than anything their own tax authority is ever likely to want. To respond to the questionnaire that the antidumping unit sends out when it has decided to take on a case, the exporting firm often has to assemble a team of thirty to fifty people and set them to work for weeks or even months. The response, which the firms must send in a Community language rather than their own, can often be five hundred or one thousand pages long. In some cases, the investigators have looked at more than 1 million different transactions; in others, in an attempt to find out what the exporter's domestic sales costs are, the investigators ask for details of the names, salaries, and pension rights of every single domestic salesman. One antidumping lawyer estimates that an exporter can easily spend, in meeting the direct and indirect costs of replying to an antidumping complaint, over $1 million.

In August 1986 the antidumping unit unveiled its provisional findings from the investigation of trade in plain-paper copiers. Each of the twelve Japanese exporters it had looked at had been dumping, it concluded; and the "dumping margin," or the extra the firms were charging at home in order to subsidize low-priced exports to Europe, ranged from 13.7 percent in the case of Mita to 69.4 percent in the case of Kyocera. To work out what duty would be necessary to redress the injury to the European firms whose profitability had been hurt by the dumping, the unit decided that a reasonable rate of return on assets before tax was 18 percent, and that a reasonable net profit on revenue was 12 percent. The investigators therefore calculated the increase in revenue that would be necessary for the European firms that had complained to earn that 12 percent pretax profit, and extrapolated from that the prices that would have to prevail. Early in 1987, the Community's council of ministers approved a flat antidumping duty of 20 percent on copiers from all the twelve producers but one. Kyocera, the firm that it had found to be dumping by the highest margin, gave a secret guarantee to the Commission not to sell its machines in Europe below certain agreed prices, and the case against it was dropped.

> The Commission accepts [argued the antidumping unit in its report on the investigation] that these measures may result in a price increase in the short term. However, in view of the extent of the injury caused by dumped imports and the importance of the Community industry injured, it is considered that in this case, the necessity to ensure the stability of the industry in question is more important. Indeed, in the long term, it is in the consumers' interests to have a viable Community industry which will compete with and offer an alternative to imports.[5]

Perhaps one might quarrel with the use of the expression *short-term* in the Commission's justification for its decision.

In late 1992, six years after the publication of the provisional findings, the antidumping duties were still in place; and the unit was in the middle of a follow-up investigation, expected to last well into 1993, to address the question of whether the duties should be removed or not. But the more important question was whether it had been right to impose them in the first place. There is a difference between a procedure that is legally defensible and one that makes sense commercially or economically.

To start with, the methods used by the investigators were highly unfavorable to the Japanese exporters — even according to the account of the investigation published in the Community's *Official Journal*. One difference between the copier business in the Japanese market and that in the European one was that in Japan, it was common for firms to offer trade-ins on old machines when customers bought new ones. It clearly cost the copier manufacturers money either to resell the old machines for less than they bought them for, or to throw them out altogether; yet the investigators disputed the firms' claims that this counted as a discount to buyers which had the effect of making machines less expensive than they seemed at first sight in Japan. The investigators also judged that Japanese firms were making higher profits on spare parts and toner than on the copiers themselves, and insisted that the machines' price in Japan for the purposes of calculation should be raised to reflect this. And they refused to take into account the prices for copiers that Japanese companies charged their importing subsidiaries in Europe, arguing that these were not free-market transactions. All of these three decisions — perhaps defensible one by one — had the effect of increasing the price of copiers in Japan for the purposes of the calculations, and thus increasing the dumping margin produced in their conclusion.

On closer inspection, however, the entire philosophical basis for the calculations seems doubtful. For instance, the investigators decided to calculate the injury to the European makers by "assuming" that they ought to have made a rate of return of 18 percent. On what basis could this assumption be made? Given that Japanese firms were at the time paying less for borrowed capital and paying out less of their profits to shareholders in the form of dividends, they could afford to tolerate lower rates of return. Were they not entitled to pass on the benefits of that to their customers? Even if the figure had been right, there was another problem. The investigators had asked themselves what level of prices would be necessary to earn the European makers profit margins fat enough to achieve that rate of return. Had prevailing prices been higher, the European makers would have made higher profits per machine sold. But those very same higher prices might have reduced demand for copiers. Or they might have increased supply by attracting firms from abroad that had previously not thought it profitable to enter the European copier market. Either way, the reasoning was rather tenuous.

Another problem in the reasoning was the claim by the European plaintiffs that there was a direct causal link between competition from Japan and their own problems. This link too was far from clear. The European makers were indeed doing badly, the Japanese exporters argued, but it was their own fault. Like Xerox itself, they had failed to see the significance of the move toward simpler and cheaper plain-paper copiers. Although they had moved into the market with belated research programs, they had not managed to get finished products onto dealers' shelves quickly enough. What made their claim more doubtful still was the fact that although there were five firms named as victims — Develop of Germany, Océ of the Netherlands, Olivetti of Italy, Rank Xerox of Britain, and Tetras of France — there were other European copier makers who had not participated in the complaint. That, presumably, was because they did not believe themselves to have been injured. Yet the investigators did not appear to ask themselves whether the fact that some European makers were doing quite well in the face of Japanese competition might not cast doubt on the claim from the others that the Japanese were the source of all their problems.

Who, in any case, were the complainers? Of the five, the French firm was effectively a start-up company with little experience in the industry. Three more, despite their complaints about the Japanese, were themselves buying small photocopiers from Japanese companies and selling them in Europe under their own names — at prices up to 14 percent higher than those charged by the Japanese for the same machines. Olivetti actually had two parallel businesses of roughly the same size, one selling its own models, the other selling Japanese copiers with Olivetti labels. Did this not cast a little doubt on their attempt to portray themselves as courageous European firms trying hard to innovate and win business in the face of unfair competition from abroad? When the Japanese firms made a countercomplaint, insisting that the firms in question were too tied up with importing Japanese machines to count as part of the European industry anyway, the investigators took a narrowly legal view in their reply:

> The question of whether the term "Community" should include Community producers who import dumped goods is a matter which can only be decided on a case by case basis and in the light of all the relevant facts regarding the nature of the links between Community producers and the exporters concerned. As a general observation, however, it should be noted that it is now entirely normal for large firms engaged in international business to buy part of their range of models from other producers . . .
>
> Overall, and in the light of the facts available to it, the Commission considers that, in importing plain-paper copiers on an OEM [original-equipment manufacturer] basis, Océ and Olivetti can be considered to have done nothing which caused them to suffer losses greater than they would have suffered if they had attempted to base their own PPC [plain-paper copier] business on the marketing of a more limited range of models.

But that was not the question. No one was suggesting that the European producers were doing anything illogical in abandoning the lower end of the copier market to Japanese competition while trying to retreat into the more profitable niches of upmarket, expensive machines. The question that the Commission ought perhaps to have asked was a different one. The crux of the European firms' case was that the photocopier industry was strategic to the Community's future, but in danger. Could they with a clear conscience ask consumers inside the Community to put up with paying higher prices for photocopiers, while at the same time admitting that they themselves had been among the most enthusiastic buyers of Japanese copiers — even going so far as to take advantage of their high quality and low price by selling them to the consumer under their own names at fat markups?

Officially, antidumping investigations are a matter of narrow trade policy. The Commission denies the widely believed view that they are a tool of industrial policy, used to keep Japanese products out of the Community so that European firms can enjoy higher profits. Only one of the officials I spoke to would admit even partly the truth of this view of antidumping as a tool of industrial policy. "Technology is not at the top of the list of objectives of antidumping policy," he said. "But one has to consider that the possibility to keep a certain technology inside the Community may be one element of the public interest test."

Outside the machinery of the Community's bureaucracy, others are willing to call a spade a spade. Ian Forrester, the senior partner of a Brussels legal practice and one of the leading specialists in the field who has fought cases on both sides, talks of an "orgy" of antidumping cases against Japanese electrical products, from typewriters to outboard motors to miniature ball bearings, which began in the early 1980s:

> That's where the Commission fine-tuned the antidumping gun so that it was particularly apt for shooting at Japanese companies . . . In each case, it would be wrong, wrong, wrong to say that the investigators added "2 + 2" on a rigged calculator and made "5." They didn't; they were arithmetically honest.

But the technique they used to construct the numbers and to compare them was, I admit, deeply unfair. It didn't yield a fair comparison. The technique of dumping investigation was constantly changing to the detriment of exporters, particularly those from countries with an elaborate distribution structure . . .

In virtually every case, the Japanese lost. And the European Court of Justice said when examining the process that it would use a minimalist standard. It would only look for gross breaches of authority . . .

Dumping has a connotation like pollution, divorce, unemployment, decay: it's a loaded word. No matter whether you get off or not, you assume that a proper well-adjusted person would not get himself into a situation where he could be accused. It's as if the investigation were a litmus test: you dip your accounting rod into the pool and it comes out red for dumping or blue for not dumping. Those two assumptions are both quite false.

The Commission's own reports on antidumping policy show just how carefully its use has been targeted. In the 1980s more antidumping investigations were carried out against exporters from Japan than against those from any other country. And in 1989, the latest year for which figures are available, the share of the Community's imports from Japan that were affected by antidumping measures was seventeen times higher than the affected share of its imports from any other industrial country.

The direction of the policy and its purpose seem clear. What have its effects been, however? Has the imposition of such stiff import duties in the case examined here given European firms the breathing space they asked for? Has it allowed them to close the gap between them and their Japanese competitors? Apparently not. Sir Leon Brittan, one of the members of the European Commission, admitted as much in a speech in late 1991.

In 1986, the European Community applied very high antidumping duties against twelve Japanese exporters of photocopiers. In due course the Community also introduced anti-circumvention measures. Yet it has been estimated that the cost of this policy for European consumers — that is, European companies, for the most part — is over 400m ECU ($537m) a year, which is twice the value of the total production of the European companies which had sought protection. Since the case was opened, the market share of those companies has dropped from 16% to 10% and a greater and greater part of their business involves the mere distribution of Japanese photocopiers which are more expensive than they need be because they have paid the additional duty. In short, the duties have been ineffective in protecting the original complainants; yet they have been hugely costly to European business and to consumers.[6]

When I left the antidumping unit, I carried under my arm a fat pile of helpful documents provided by its officials. The copier on which they had been produced, like most of the copiers in the various offices of the European Commission, was made by Canon.

The most trenchant objection against the Community's antidumping policy, therefore, is that it is costing consumers money but failing to benefit producers. But other complaints, too, have been made about it. European firms, in particular, have argued that the procedure is too slow and cumbersome to offer them effective relief from a sudden surge of dumped goods. In markets for high-tech goods like photocopiers, computers, and consumer electronics, firms often bring out two new product generations every year. Most products yield the bulk of their lifetime profits in the first three months that they are on sale, when their novelty value is highest and when they offer the sharpest improvements upon what is already available. A procedure that takes a year or more to come to a decision — and then imposes duties not on the goods that have already been sold but on goods to be sold in the future — is therefore far from satisfactory.

To make things worse, it is quite possible that a foreign firm should actually be guilty of dumping at the time an investigation begins, but that it should have achieved sufficient improvements in productivity and economies of scale to be selling at far above the product's "normal value" by the time the investigation comes to its conclusion. There are other wrinkles in the system as well. One is that the Commission reserves the right to impose extra punitive duties if an exporter simply absorbs the duties it has imposed by cutting its prices; but under the present arrangements, an exporter can "eat" the duty for four years with impunity, provided he takes care to increase his prices in the fifth year, when the duty is likely to come up for review.

Yet faced with these problems, the first response of the antidumping experts at the Commission has been to use a short cut. To avoid the longer judicial procedures involved in an imposition of duty, they have accepted "price undertakings" — promises from exporting companies not to sell their products inside the Community below a certain agreed price. At first sight, a price undertaking is an easy and convenient way to solve the problem of dumping. The unit can accept an undertaking without having formally to win the agreement of a meeting of ministers of the Community's member states. Importing companies are happy with undertakings, because they raise prices in the market just as effectively as duties do. Exporting companies may not like them, but they dislike them less than they dislike duties because the exporters themselves are allowed to keep the difference between the new high price after an undertaking has been given and the lower price beforehand. In the case of a duty, of course, it is the European Community that pockets the difference at the border when the goods are imported.

But exactly the same evidence explains why, for the European consumer, price undertakings are if anything *less* desirable than duties. Buyers have to pay the same higher price — but they are paying to line the pockets of a Japanese or other foreign firm, not for the greater cause of European competitiveness. And it is in the nature of undertakings that they must be secret: if a competitor finds out that a certain firm is not allowed to sell below a certain price, he can with impunity raise his own almost as high. At least a duty is known and measurable, so the public can find out what has been done in its name, and exactly how much it is paying for the privilege of keeping an uncompetitive European firm in business. The only evidence of undertakings is that the Commission announces when it has accepted one and from whom. It is quite impossible even to attempt to measure whether they have served their purpose.

Perhaps the single most important case of a price undertaking occurred in January 1990, when the unit successfully demanded promises from eleven different Japanese companies not to sell below certain agreed prices their dynamic random-access memory (DRAM) chips. DRAMS are essential components not only in computers but also in cars and in a growing number of consumer products, ranging from electronic diaries and miniature CD players to intelligent washing machines and vacuum cleaners that use fuzzy logic to differentiate automatically between polished wooden floors and shag-pile carpeting. Only three European firms have a solid background in the memory chip business: Philips of the Netherlands, Thomson of France, and Siemens of Germany. It was in order to keep these firms in the chip business that the Commission thought it necessary to intervene.

The decision came in for widespread criticism. In the first place, it was four years too late. The sudden entry of the Japanese into the chip business had begun at the turn of the 1980s after the successful conclusion of government-prompted cooperative research into very large scale integration of electric circuits; and it was all but complete by 1986, when Japanese firms had displaced American chip makers from their dominant hold over the market. In 1986 Washington had persuaded Tokyo to sign a semiconductor agreement that established floor prices for Japanese chips in the American market and, in a secret side-letter whose very existence was to prove controversial in the years ahead, laid out "expected" increases in the Americans' market share in the Japanese chip market.

The U.S.-Japan Semiconductor Agreement has been held up in the United States as a paradigm of how not to carry out trade policy. It was ineffective in preventing the exit from the industry of a number of the proudest names in the history of American chip making, and yet it increased prices for the American computer makers that buy memory chips. The result was that big Japanese makers like Toshiba, Hitachi, Fujitsu, and NEC were able to profit enormously as chip makers when DRAM prices later rose (Toshiba made over $1 billion in profits from its chip business alone during 1989)[7] — and at the same time win a significant competitive advantage in their computer businesses because their American competitors were paying much more than they for a key component. It was no wonder that the floor prices were abolished in 1991 when the pact came up for renewal. In only one sense was the agreement on the right track: it correctly identified the system whereby a computer company "designs in" a particular component into its product as the moment when the buying decision is actually made, and it encouraged Washington to put much greater pressure on Japanese firms to consider buying American chips. Although the U.S. market share of the DRAM market remains far below what American manufacturers consider fair, sales have risen spectacularly all the same.

Europe was starting from a different position from that of the United States, however. Its makers had never been world leaders in their fields; Siemens, the strongest European company in the chip business, was thought to be losing money heavily in 1991 and 1992 in the market for 4-megabit DRAMS. The sharp rise in Japanese penetration of the European market that took place in the first half of the 1980s was nothing more than a smaller example of a wider trend taking place in a global market. So the antidumping unit in Brussels might have been expected to take a more circumspect view than the U.S. Commerce Department. Sadly, it seemed determined to make the same mistake. It is still too early to judge the results, but the decision in 1990 to institute floor prices by formally accepting the undertakings signals a period in which European computer firms will be hobbled in their attempt to compete with American and Japanese makers. One leading

European computer maker, as noted earlier, observed with wry disappointment that the undertakings had not caused him to alter his procurement patterns at all — he had not bought a single extra chip from Siemens, but was forced to pay more to his existing Japanese suppliers.

To make things worse, the underlying reasoning behind the decision to accept the undertakings no longer seems so certain as it was before.

> The Commission took the view [argued the antidumping unit in its annual review of 1990] that a viable Community DRAM industry would contribute to a strong Community electronics industry overall. This was because DRAMS served as a technology driver for other more complex semiconductors which are key components for the data processing, telecommunications and automotive industries.

This is the classic defense of high-technology protectionism. It is a view of semiconductors and their strategic importance in the wider industrial economy that is perpetrated by the Japanese themselves above all, by their habit of referring to memory chips as the "rice of industry." Yet such a sweeping assertion of the importance of the chip industry seems less convincing in the 1990s than it did in the 1980s. With the latest fall in the the "silicon cycle" — the apparently inexplicable roller coaster of chip prices determined partly by demand from the wider economy, and partly by factors inside the business itself such as the number of makers and the amount of money they invest in new plant and equipment — pundits in the semiconductor business are for the first time beginning to wonder whether the development costs are just too high to justify the returns. Many Japanese firms, even those that made fat profits like Toshiba, have found themselves suffering painfully from overcapacity in the latest 4MB chip generation; it is in response to this that they have attempted to spread the risk by entering strategic alliances with other companies to share development of future advanced chips. Some companies (like Sharp) have decided, more radically still, that rather than trying to do everything themselves, they can prosper quite adequately by buying chips from the firms that make them most cheaply.

Developments in 1991 and 1992 in a new kind of semiconductor technology called "flash memory" made a stronger point still. Intel, one of the leading chip makers in the United States, has for some years made heavy profits from its successful series of microprocessors, quite impervious to the increasing Japanese dominance of computer memory. Yet soon after Toshiba, with its specialty in memory technology, found a way of making flash memories that can store data while a computer is switched off in a far more compact space than a traditional rotating disc drive, Intel made an aggressive move into the market and now dominates it. Experience in DRAM manufacture may make a company strong, but it is by no means the be-all and end-all of industrial competitiveness.

The next big technology trade issue facing the Community may well be the question of flat-panel screen technology. This is one of the areas where Japanese businesses have most power in a global market. After years of careful practice making liquid crystal display calculators, Japanese firms began at the end of the 1980s to put serious work into turning liquid crystal into something more spectacular: full-color, flat replacements for the traditional television or computer monitor. Led by Sharp, the firms came up with a new approach called active-matrix thin film transistor (TFT) displays, in which each one of the million or so "pixels," or dots on the screen, is a liquid crystal controlled directly by its own electrical circuit encapsulated between two thin sheets of glass.

The new screens are made using methods learned from advanced semiconductors: they have to be made in ultraclean conditions, with the tiniest dust fragments carefully filtered out of the air and the staff involved dressed up as if going to work in an operating room. Given the fact that a single malfunctioning element can ruin an entire display, they are extremely difficult to manufacture. At the moment, a ten-inch color LCD screen can cost well over one thousand dollars; that is why they are being used so far only in high-value applications whose price tag can justify such a cost, such as top-of-the-line notebook workstations or personal video systems that allow first-class passengers on long-haul airplane flights to choose their own film instead of seeing the same one as everyone else.

The new screens share with the latest generation of memory chips the characteristic that developing them is a billion-dollar business that is unpredictable as well as expensive. No less a firm than IBM felt itself obliged when getting into the market to find itself a partner. In late 1991 a joint-venture company called Display Technologies, half owned by Toshiba and half by IBM, began making flat-panel screens at the Japanese castle town of Himeji.

Just as the Himeji factory was getting into its stride, however, the U.S. government did an extraordinary thing. In response to a complaint from a handful of small, mainly start-up, firms, the government decided to impose a hefty anti-dumping duty on color LCD screens imported from Japan. In an attempt to prevent the duty from immediately feeding through into a sharp increase in the price of the computers that have them, the government decided to impose the duty only when the screens were imported separately, not when they formed part of a fully assembled computer.

Unfortunately, the trade specialists in Washington had failed to consider the effect their action would have on U.S. companies that were buying the screens from Japan. Unable to pay the cost of the duty, and unable to buy the screens in the United States, since none of the firms that had successfully demanded the duty was yet able to manufacture the screens in quantity, they were forced to stop making their most sophisticated portable computers in the United States, and to move their manufacture and assembly entirely abroad — to Taipei, to Singapore, to Seoul, to Tokyo, or to any place where the government did not make such a misguided attempt to protect a fledgling technology industry. Could such a thing happen in Europe, given that Philips is trying to get back into the market for flat-panel displays? Sadly, the history of the Community's antidumping policy raises the risk that it might.

Filippo Maria Pandolfi smiled. At 850 million ECU ($1.06 billion), it was one of the biggest handouts that had ever been proposed to the television and film industry. Yet the paradox was that while European filmmakers had begged for years for subsidies to help them drown out American imports with homegrown culture, this money was not in the end intended for them. The ultimate beneficiary of this proposed gift from the European Commission was supposed instead to be a handful of big electronics firms: Philips of the Netherlands, Siemens of Germany, and Thomson of France.

The background to it was straightforward. The European electronics industry, still smarting from the embarrassment of Japan's rise to power in the market for CD players and Walkman tape decks, had noticed with horror in late 1990 the publication of a handful of articles in Japanese newspapers showing that the big Japanese firms had taken another giant step forward. Sony and Matsushita, later to be followed by other big names, had put on the consumer market the world's first high-definition televisions (HDTV). Like most other electronics products at the beginning of their commercial lives, the new Sony televisions did not seem very practical. With a thirty-eight-inch picture and a large black case containing all the gadgetry necessary to work them, the machines cost over ¥4 million ($33,216) each — and weighed almost exactly a metric ton.

But that was not the point. For more than a decade, high-definition television has been the Holy Grail of the electronics industry, the new "star product" to replace the videotape recorder as something that hundreds of millions of households all over the industrial world can be persuaded to buy. It is a television system with CD-quality sound, with a long, narrow screen whose proportions are much more like those of a cinema picture than of today's televisions, and with much higher picture quality than even the best of today's color models. And although American and European firms had been talking about it and working hard at developing prototypes for it, the Japanese had actually done it. True to their traditional methods, they had taken the courageous step of making a few and putting them on the market to see what consumers thought of them. In doing so, they had been greatly helped by NHK, the Japanese state-owned broadcasting company, which had not only done a great deal of its own research into the technology but had also started up, first at two hours a day and later much more, regular daily high-definition television broadcasts. Not only could Japanese consumers buy an HDTV: they could also use it to watch something.

Early on, the European electronics industry realized that although it might have managed to win some taxpayers' money toward the research and development of the new technology, it had no chance of persuading Brussels to give out large subsidies for the mass production of the new televisions. The European Commission's critics would find such an idea just too tempting a target. Instead, a more subtle approach presented itself: the industry decided to ask the Commission to fight its battle by means of standards. (A standard is a set of agreed broadcast and reception specifications, including such things as the number of lines in a television picture and details of how the information will be encoded.) The Japanese had invented their own HDTV standard, known as High-Vision, and they tried to persuade the European and American authorities to accept it too. In principle, the logic of a single world standard was faultless: it would cut costs for both consumers and producers, and it would speed up the spread of the new technology by making programs exchangeable all over the world. But accepting others' standards raised the risk of allowing them to get in early, to build up production and cut costs, and then to exclude latecomers by controlling the patents necessary to produce machines that work to the standard. It was no wonder that a joke was making the rounds in Europe in 1991 as the lobbying battle took place: "*Q*: How many television standards will there be in the European Community? *A*: Just as many as are necessary to keep the Japanese out."

Luckily, Philips had already developed its own HDTV standard, known as HDMAC. In doing so, it had pursued exactly the same strategy as it followed over the introduction of the digital compact cassette. While its Japanese competitors were keen to make a dramatic technical jump forward with a new digital tape format, and thought that consumers would be willing to throw out all the tapes in their old collections, Philips had been much more conservative. As explained in chapter 6, by making technical compromises, it had come up with a digital tape called DCC that could play old-style tapes too. With HDMAC, however, the compromise had to be different — for high-definition technology was just too different from existing television technology for anyone to come up with a television set that could display both.

Yet Philips's marketing experts doubted that they could just follow the Japanese and put a $33,000 high-definition television on the market right away. A group of pioneering Japanese consumers large enough to set the ball rolling toward falling prices and increasing volume might be willing to pay such a sum for a television set without quite knowing what programs they would be able to watch on it. Europeans, being much more conservative, certainly would not. It was a high-tech version of the chicken-and-egg problem: without programs to watch on it, nobody would buy the new machine. But without machines in the market, there would be no viewers for any new programs that broadcasters might put out in the new standard. No broadcaster would be willing to go to the extra expense of converting editing equipment and cameras to make programs that nobody could watch.

The Dutch company realized that it had to bring about the change to HDTV in two stages. So along with HDMAC, it devised another technology known as D2MAC, with the same 16:9 width-to-height ratio as true high-definition television (the ratio of a traditional model is 4 : 3), but without the improved picture quality. It could thus put D2MAC televisions on the market almost immediately for only twice the price or so of existing models, and it could persuade consumers to buy them to watch television films in wide screen. With some D2MAC machines in the market, television stations would then have a reason to start transferring over to high-definition broadcasting. D2MAC owners would be able to watch the new high-definition programs on a wide screen but without their full picture quality. Some years later on, Philips could then introduce fully fledged HDMAC.

It was an elegant solution to the problem. But even so, it faced an obstacle. At first, there seemed a chance that the European Commission might be willing to force satellite or cable broadcasters or program-makers to work partly in HDMAC. When it became clear that such *dirigisme* was politically unacceptable, the question then arose, would the broadcasters invest in all the new equipment voluntarily? The answer was a resounding no. Satellite channels and filmmakers insisted that they would require large subsidies from Brussels if they were to cooperate in the project of creating a new market for Philips and its friends.

Thus it was that Pandolfi, the member of the European Commission responsible for promoting research and development, found himself trying to persuade his fellow commissioners to offer some 850 million ECU to the broadcasters. It was a thankless task. Signing a memorandum of understanding with the industry proved to take months longer than he had hoped. The sweeteners needed had started at 200 million ECU, then risen to over 1 billion ECU, then fallen back again. And the final hurdle — persuading the rather less sympathetic ministers from the Community's twelve member states to agree to the disbursement of the money — remained to be surmounted.

His proposal certainly had some arguments on its side. The money was not to go directly to Philips or to any other electronics maker, nor, directly, was it to featherbed the broadcasters. Instead, filmmakers and broadcasters would have to come to the Commission with carefully costed ideas for specific programs or entire television services — satellite, cable, or terrestrial — and explain how they would help to promote the new standard. There was a little minor pork-barreling going on: under pressure from the commissioner in charge of culture, who had raised the bogeyman of a "two-speed technological Europe," money from the project was to be diverted toward the promotion of high-definition television in some of the Community's lesser-known languages — a provision that was certain to make sure the taxpayers' money was less successfully spent than it would otherwise have been.

Some of the EC governments wanted to look much more closely at what the money would be spent on. "There are some things we would agree with," said a top British official concerned with the matter, "where we think Community funding would be helpful. For instance, it would obviously be a good idea to help with the conversion of films from the old television format to the new. But when Pandolfi goes on to recommend subsidizing simultaneous broadcasting in two different standards, that's much bigger bucks. That's not what we see as the way ahead." Even inside the Commission itself, people admitted that there was no great enthusiasm for the Pandolfi plan.

The sceptics had good reasons for concern. Underlying the whole argument about HDTV lies an assumption that has only been called into question since the Japanese firms started putting consumer sets on the market. Until 1990 it was taken as given that HDTV is important — perhaps even strategic — because it brings together so many other industrial skills. The American Electronics Association published a list of seventeen different technologies involved in the project, ranging from video and audio compression to fiber optics and microelectronics, from flat-panel displays to charge-coupled devices and new materials. A widespread assumption was that mastery of the new market for HDTV would give the already powerful Japanese electronics industry an irresistible stranglehold over the world market. People had begun to talk of winning the HDTV battle as a national priority.

Yet since the first consumer sets appeared, even Japanese firms are having second thoughts. Several of them are no longer nearly so convinced as they were that HDTV is the key to future success. Startlingly little prominence was given to HDTV sets at the 1991 Tokyo electronics show; meanwhile, the Japanese makers were keen to push EDTV, a steppingstone technology of their own. Combined with the miserable financial results that most of the big Japanese makers turned in for the recession-hit financial year that ended in spring 1992, these hesitations over HDTV have made the whole question much less certain. Just before the European Community was on the point of making its big investment in this technological mascot, studies began to appear in the United States which pointed out that HDTV, even if it becomes a mass-market product, is unlikely to prove the last word. Today's high-definition television, for all the huge amounts of computer memory it requires to process its picture, is an analogue technology like today's televisions. A fully digital television that formed a picture dot by dot rather than line by line, on the other hand, would bring a number of important advantages. Broadcasts could be stored, manipulated, and reproduced digitally; and the move to digital would also finally bring television and computer technology together. The problems of compressing and managing the huge amounts of data required for digital television, however, mean that it is likely to be some years away.

Even setting aside the concerns over digital television, one specialist is skeptical about the case for pouring huge amounts of public money into HDTV projects:

> This study asked two questions: is HDTV a strategic industry in economic terms, and is strategic industry promotion necessary? The first issue remains at best an open-ended question among technology experts, and even if there were a consensus on the strategic importance of HDTV there is little evidence to suggest that strategic industry targeting would be a cost-

effective approach for the nation. The HDTV debate has furthermore demonstrated that the mere possibility of strategic industry promotion distorts incentives by encouraging firms and trade associations to lobby for special treatment on the grounds that they, like previously favored groups such as semiconductors, are critical for the nation. Although consumer HDTV will generate spillovers for the linked industries, its importance as a strategic industry has been overstated and the threat of foreign targeting exaggerated.[8]

Much less controversial in Europe, despite the far greater sums of money involved, are the Community's plans for a dramatic increase in public subsidies for European companies' research and development (R&D).

The underlying statistics are alarming enough. During the 1970s companies from the European Community accounted for about twice as many patents in the United States, the world's biggest single market at the time, as Japanese firms did. Now the position has changed: not only were Japanese companies the four top winners of new U.S. patents in 1991, but also the total number of patents awarded to Japanese companies was more than all the number awarded to firms from all the twelve members of the Community put together, with three times the population and almost twice the size of economy as Japan. Bizarrely, considering the myth that Japanese firms are good only at copying the ideas of others rather than coming up with ideas of their own, Europe's balance of payments in ideas — its trade in payments for intellectual property and patent fees — is more sharply in deficit than Japan's. While the United States, as the world's biggest exporter of technology, receives 2.6 times as much as it spends on such fees, Japan receives 0.8 times what it spends, and Europe only 0.7 times.

Perhaps more worryingly still, Japanese companies have increased their lead over Europe at making high-technology products (goods whose value is far greater than the cost of the raw materials that went into them). In the 1970s Japan exported three times as many high-tech goods as it imported, while the United States exported twice as many, and Europe's trade was in balance. By the end of the 1980s, both the United States and Europe had become net importers, while Japan's exports had risen to five times its imports. Measured in straight numbers of engineers and researchers, the picture is similar. Japan has about 600,000 engineers, almost exactly the same number as the European Community; measured as a percentage of the population, therefore, there are more than twice as many in Japan.

With these figures in mind, it is perhaps not surprising that the ministers who met at Maastricht at the end of 1991 to negotiate a treaty to change the future course of the EC should have given top priority to improving Europe's performance at research and development. Public spending had been rising for some time before Maastricht, but the ministers agreed specifically to seek a common approach to R&D and to give it more generous resources. Accordingly, Jacques Delors's proposals for the Community's five-year spending plans between 1992 and 1997 penciled in a rise in real terms from 2.4 billion ECU ($3 billion) to 4.2 billion ECU ($5.3 billion) during the five years. Even that increase will do little to close the huge gap between the proportion of its total economy that Europe spends on research and development and what Japan spends. According to the Organization for Economic Cooperation and Development (OECD), the United States spent 2.8 percent of its gross national product on research and development in 1991, while Japan spent 3.5 percent, and the Community 2.1 percent. "The Community's current level is similar to that of Japan ten years ago," a recent working paper on the subject from the European Commission observed dryly.[9]

Extra public spending on R&D or on training engineers is like motherhood: who can be against it? Yet it is far from clear that this proposed increase in central spending from Brussels — or the much greater increases that would be necessary if the European public sector were to attempt single-handedly to raise Europe's R&D intensiveness — would be well used. Even the sums that the Community has disbursed so far have drawn criticism for their concentration on "big science" projects, too easily turned into subsidies to big business, which continue for years with all too little reference to the technologies that European companies need to fight in the world market. The reforms proposed for EC science and technology programs in the 1990s look better on paper, and more likely to direct resources to where they are most sorely needed, but it is hard to tell how they will turn out in practice.

Many of the most earnest European protagonists for greater central government spending on research take too seriously the idea of Japan as a place where government-sponsored research, done by carefully marshaled consortiums of companies, is responsible for a large share of the spending. In fact, the opposite is the case: the public sector accounts for only about a fifth of Japan's R&D spending — compared with a half in the United States, where the Department of Defense and other government bodies channel huge amounts of money into military R&D. Much of the research that comes under this heading is not what most observers would imagine. Computer software, for instance, an industry that is one of the United States' most prolific technology exporters, absorbs many millions of government dollars. The overwhelming bulk of Japanese R&D, by contrast, is done by well-known private companies such as Toyota, Matsushita, Hitachi, NEC, Toshiba, Fujitsu, Nissan, Sony, Mitsubishi Electric, and Canon.

As for the engineers and researchers, it would be truly worrying if the universities and technical centers of the Community were proving unable to supply those that industry needs. Yet despite the regular cries from European companies that they have trouble recruiting, there are no signs of the first effect one would expect to see from an imbalance between supply and demand: a rise in the price, or, in other words, the salary, of engineers. On the contrary, European engineers, who are far more mobile than the average European worker, still complain that they can win not only more money but also better working conditions and higher prestige in the United States.[10] There are two more likely reasons for Europe's apparent "shortage" of engineers. One is that the social status of the job is not high enough (a phenomenon observed in almost all EC countries except Germany, where an engineering rather than legal qualification seems almost a sine qua non for joining the board of a big industrial firm). The other is because European companies cannot pay high enough salaries to attract more people into engineering. That is likely to be because the value that European businesses derive from their researchers' work is less than that derived by their competitors in the United States and Japan — which in turn is probably because they are less good at turning ideas into profitable commercial products. Perhaps surprisingly, the force of this argument is recognized in the European Commission's analysis of the problem:

> Whilst European research is not sufficiently reflected in international competitive advantage, this does not mean that it is inferior in quality to that of Japan or the United States. The examples of Ariane and Airbus, telecommunications, chemicals, the Scandinavian robots, all prove this point. However, the problem is Europe's weakness in integrating [R&D] and innovation in an overall strategy . . . It is simply not enough to innovate in order to produce efficiently, even less so in order to respond to the needs and aspirations of consumers. In other words, it is not [R&D] which directs the strategy and organization of a company, but rather the opposite. In this respect, Europe has much to learn from its competitors, primarily Japan.[11]

There is one area, however, in which government help to the private sector leaves a great deal to be desired: where it condemns companies to using a low-quality input into their processes, makes it harder for them to make their businesses more efficient, and increases their costs. This is education. In many European countries, not enough of the young adults who leave schools and colleges have even basic skills, let alone the high degree of literacy and numeracy that is demanded of people by the new flexible production. In organizations where workers themselves have to take the initiative to make things work better, everything depends on the workers themselves. And not even the best efforts of the best European companies to train can overcome a lack of the straightforward tools necessary for living in an industrial society.

A study published in 1992 by the Organization for Economic Cooperation and Development has made a pioneering attempt to establish the link between how well a nation's children can read and write, and how profitable and successful its industrial companies are.[12] One of the most shocking conclusions of the report was that in Canada, the only country where a sufficiently detailed study has been done, a full 38 percent of the population was not "functionally literate." Less than half of those would be people who themselves would admit to having reading difficulties. The rest may well have been able to read and write sufficiently well to satisfy the traditional measures, but they tended to avoid situations that forced them to read.

Japan is not immune to illiteracy. But its strict, regimented education system prides itself on concentrating furiously on the bottom 50 percent of the class, on making sure that the average pupil leaves equipped with all the skills that an electronics assembly line or the body shop of a car company could ask for. Educators are right to turn up their noses at such a drab, businesslike approach to the job of education. School should be more than that, they insist; it should be a preparation for life, it should teach people how to develop their own abilities, it should show them how to enjoy themselves profitably. But there are worrying signs that many European school systems are failing to fulfill even the basic job of turning out factory fodder. Correcting that is a higher priority than any other industrial policy.

EIGHT

The Reluctant Missionaries

A PAIR OF BUSINESSMEN, one Japanese and one American, once found themselves in Malaysia competing for the same valuable supply contract. After each had made his presentation to the authorities, displaying his product and explaining its virtues, the two decided to go for a walk in the country together. Some miles away from town, far from the nearest hut, they heard a growl from behind the trees. From the gloom, the eyes of a man-eating tiger glowed angrily at them. Both men froze. Then, at first slowly but increasingly quickly, the Japanese began to run away. The American looked after him in disbelief, but then started to follow.

"Are you a fool?" he gasped after the Japanese. "Do you think you can outrun a hungry tiger?"

"No," came the response. "I just have to outrun *you*."

This story has an economic as well as a social moral. Whatever the merits of a company's product, however advanced its technology, what matters is how it measures up to its competitors. In ten years' time, Europe's business landscape will be determined by the relative strengths today of European, American, and Japanese companies. Which are the fast-est runners?

Japan starts with the most obvious advantages. Japanese firms have shown in the past two decades that they are more able to respond quickly to outside shocks, such as sharp increases in energy prices or unexpected falls in demand overseas, than are firms from any other country. In the pure business of man-agement, Japanese business leaders seem to be more prag-matic and more able to think flexibly than their competitors. Their country also has an admirable thirst for the new. Just as Japanese consumers are swept by crazes for new foreign words and new products every few months, so also do Japanese com-panies scour the world to find products or processes that are better than their own, which they then set out to imitate and improve.

But there is another strand to Japanese strength that is too often neglected: the pure intellectual force of its companies' inventors, which can be seen in the fact that the four organi-zations that received the most patents in the United States during the last three years of the 1980s were all Japanese. As Japanese companies gear up to do more pure research, they are likely to start producing the dramatic breakthroughs that were the traditional preserve of Europeans before the Second World War and of Americans since.

Japanese companies also have a head start on the rest of the world in their manufacturing methods. Just as Britain was first with industrialization itself, and the United States first with mass production, it was in Japan that the new flexible production was born. In many different industries, not just in electronics, computers, and car making, Japanese firms are masterly at turning out products of superlative quality, brought to market quickly and cheaply and with numerous different models. The best example of this is perhaps Sony's Walkman, which is in effect a single technology now available in more than two dozen different products.

And underlying these things, Japanese companies have managed to harness the talents of their workers to a degree not yet achieved elsewhere. Part of this is the result of the group ethic that remains stronger in Japan than in the West, but partly too it is the consequence of sensitive management that pays attention to the wishes and to the ideas of everyone in the firm. When white-collar workers are confident that their loyalty to their employer will be rewarded in kind, they are more willing to put in extra hours or extra effort.

But Japan is by no means invincible, as we have seen. Its work ethic pays too much homage to brawn and not enough to brain. Many Japanese employees are startlingly less efficient than their counterparts in the United States. Not wishing to upset the corporate apple cart, they hold back from questioning why things must always be done a certain way. It is not just a strength but also a weakness to persist at a project long after it seems doomed to fail. This lemming mentality, the legacy of a strictly regimented education system, is sometimes so strong that citizens of other countries cannot find a comfortable home inside a Japanese firm.

Japanese companies, with their relentless pursuit of sales and market share above profits, suffer from the same malaise. They need to take to heart the old adman's slogan: It is good to be big, better to be good, but best to be both. The craving for scale for its own sake has led many Japanese firms into businesses, such as semiconductor memory manufacture, that now seem much less alluring and profitable than at first. Likewise, it has also left them alarmingly dependent on a surprisingly small number of products. In 1989, for instance, some 30 percent of the sales and 60 percent of the profits of the Matsushita group companies came from videotape recorders. When such star products wane, Japanese firms have a problem.

What about the United States? It too displays an enormous openness to new ideas, manifested in a tolerance and wide-eyed curiosity that is entirely missing from Japan. And although the leading Japanese electronics and car making firms still have the edge in terms of agility, it is important to remember that there are historical reasons for this. Today's American giants, such as IBM and General Motors, had their golden years of growth a generation ago. It is therefore perhaps little wonder that they are showing management problems that are a sign of old age. Their Japanese competitors, by contrast, have the advantage of being at a far earlier stage in their life cycles.

The Big Three car makers are already fighting back hard, trying to remake themselves in response to the challenge from Japan. But there are signs of a new flexibility elsewhere too. The Compaq computer company, for instance, brought out a new range of notebook computers in the middle of 1992 that were dramatically cheaper and offered significantly better performance than the machines the company had been selling only a few months before. How? The company had sent two engineers to a components trade fair, and they had knocked together a cut-price working prototype in only three days to prove to their colleagues that the firm could turn out good computers at sharply lower costs than before.

On top of these strengths, American firms retain the intellectual high ground. It is in the United States, more than in Japan and in Europe, that most of today's most important discoveries are being made. Although this advantage is increasingly coming under threat from the other side of the Pacific, the stream of good ideas that is coming out of American universities and corporate research laboratories is a key raw material for U.S. firms in competition for tomorrow's markets. Motorola's success in making tiny cellular telephones is not just the result of its marketing skills and its ability to make products of good quality the first time around; it is also because of the firm's proven scientific edge in developing the computer chips and the programs on which the telephones depend.

The final high card in the American hand is service industries. It has become fashionable to decry the replacement of manufacturing by services, and to talk disparagingly of an economy in which people make their money by flipping hamburgers rather than by making things. But the truth is that there are services and services: the mirror image of the low-wage, low-skilled services like the fast-food business or domestic cleaning is that of the service industries that provide software for high-technology goods. More and more of the value inside computers, cars, VCRs, and telephones is coming from the weightless, invisible, intangible software — and that is an industry in which the American lead over the rest of the world is greater than in almost any other.

But the problems of the United States are daunting indeed. There is the creaking high school system, which threatens to leave the country with a vast underclass of unlettered people, whose work can never be worth more than a few dollars an hour and who are likely to be thrown out of their jobs by equally skilled competitors from Mexico or Malaysia. There is the inability of Washington to deal with a vast and still growing budget deficit, which threatens to produce at some time a collapse of confidence in the creditworthiness of the federal government which would drive interest rates and therefore taxes skyward and would bring down a slump that would make the early 1990s recession seem mild by comparison. And there are the shenanigans of the capital market in the late 1980s, which left too many companies leveraged with debt up to the eyeballs, barely able to continue servicing the loans they had taken on to prevent themselves from being acquired by Wall Street predators. Thankfully, a growing number of defaults on junk bonds in the early 1990s should make investors more wary of lending money to takeover artists, which in turn will reduce the risk that good firms will be broken up in order to pay back the excessive prices that were bid for them. But the bad effects of the junk boom of the 1980s will take a decade or more to wear off — a period of time during which American business will be unnecessarily hobbled in competition with European and Japanese firms.

Turning to Europe, one is reminded of Dr. Johnson's sexist

view of women preaching: surprising not that they do it well, but that they do it at all. Given the difficulties that European firms have labored under, their present position in world markets is better than might have been expected. Take Siemens, for instance, continuing to participate in the race to make high-capacity computer memory chips when all but a handful of American, Japanese, and Korean giants have dropped out. Or Renault, producing cars of undoubted style and innovation with a discontented work force and outdated machinery. Or Olivetti, hanging on by the skin of its teeth as an independent computer maker in a market increasingly dominated by international conglomerates spreading their sales over three continents.

Europe's strengths lie partly in its past — its role as the cradle of most of the technical innovation of the twentieth century, and the marketing and manufacturing prowess that gave it dominance years ago in markets that it still occupies today — but partly also in its future. One of the results of the European Community's single market program is that cozy cartel arrangements all over the continent are being broken up. Consumers are beginning to benefit from lower prices; companies, too, will benefit in the long run, as the more efficient European makers take market share away from the less efficient. But the dismantling of European government monopolies is likely to be even more important. At the moment, businesses in countries like Belgium and Italy have to pay very high prices for basic services, such as road distribution, telecommunications, and mail service, that American and Japanese firms can take for granted will be prompt and cheap. As many of these prices fall, European companies will discover a small but significant fillip to their competitiveness.

There are problems ahead, however. If it is to have a single currency by the end of the century, Europe faces a sharp recession as its free-spending economies have to cut back on subsidies and handouts. Although many of the savings will come from cuts in state-owned industries that ought to have been subsidized long ago, the dislocation and resulting unemployment will not be any less painful for that.

And there remains the problem of Europe's social welfare traditions. While achieving less social cohesion and a weaker sense of community than can be seen in Japan, the European economies have succeeded in spending huge amounts of money on benefits to the unemployed and to the sick, and on direct government spending for schools, hospitals, and many other things. The result is that while wages in Germany are comparable to those in Japan, when nonwage costs are included it costs almost twice as much to employ a German worker as a Japanese. That high price must either be justified by higher productivity, or in an open trading system German products face a certain loss of market share to their Japanese counterparts.

Above all, however, European business has developed a dependency culture, looking to government for solutions that ought to be found inside itself. Such dependency is already well known and documented in Japan, with its methods of "administrative guidance" and more direct government fiat. But it is alive and well in Europe, and it is one of the obstacles to the salvation of many ailing European industries.

What if Europe, faced with the challenge from Japan, were to do nothing at all? To put it another way, the Community could avoid the restructuring that has been forced on the United States' car and electronics industries by a simple device: protection. It could raise higher tariffs against Japanese imports. It could place quantitative limits on production by Japanese factories in Europe. And it could affirm that these measures — contrary though they might be to international trading rules — would be permanent rather than temporary. Far from aiming to give European industry time to catch up, they would be designed to keep the more efficient Japanese industrial organizations out for good.

At first sight, such a strategy appears to have advantages. It would safeguard jobs at car factories in France and Italy, in television plants in the Netherlands, in computer companies in Germany. And it would provide the psychological reassurance that however inefficient or unsuccessful they were, European businesses would be both run and owned by Europeans. But it would bring powerful disadvantages with it too. First, it would make European consumers poorer: the products imported from Japan or made in Japanese-owned local factories to which Europeans would be forbidden access by such a strategy would, by definition, be cheaper or better (or both) than those already available on the market. (If they were not more competitive, there would be no need to keep them out.) To a degree, this is already true: cars, computers, CD players, and fax machines already cost significantly more in Europe than in either the United States or Japan. But the trend would continue, and the gaps would widen.

There would be a second penalty too. One of the most important strengths of Japanese companies — both in their operations at home and in their factories abroad — is that they have managed to find ways to improve productivity year after year, faster than their competitors. Car companies look for ways to use the same number of hours of work to make more cars, and pressure their suppliers to produce the same components for a price that falls, rather than rises, over the life of a model. Audio and video products get smaller and more full of gadgets every year. Computer screens get brighter; batteries last longer. One of the results of this process is that growing productivity translates into higher wages. It also translates into shorter hours: although Japanese workers still put in more work every year than either their American or their European counterparts, their working hours are falling fast. If Europe closes its doors to the pressure that makes companies use their workers more efficiently, then it will be forced to forgo those benefits. Under such a policy, it would become increasingly hard to cut hours and raise wages.

There would also be a third effect, which is perhaps the most chilling. Japanese firms are already offering stiff competition to European and American goods in markets all over the world. In the fast-growing markets of Southeast Asia, they dominate overwhelmingly. Even if autarky were to work at home, European firms would see their Japanese competitors pull farther ahead in the markets of the rest of the world. And as their sales there increased, increasing economies of scale would help Japanese costs to fall again. The gap would widen, and European workers would notice it because export sales would become tougher.

Cutting itself off from the broader changes in the world market would turn Europe into a twenty-first-century version of the Brazil of the 1970s: determined to develop on its own, suspicious of outside methods, insistent that inward investors should come in only on its own terms. The results might appease nationalist feelings. In the end, however, they would lead to certain decline.

Interestingly, many Japanese believe that Europe is already in decline, and refuse to take the single market project as a sign that the future will be any different. This is partly a symptom of Japan's preoccupation with the United States since the war — a preoccupation that can be seen in the main entrance of the Keidanren, the country's leading employers' organization, where a prominent digital display bearing the words EXCHANGE RATE shows the number of yen needed to buy a dollar at that minute on the foreign exchanges.[1] But it is also partly the result of a Japanese view that Europeans take too many holidays, do too little work, spend too much money on health care, pay too little attention to quality, and believe their superiority to Americans and Asians alike is proved by the crumbling beauty of European urban architecture and the continued popularity all over the world of German opera, Italian clothes, and French food. At least the United States can set against its rising crime and collapsing institutions a genuine openness to new ideas, a technical excellence, and a social mobility that are missing from Europe.

Such prejudices are likely to be proved wrong. For although the differences between Japanese companies and their European competitors described in the earlier chapters of this book may seem too vast to be closed in a short time, the same appeared true twenty years ago when Europe was faced with the apparent threat of colonization by more efficient American businesses. Techniques that then seemed alien and incomprehensible — secret weapons, almost, that American firms knew how to use — are now universal. Who today would place the same wide-eyed belief in market research and basic accounting as Europeans did when they saw Americans using it in their market for the first time? "According to an American executive in Frankfurt," Servan-Schreiber recorded in 1967,

> "If a German manager wants to increase his production, he studies all the factors that go into the manufacture of his product. But if I want to increase my production, I add to these same calculations our research and market predictions so that I will know not only *how* to produce, but how to produce the desired quantity at the lowest cost. What interests me is my profit margin. What interests my European competitor is a factory that produces. *It isn't the same thing.*"[2]

The question that lies ahead for European business is a crucial one. If it is to accept the challenge of competition from Japanese manufacturing methods, what is the best way to assimilate them with the least industrial dislocation? In short, European business may know where to go. But how does it get there from here?

One answer, of course, is that it may not. Faced with a challenge from more efficient firms across the Atlantic, European businesses only caught up halfway. That is why the biggest computer company, and the second- and third-biggest car makers, in Europe are American. In twenty years' time, if European companies find themselves unable to reform in the face of the still greater challenge from Japan, the combination of exports and direct investment by Japanese companies may well be enough to satisfy a large slice of the demand in Europe for cars, electronics goods, and microcomputers. In short, Japanese manufacturing methods may be diffused into Europe, but only by replacing existing businesses.

That may be less of a bad thing than it seems: even without any prodding from European governments, the Japanese would still need to employ hundreds of thousands of Europeans. Quite apart from those who would work in Japanese-owned factories, there would also be sales and distribution people, managerial staff, technicians to repair products that go wrong (though there are likely to be increasingly few of those, as quality continues to rise), researchers to develop new products, and so on.

Consider, for instance, the state of the British car industry. Before the Second World War, Britain had more than six independent car makers, many of them leading the world in technology and engineering quality. By 1992 the two leading names in Britain were Ford and General Motors. Jaguar had been sold to Ford — in a transaction that turned out to have been highly favorable to Jaguar's former shareholders, as the collapse of the British firm's sales in the United States drove it into loss. Bristol and Morgan remained tiny niche players. The Panther Car Company, started up by a British engineer and specializing in quirky ideas such as a six-wheeled two-seater with a top speed of over 200 miles an hour, was in the hands of a Korean businessman whose family dominates the world market for fur coats. Rolls-Royce Motors, which sold 1,723 cars in 1991, had become a maker of mere luxury goods; its sales fell by half in a single year, and it was reduced to a three-day production week. The only remaining British mass-market car maker was the Rover Group, by then a subsidiary of British Aerospace, which owed its continued British ownership only to the political storm that had blown up when Ford tried to buy it. Rover's future appeared to lie in a fragile dependence on Honda for new designs, at a time when Honda itself was on the point of opening up its own factory in Britain.

All the same, the total number of cars being made in Britain was rising. It dipped below 1 million in the 1981 recession, its lowest figure since the Second World War, but then began to recover, thanks first to the revival of Vauxhall Motors under General Motors management, and then later to the arrival of Nissan. By 1992 Nissan was planning to increase its Sunderland output to 250,000 cars a year (more than Rover); and Toyota and Honda were both preparing to start production at their own British factories. The two firms' planned capacity was to be 300,000 by 1995. As a result, analysts were predicting that the car business could return to trade surplus, and the total number of cars made in Britain could rise above 2 million for the first time since the 1950s.[3] And with Nissan already operating a technical center and Toyota preparing to manufacture engines in Britain, it was clear that both research and development capacity and the parts of the production process that add the greatest value were beginning to flow back into the country. In this respect, the British car industry was in a situation similar to that of American consumer electronics: although only one domestically owned firm (Zenith) was left, plenty of television sets and audio equipment continued to be made in the United States by foreign companies. Both industries are in fine shape; they are just in different hands.

Europeans would be forgiven for being less than entirely satisfied with such a state of affairs. Japanese direct investment in Europe and the United States has progressed furthest in the car industry, where the final stage of putting all the components together has remained obdurately labor intensive, resisting efforts to automate all but a few parts of the process.[4] In industries where labor is a less important part of total cost — electronics, semiconductors, computer design — skilled jobs will be much slower to move out of Japan, so the balance will be tilted for some time away from local manufacture and toward direct exports. There is also less pulling Japanese firms toward manufacture in Europe in those industries — for while the car industry is still sharply differentiated between markets (the idea of a "global car," a single model that would sell equally well all over the world, has proved a chimera), the computer industry and the electronics industry are not. Notebook PCs are gray in Japan and white in the United States, but identical inside;[5] portable stereos are identical all over the world. As a result, the aim of being "closer to the customer" is rather less urgent. Furthermore, Japanese firms tend to keep control of the newest (and therefore most difficult to produce) products at home, releasing them for overseas manufacture only when their technology has matured and profit margins on them have fallen. (For instance, Sony makes camcorders and digital audiotape machines in Japan; jumbo rolls of audiotape, however, are manufactured in Europe.)[6] These three factors combined will reduce the number of jobs that it is economic to do in Europe, the level of skill they require, and consequently the wages they command.

Luckily, it is unlikely to come to that, for the arrival of Japanese firms in Europe has already begun to prompt sweeping changes in the way local companies do business. At Renault, the Institut de la Qualité is a clear sign that the company has woken up to the gap between its methods and best practice in Japan. It will be some years — perhaps even two full model cycles — before the results can be seen, but the outlook is promising. At Philips, the new digital compact cassette project shows that the firm has left behind the belief that technology alone will win it customers; the company is now thinking not just about how to establish it as a new standard, but more importantly how to make money from the standard if it succeeds. There are fewer promising signs in the European computer industry, which was lagging far behind its American competition even before the Japanese entered the market for portable machines, but the beginnings of a turnaround are evident at Olivetti: the firm claims that it now knows which products make money and which lose money, and it is also beginning to think more clearly about how it can find a place for itself in a computer industry where it no longer remains a competitive manufacturer of machinery.

Yet there is a worry. It is easier for European business to learn from abroad when it has a nearby example to emulate, when a competitor next door proves that its advantage comes not from lower labor costs or a different language, but simply from a better management of the production process. But competition is still a slow way of transferring know-how. Process technology — a term that can be applied to everything from the smooth running of a factory assembly line to the more general processes of developing and bringing to market new products — is by its very nature harder to copy from outside than a new piece of machinery. Its strengths are harder to measure, and its secrets easier to conceal. It is no coincidence that although Toyota has been forthright in patenting the detailed improvements it has come up with in car design, the firm has found it neither necessary nor possible to patent its entire production system. If it took a team of researchers from MIT five years and many millions of dollars to understand its subtleties, what hope is there for a single European business in electronics or computing, for example, to learn in detail how Sony develops new camcorders or why Toshiba notebook computers are leading the world?

At first sight, Japanese companies that invest in Europe and the United States behave in a very puzzling way. Setting up a brand-new factory in a faraway country with a different language is a project to tax the managerial skills of even the best company. Why, then, should Japanese firms choose to start from scratch on "greenfield sites," and often in areas far from the traditional centers of the industry in question? Acquisitions do occur, of course, and are sometimes successful. In 1974, for instance, Matsushita took over Motorola's moribund television factories in the United States, paying $50 million for a business that was losing $19 million a year; after two years of drastic change, productivity at one of them was up by 30 percent and defects had fallen to a fraction of what they were before.[7] But in manufacturing industry, acquisitions are the exception rather than the rule.

This is because the advantages of buying an existing business — a work force, equipment, communications, and infrastructure and management already in place — have to be weighed against the problem that it may be hard to bring about change there. The fact that many of the biggest transplants have not merely built up from scratch but have also deliberately chosen sites far away from other companies in the same business is chilling: it shows that Japanese firms consider the problems of the existing industry so deeply ingrained that they outweigh all the advantages of joining it. There could be no more powerful reminder of how much European firms will have to unlearn when they try to reform themselves from within.

Only one significant attempt has been made by any Western company to replicate the greenfield-site advantage of the Japanese: it is in the car industry, at General Motors' Saturn project in Tennessee. There, the resemblances with Japanese practices are uncanny:

> The philosophy that people are capable of achieving extraordinary results when they are directly involved in decisions that affect them is the foundation of Saturn's approach to teamwork. In the manufacturing and assembly complex men and women are organized into self-directed work teams consisting of six to 15 members. They are responsible — both personally and as a team — for maintaining quality through their work process.
>
> At Saturn, quality isn't a habit, but a way of life and a team responsibility.[8]

This most sincere form of flattery is echoed at the nearest airport, where arriving passengers are greeted on one side by a Nissan car made at the Japanese firm's Smyrna plant, and on the other by a Saturn from Spring Hill. Behind the public relations hoopla, however, is a deadly serious issue: the new GM plant stands only by the grace of the United Auto Workers union. Not only was GM forced to make a number of important concessions in the management of the factory (such as a slow line speed and an unprecedented degree of union involvement in decision making); it also had to concede that the success of the Saturn project would not be a signal for the company to fire workers at its less efficient plants in Michigan and replace their output with cars built by young Tennessee enthusiasts. Its Opel subsidiary had a freer hand in introducing Japanese-style practices as it was preparing the new Eisenach plant in what used to be East Germany for production in 1992; but nobody pretends that existing capacity can somehow be willed out of existence. Like the Americans before them, European companies will have to work with what they have themselves created.

An obvious obstacle is the age of their factory equipment. For four years at the end of the 1980s, Japanese firms invested staggering sums on new plant and equipment — so much so that total industrial investment in Japan actually exceeded that of the United States, an economy twice the size. The gap between Japan and Europe was even greater. In 1991, for instance, Ford of Europe found itself faced with a short-term boom in demand for its products in Germany but with a matching slump in Britain. Yet one of its two main factories in Britain had been set up so that it could only produce cars with the driving wheel on the right-hand side — an equipment problem that cost the company dearly, and was one of the factors that contributed to the unprecedented loss that Ford's British subsidiary showed that year. This is evidence of a wider problem in the automotive industry: because Japanese companies recognized much earlier the benefits of making their factories able to switch flexibly between production of one model and another, Europeans are handicapped from the start when they try to catch up by the rigidity of their own factories.

The same is true of their human beings too. When Japanese companies have come to Europe and the United States, they have had the advantage of being able to set up from scratch. Often recruiting in areas of high unemployment, they have been able to staff their plants with highly skilled and highly motivated workers at relatively low salaries. When Nissan first opened its car plant in the north of England, sixteen thousand people applied for the first four hundred jobs. Today, many of its workers are in their mid-twenties; at Renault's vast plant at Flins, the average age is forty-five. As the European car industry runs to catch up, it will have to drag behind it the weight of higher pension and health costs for its older workers.

There is also the job of winning back the hearts of consumers. It has already been observed that the Japanese had to labor for years in order to do away with the reputation of their products as cheap and of low quality. (Proof of how much it rankled can be noted in a story told by Makoto Kikuchi, head of Sony's research laboratories and formerly a distinguished technologist in government service, and recorded in his memoirs. On a business trip to the United States in the 1960s, he was brought a drink with a paper umbrella in it. "Here," said the waiter, pointing to the umbrella, "is something from your country." The remark was obviously kindly meant; the Japanese scientist, however, took deep offense at it.) In the United States, the Japanese have progressed so far that cars made in joint-venture factories in the United States sell better when they bear the name of the Japanese partner than when they bear the U.S. car maker's name. And in Europe, one enterprising electronics chain dreamed up the idea of putting a Japanese-sounding name on its products.[9] But in general, European companies have been less slapdash, and European consumers have not yet had enough experience of Japanese goods at free-market prices to lose their faith in European goods; in Europe, therefore, the job is likely to be less difficult.

It was a sign that the British are far less phlegmatic than foreigners often take them for. At the September 1991 Trade Union Congress, the annual conference of Britain's labor unions, a group of left-wing labor leaders pushed through a resolution that deplored the spread of "alien" and "feudal" labor practices from Japan. Although the congress is notorious as a talking-shop where activists from up and down the country come to vent their frustrations, the passing of the resolution by an overwhelming majority alarmed the right wing of the movement sufficiently for them to disavow it outright, and for one prominent trade unionist to dismiss the resolution as "racist."

Racist it may have been; it was also probably right. For although they are keen to hear their employees' views on how the manufacturing or design process can be improved, on how quality can be raised and costs cut, Japanese firms are unequivocal in insisting that it must be management, rather than the work force or the labor union, that decides basic things such as the way work will be organized at the plant, the hours it will open, and the suppliers it will deal with. To that degree, Japanese business certainly fits the description of feudal.[10] British unions, by contrast, particularly in manufacturing industry, have been used to acting as surrogate managers. As for the allegation of being "alien," the idea that a factory general manager would wear the same uniform as the office cleaner, or that both of them would eat in the same dining room, was unheard of in Britain before the first Japanese investment wave of the early 1970s.

Paradoxically, the extreme left may well be right in believing that the spread of Japanese methods threatens the British labor movement with extinction. For British unions have traditionally had two functions: to fight for workers' rights against the wishes of their employers; and, equally importantly, to fight for their rights against those of other workers in the same organization. (That is why they are known as "trade" unions in Britain; many of the most damaging disputes in British industry in the 1970s were the consequence of "demarcation" disputes, or arguments between the members of different trades about who should do what.) In demanding that their workers behave as part of a single team, not as competing groups of different specialists, the Japanese-style factory renders the second function entirely redundant.

As for the first function, the idea that workers need to fight with their employers for their rights is the legacy of generations in which unscrupulous factory owners tried ruthlessly to exploit their employees. Essentially, it consists of an attempt to have the division of the profits of the business slanted more favorably toward employees, and less toward managers, shareholders, and banks. Arguably, the history of organized labor in Europe since the 1970s shows that unions have failed in this attempt: by concentrating on how to slice the cake, they have neglected the more important question of how big the cake is to begin with. While organized labor in the West has resisted attempts to improve productivity by making factories more flexible and by increasing automation, Japanese workers have allowed their employers almost complete freedom to change methods of work. The results speak for themselves: higher wage rises in Japan.

This is partly because Japanese workers are organized into company unions, while in most other industrial countries, unions contain workers of the same skill or of the same industry. There is no question that Japanese unions are mere poodles by comparison with their Western counterparts. (In 1990 a Japanese railway union called a strike in support of a wage claim, but decided that the strike should last about forty-five minutes and start just after 5:00 A.M., so as to inconvenience the smallest possible number of passengers.) They have puzzlingly neglected some aspects of working conditions that many foreigners would find insupportable — such as a common practice in Japanese industry either to make workers change backward and forward between a night shift and a day shift every week, or to work absurdly long shifts, such as twenty or more hours in succession.[11] But in a capitalist system in which firms grow by producing goods at higher quality or lower cost than their competitors, the primary source of higher wages for workers will be higher profits in their firms — so it is understandable that workers should have more interests in common with people who do a different job in the same company than with people who do the same job in a different company.[12]

In the United States, many Japanese firms have been hostile to organized labor; they have seen, quite correctly, that unions are often an obstacle to any change that increases productivity. In Britain, they have generally been more circumspect: hence the decision at Nissan to admit the Amalgamated Engineering Union into its plant, and the "beauty contests" that Toyota was holding in early 1992 to decide which union would win the right to represent workers at its new plant in England. But even when a union is admitted to the factory, its job is unquestionably far more limited. (Even in the central job of bargaining for pay, it can sometimes be outmaneuvered. In one of its early years, Nissan awarded its factory employees a *higher* pay rise than the one their union representatives had asked for.) Pay bargaining apart, unions are increasingly likely to find themselves turning into minor sections of the personnel department. For in a well-managed company, the firm's own internal communications system ought to solve grievances long before they grow serious enough for workers to want to resort to an outside agency. A union may happily collect dues from its members, therefore; the services that it can hope to provide in return — and thus its long-term future — remain in doubt.

The speed with which Japanese firms in Europe and the United States have managed to meet (and sometimes surpass)[13] the productivity of their factories at home shows that far from being obstructive, European and American workers themselves are actually quick to respond to the challenges of more flexible manufacturing. Only partly can obstruction from unions be blamed for the problem. It is in fact management that is the single biggest obstacle to catching up. As one European component manufacturer admitted sadly, "For too long, we in the West have divided the production process into simple, repeatable tasks, and invited people to bring their bodies to work but not their heads. Japanese manufacturing industry has not made that mistake."[14]

The difficulty is that the larger the firm, the more scope there is for bureaucracy and rigidity. General Motors, the gi-

ant that towers above them all, is perhaps the worst case. Its
faults have already been dealt with in detail. But in general,
the difficulty is not that the firm's top management fails to
understand its own problems; rather, it is that the organization has just grown too large to be able easily to implement
solutions to them. In a speech in October 1991, John F. Smith,
the corporation's vice chairman, gave a lucid analysis of the
issues that faced him and his colleagues. After explaining in
detail the reasons why GM had fallen behind its Japanese competitors, he concluded:

> Lean production involves fundamental change for everyone, in
> ways of thinking and working, and in the roles and relation-
> ships. That's why it's so tough to get it going. Change is never
> easy. We have to overcome a long history of adverse relations,
> authoritarian practices, poor communication, and conflicting
> values and motivations . . . We've still got a ways to go, and
> it's going to take a lot more energy, talent, money and
> perseverance.[15]

That was an understatement, to put it politely. Smith was
speaking only four months before the firm turned in its 1991
loss of over $4.5 billion, and announced the details of its sec-
ond major restructuring in a decade.

For years, outsiders had been convinced that GM's very size
made it impregnable. Its market power, they believed, was so
broad that it was able to dictate prices and the pace of innovation in the car industry. So strong was this belief that many
felt the firm should be broken up, a fate that had already be-
fallen Standard Oil and was soon to come to AT&T. Yet the
truth turns out to have been the opposite: after a certain
point, size becomes an obstacle to change, rather than a way
of keeping competitors at bay. The fate of General Motors is
a dire warning not merely to Europe's car makers, therefore,
but also to its big electronics and computer firms.

The biggest and most important management study ever
of the European car components industry was carried out

between 1989 and 1992. Not a single university professor was involved, however. The research team consisted of 140 people, some British, some Japanese, from the Toyota Motor Corporation. Toyota's researchers collected data on 2,000 companies from fourteen European countries. Over a period of eight months, specialist teams of five or six people — usually containing an engineer, a quality controller, a purchasing specialist, and a production expert — visited 400 different factories. They even went so far as to ask the top 230 firms to come up with specifications and quotations for prototype parts.

Despite the monumental effort that went into it, the study will never be published. For it had a more straightforward commercial purpose: Toyota was trying to choose some 150 suppliers from which to buy parts for its new factory in Britain. Since the company's parts purchases are likely to reach about $1.2 billion a year when production at the factory reaches the planned total of 200,000 cars a year, the firm could claim with some justice that it had a right to be a choosy customer. For rather than importing most of its parts from Japan, the firm planned to buy in Europe 60 percent of the parts needed at the factory's planned opening in late 1992, and 80 percent by the time it was up to full capacity. Some, of course, would come from factories built in Europe by its traditional Japanese components suppliers: Nippondenso, for instance, was to build air conditioning and heating systems at a nearby greenfield site in Telford.

Toyota's painstaking survey, before formal parts procurement had even begun, showed something dramatic. Its aim was not merely to find the firms that could deliver a given part at the lowest price. Rather, Toyota was looking for firms that could do much of the necessary design work — something that is standard in Japan but remains much less common in Europe — and, more important still, could undertake to make small improvements in its operations every year. It was looking, in short, for firms that might not have been world-class suppliers in 1989 but have the potential to become world-class suppliers in 2009.

Toyota was by no means the first Japanese company to be doing this. Sony and Matsushita had been doing the same thing in the electronics business for more than fifteen years; the former now has special technical centers at Basingstoke and Stuttgart that are helping to encourage local procurement. In the car industry, Toyota's competitor Nissan actually led the way by establishing a supply development team — something unknown in the European components industry when it was first introduced. Ian Gibson, who runs Nissan's plant in Britain, explains:

> We took a number of . . . senior people; we trained them here in the UK; we trained them in Japan. We also shipped them to the US so that they could look at what happens there. They work with a supplier at a time, spend some weeks with him in order to teach him techniques and technologies and means of improvements, so that they do improve. That has been extremely successful. When we first asked our suppliers if they wanted to become involved, we had 12 volunteers; now we have a five-year backlog [of suppliers waiting for a visit from the team]. They can see what can be done once they have those skills and experience.[16]

It is hard to overestimate how profoundly significant this is. Not only is Nissan acting in effect as a miniature consultancy that offers management advice to its suppliers free of charge. More important, it is acting as a powerful force for change in the European components industry. It is encouraging firms that have made things the same way for years to take another look at their production processes and to ask how they can be improved. By the process of *kaizen*, or "continuous improvement," the company is forcing its suppliers to raise productivity, reduce the number of defective parts they turn out, and invest more in design and new product development.

This "service" only appears to be free of charge, of course. The car maker's aim, as in its relations with suppliers in Japan, is to save money on its components; it will therefore expect to receive the vast majority of the money it saves its suppliers back by means of lower component prices. But the process set in motion has two powerful side effects: it puts the suppliers' management in a frame of mind where they can look for improvements themselves and see the results in their own profit margins; and it allows them to take advantage of the efficiencies they pick up from their Japanese customers to cut costs when they do business with other less demanding firms. The full effects of this phenomenon will continue to develop for years, if not for decades. At present, the gap remains wide. Toyota has complained in public, for instance, that its components bill is likely to be more than 50 percent higher than it expected because of the inability of its new European suppliers to meet the price and quality specifications of their Japanese counterparts.[17] But over the long term, the process will transform component industries all over Europe that do business with Japanese assembly companies. Even firms that do not do business with Japanese makers will be affected: when they tender for supply contracts with American or European firms, they will be under competitive pressure to match the bids of leaner, more efficient European component companies that have done.

Since a more efficient components industry will in the end benefit all the firms that are its customers, this learning process is likely gradually to begin to close the gap in the car industry between the Japanese makers and their European counterparts. The American makers in Europe, with the benefit of earlier experience of Japanese competition in their home markets, have already begun to imitate Japanese methods. In 1981 Ford of Europe had three thousand suppliers; by 1991 the number was half that, and they are rated more broadly than simply on quantity and price. General Motors abandoned its old-style procurement policies in Europe in 1987 and replaced them with a new system that favors suppliers who are good at developing their own ideas and able to deliver defect-free parts on time.

The components makers will not have long to catch up. In the United States, where the Henry Ford tradition had led car makers to try to make as much as possible themselves, the components industry was weaker to begin with. Unable to buy high-quality components at the right prices from local suppliers, the Japanese assemblers were forced to bring their long-term suppliers from Japan with them. By 1991 there were some four hundred Japanese component factories in North America. In Europe the car makers have been more circumspect — partly because the clamors for protection in the auto industry are more strident than on the other side of the Atlantic, partly because there was more to work with in the first place. But the announcement of the building of a new Nippondenso parts plant in Britain brought a chill to the spines of local firms, especially when it was revealed that the firm had won an important contract to supply air conditioners to Jaguar before its factory was even finished. In the electronics business, it is the Japanese firms themselves that have been the inward investors into components: Sony's laser pickup facility in France and Canon's planned $21 million factory in Scotland to make photocopier parts are likely to prove strategic examples.

In one way, however, European firms find themselves at a substantial disadvantage to their American counterparts. In the American car industry, the Big Three were not reduced to learning from Japan only by imitation or by benefiting from leaner parts supply. They had direct links with Japanese assemblers too in which they were able to learn intimately how Japanese firms build cars in return for helping the Japanese gain access to the American market. The alliances are cemented by shareholdings: General Motors owns more than a third of Suzuki and 3 percent of Isuzu, two of the minor Japanese assemblers; Chrysler owns 10.3 percent of Mitsubishi; Ford owns almost 23 percent of Mazda. But more important than that, the U.S. and Japanese car makers have set up dedicated joint-venture companies — Diamond Star Motors, NUMMI, and CAMI — in which Japanese methods and American managers and workers have proved a rejuvenating mixture for the industry.

Partly because their experience of business in the United States has made them more confident that they can go it alone in Europe, Japanese firms have less desire to do the same again. Worryingly, however, the Europeans do not even appear to want to join up. As noted earlier, the two most important cooperative ventures are the agreement among Mitsubishi, Volvo, and the Dutch government to build cars in the Netherlands from 1995,[18] and the link between Honda and Rover Group in which Honda's British subsidiary and Rover have exchanged 20 percent shareholdings. Fiat, Peugeot, Renault, and Volkswagen remain largely unexposed to the chapter-and-verse detail of how the Japanese make cars. Not even Mercedes-Benz has yet found a way to learn from the Japanese: despite the widely touted strategic alliance between the Daimler-Benz group and the Mitsubishi *keiretsu*, the two sides were unable to agree on any important joint production venture in the car industry, and the Volvo venture is seen in Tokyo as Mitsubishi's key investment assuring its place in the Europe of the 1990s. Hiroshi Nakamura, president of Mitsubishi Motors, explained to the *Nihon Keizai Shimbun*, Japan's leading financial paper:

> Q: *Your company has also formed a tie-up with Daimler-Benz AG of Germany to sell imported passenger cars in Japan and develop commercial vehicles. Why then have you decided to link up with Volvo to produce small cars in Europe?*
>
> A: Our company and Benz have different conceptions of production technology. Volvo thinks highly of Japan's development and production technology, while we strongly desire to learn Volvo's high-level safety technology. Japanese car makers possess outstanding technology in efficiency of production, whereas Sweden is better at creating good working conditions.[19]

That was a polite way of saying that Mercedes-Benz did not think it had anything to learn from Mitsubishi. Interestingly, the MIT study concluded that Mercedes's quality was slightly higher than that of competing Japanese luxury cars, but only because it put four times as much effort into making each car.

In the consumer electronics sector, a similar but much quieter strategic venture between Matsushita and Robert Bosch appears to be bearing fruit. In 1982 the two firms established a joint venture in Europe called MBV (Matsushita-Bosch Video GmbH), which sells videocassette recorders under the Blaupunkt and Panasonic brand names and CD players under Matsushita's. By 1993 the firms planned to have a fully local development, sales, components, and manufacturing facility based at Peine and Osterode in Bosch's home territory, turning out 1 million video decks and CD players a year.

In the computer industry, however, the field is almost bare: despite the plethora of OEM (original equipment maker) deals, in which European firms put their labels on machines manufactured in Japan, there is not a single current European equivalent of the many joint ventures and technology-sharing agreements between Japanese and American firms in semiconductors, RISC technology, screen display technology, or magnetic or optical memory devices. Partly, of course, this reflects the depressing fact that Japanese firms see little computer-industry technology in Europe for which it is worth bartering their own secrets.

It was a daring thing to do, to try to bring a friend illicitly into an old-style car factory at the heart of the General Motors empire, to see how it really worked. But Ben Hamper had laid his plans carefully. He warned his visitor to make sure he looked scruffy, and if stopped by anyone to give a false name, to claim his ID was upstairs, and "at all times, act surly and miffed." Only when the friend arrived in the parking lot did Hamper realize he had forgotten one thing: to remind him to leave his Honda at home and come in an American car.

> Uh-oh. Rare was the time you gazed upon a Japanese import in this sprawling car kennel. When you did, they were usually

very easy to identify — busted-off antennas, boot heel indentations on the quarter panel, key scrapes along the paintjob, broken mirrors, broken windows. Freedom of choice in one's particular mode of transportation ended rather abruptly at the entrance gate to most GM assembly plants. There were plenty of flag-totin' vandals still takin' night classes at the John Wayne Institute of Insecure Bigots.[20]

It is in the car industry that anti-Japanese feeling has erupted most aggressively. In one tragic case, a group of drunken Detroit residents on a binge attacked and killed a passing Chinese man, under the impression that he was from Japan. Even in intellectual circles, it has become acceptable to say things about the Japanese that would immediately be condemned as racist were they applied to Jews or to any other ethnic or national group. Japanese investors are characterized by their detractors in the United States as secretive, sinister, and prejudiced. They are accused of reserving the key jobs in their American operations for their own nationals. They are accused of downgrading the United States by offering only unskilled assembly jobs, and at the same time of pinching the nation's crown jewels by buying up high-tech start-ups in California. (The apparent contradiction of these last two accusations remains unresolved.) And their attempts to win influence in Washington by hiring former government employees and engaging the most prominent law firms and lobbyists — exactly what one would expect them to do, given the importance of their economic interests in the United States and the political nature of the threat against them — have brought more accusations against them than against the American officials, professionals, and politicians who put themselves so brazenly up for sale.[21]

So far, there are few signs of such feelings in Europe. But that is more likely because European workers and managers remain unaware of the onslaught that is to come than because they are sanguine about it. The recent history of racial tension in Europe — anti-Algerian feeling in France and anti-Turkish feeling in Germany in the 1960s, riots of inner-city blacks in Britain in the 1970s, the return of the Nazi right in France and Germany in the 1980s — shows that Europeans can be as xenophobic as Americans. The first stirrings of anti-Japanism were visible in Britain in 1991, when workers from the car assembly lines demonstrated against changes in working practices with placards bearing the words WE'RE BRITS, NOT NIPS! And the tone of comments from the top of European industry is barely more reassuring. Against the equanimity with which politicians and business leaders met Fujitsu's move to take control of ICL has to be set the vivid attacks made on Japan by the leaders of the French car industry.

There is clearly a worrying potential for a political backlash against Japanese investment. It would, of course, be a different kind of backlash from that created by the arrival of immigrant workers; the thirty-five thousand or so Japanese who live inside the European Community are noticeably richer than the average European — and they are more visible in the continent's top restaurants and golf clubs than in the queues at its unemployment benefit offices or in the cells of its prisons. But the backlash, when it comes, is likely to have two prongs. When a wave of mergers and contraction hits the European car industry, for instance, the tabloid newspapers and television are likely to attack Japan simply for putting Europeans out of work. Specialists, by contrast, will look beyond the natural process by which inefficient European firms are forced to contract, and ask searching questions about the quality of the jobs that are to replace those of the displaced European workers. Critics are already beginning to charge that Japan is hollowing out Europe from the inside by replacing "real" industry with screwdriver plants in which low-skilled workers assemble products from kits, with the design and development and the manufacturing work that yields the high value added being done in Japan.[22]

Against that last charge, Japanese firms have a stronger defense than is usually realized. Japanese investment in the continent has grown so suddenly that the companies simply have not had the time to move to Europe all the functions that would be part of a mature European subsidiary. It is a hard enough job, they insist, to design and set up a factory halfway across the world and to staff it with workers who speak a different language and come from a different culture, without compounding the difficulty by starting work at the same time with an entirely new set of suppliers or a new design process. That, after all, is what it means to demand that Japanese investors buy a high proportion of their parts locally or do a high proportion of their research locally from the very beginning. Comparing Japanese factories in Europe with those owned by American companies is sharply unfair: the Americans have often had a generation or more on European turf, learning the ways of the market, and finding top-quality managers to run their local subsidiaries. "We don't ask a generation," says one Japanese manager in Spain. "Just give us a decade: that is when you will see the localization of supply and of research and development that you are looking for." This book has already described several examples of how Japanese operations that began almost as screwdriver facilities are on the road to becoming independent regional subsidiaries that take their own products all the way from development to market.

This defense would be more palatable, however, if there were less evidence that Japanese companies routinely discriminate against their foreign employees. There are a handful of Japanese firms, it is true, in which American or European managers get a real chance to influence the company's policy. One example might be Nissan: Jerry Benefield, a former Ford executive, runs his own fief from the company's factory in Tennessee; Ian Gibson, a Briton, has been entrusted with wide-ranging powers in the company's European manufacturing operations. Another would certainly be Sony, which even before its purchase of Columbia Pictures and CBS (businesses that, by their nature, had to be left to locals) had handed over control of its American hardware operations to

Michael Schulhof and those in Europe to Jack Schmuckli, the Swiss national who came to the firm after dealing with it for many years from inside Polaroid.

But for the most part, the situation is pitiful. Japanese companies with tens or even hundreds of thousands of employees throughout the world employ only a handful of foreigners who have reached the ranks of middle management. Toyota and Honda, for instance, have only in the past few years started allowing Westerners to join them on the same terms as Japanese graduate trainees, starting with a grueling half year divided between working on the production line in the factory and trying to shift metal in a car dealership in provincial Japan. The insecurity these new employees feel, however, is evident from the fierce way they defend the company against the slightest criticism even in private, and the exaggerated deference with which they bow and use honorific language when talking to their corporate superiors. This is no surprise: to survive, they have to be more royalist than the king.[23]

And in many cases, it is quite evident that Japanese firms have often deliberately avoided hiring the most talented candidates that present themselves. Rather than risk the disruption that might accompany the stimulative effect of a dissenting foreign voice, many Japanese firms appear to prefer to choose Americans and Europeans who are as submissive and unthinking as the most malleable of their Japanese employees.[24] In the United States, whose legal system (for all its faults) exposes and remedies such practices more readily, this subtle discrimination has on occasion turned into out-and-out illegality when Japanese employers have avoided hiring ethnic minorities, failed to treat their women workers the same as men, and transferred to other businesses Japanese nationals working in loss-making subsidiaries while the American workers in the same subsidiaries were sacked outright. The sad fact is that most Japanese managers, and even some who have been extensively exposed to Western ways, simply refuse to believe that their foreign employees can be trusted as much as their Japanese employees. Almost all multinational companies have a mild bias toward the citizens of the country where their head office is, but in this respect Japanese firms are far worse than their American and European competitors. No number of sponsored opera productions, no degree of involvement with the local football team, no commitment to environment-friendly packaging can compensate.

It is unfair to put the blame for this on the individual managers of Japanese firms in Europe or the United States. They are victims of their country's education system, with its exaggerated emphasis — an emphasis that is unfortunately intensifying, rather than weakening — on what makes the Japanese different from others, rather than similar to them. Any prejudices they might have are reinforced by the inescapably large differences between Japan and other industrial societies, in attitudes to work, to hierarchy, to shyness and articulateness, to perspiration rather than inspiration, to the individual rather than the group.

Japan is not unique in being so different from the West; on the contrary, sociologists find many similarities with other Confucian civilizations. Korea deliberately kept itself closed off from outside influences. The Chinese are as dismissive of foreigners as the most nationalist Japanese. The Thais take a similar view of women. The Burmese are as intent on preserving a façade of dignity, no matter what the reality underneath. Foreigners can expect to be goggled at in other Asian countries. The difference, however, is that none of these other countries has ever had such a dramatic effect on the lives of people in Europe and the United States. The level of trade and investment between Japan and the West simply demands that Japan make itself less exclusive.

It would be rash to turn such a demand into direct prescriptions. Could host countries in Europe tell their Japanese residents to stop living in upmarket ghettos? To stop eating in their own restaurants, singing in their own *karaoke* bars, and playing golf on their own courses? To start making business decisions in a transparent way rather than by vague *nema-*

washi[25] over the telephone to Tokyo? To change fundamentally their attitude to women? The degree to which Japanese businesses integrate into their Western surroundings will depend tremendously on just such things, not merely on formal rules such as how many components they buy locally and whether they are willing to help foreign firms import into Japan. But the difficulties of legislating on such matters are evident.

One of the few Japanese to have grasped this issue is Akio Morita, the maverick chairman of Sony, whose willingness to talk openly has divided the Japanese business establishment between sneaking admiration and barely disguised fury. Morita lambasts the United States with the best of them,[26] but he has also argued forcefully that Japanese companies need to do a great deal more to reassure Westerners that there is nothing sinister about working for them. Such feelings are echoed by a top British official at the European Commission in Brussels, who gives a long list of familiar things he wants Japanese firms in Europe to do. They should invest more, to create new jobs; they should make sure their investments are well integrated into the local economy and business; they should transfer more research and development power to Europeans; they should promote more European managers. The surprise comes at the end, however: "These are not conditions. They are advice: these are the things the Japanese should do if they want to avoid the risk of political difficulties like those they have had in the United States."

It was a balmy week in May 1991, and the azaleas were out. Bordered with vivid purple flowers, the drab avenues of the city's Marunouchi business district looked almost presentable. But the battles of international trade were continuing unabated. Dan Quayle, the U.S. vice-president, was making use of a visit to Japan to tell the government in Tokyo to open up its market to more car parts. Jacques Delors, the president of the European Commission, arrived to repeat the Commission's long-standing complaints that Japan should do something about its persistent trade surplus with the Community. And at the same time, a large team of American negotiators was in town, reviewing with a critical eye the progress of the Structural Impediments Initiative, a set of agreements struck between the United States and Japan the previous June to make the Japanese market more open to foreign business.[27]

Yet paradoxically, just as all these efforts were being made to prise Japan's apparently closed market a crack open, five hundred guests were sipping cocktails and champagne at the British embassy in Tokyo to toast the success of British businesses that had done well in Japan. It was a remarkable about-face. Only four years earlier, Mrs. Thatcher had banged the negotiating table and told the Japanese that she would not tolerate their refusal to give more seats to foreigners on the Tokyo stock exchange and to open their market to Scotch whisky. By 1991, only a year after the lady's departure from Downing Street, the British establishment (both Labour and Conservative) had largely come around to the view that it is possible after all to export to Japan — if only you make the effort. "There isn't really a body of industrial or business opinion in our country holding the view that Japan is impenetrable," explained Michael Perry, now the chairman of Unilever. "Now we have to improve our market share. The playing fields are level enough, the markets are open enough; henceforth, it's a battle to win markets in Japan against our competitors from other countries."

That was the year in which the gap between the British view and the attitude of governments elsewhere in Europe was at its most alarmingly wide. When Douglas Hurd came to Tokyo as British foreign secretary for one of a series of regular meetings with his opposite number, all he would say about Japanese trade barriers was that he had "a number of private business matters I intend to discuss with my Japanese colleagues." Such diplomatic politeness was a far cry from the attitude of Horst Krenzler, a top EC official who launched into a virulent attack on Japanese protectionism almost as soon as he got off the plane in autumn 1990. Krenzler chose an unfortunate ground on which to do battle: he complained particularly angrily about Japanese quotas on leather imports. Europe, too, had quotas on leather imports. More generally, Europe was more guilty of imposing quotas on imports than Japan. Even ten years earlier, before Japan had begun a substantial market-opening process, France had exactly twice as many import restrictions in force as the Japan it was so keen to criticize. And since the late 1970s, the tariffs that Japan imposed on imports had been falling sharply: by 1987 they were lower than the tariffs in either the European Community or the United States.

That is not to say that the Japanese market is as fully open as Perry would like to think. The inheritors of generations of xenophobia and decades of carefully crafted exclusionary industrial policies, Japanese customs officers and the industries they seek to protect are adept at using administrative procedures, rather than formal tariffs in themselves, to keep foreign goods out. American express-delivery companies have found that Japanese customs delay shipments as they come in, and thus put them at a disadvantage compared with their domestic competitors, by insisting that official artists draw pictures of the contents of shipments rather than photograph them. French ski makers have heard Japanese officials insist that they should not be allowed to sell their products in Japan because "Japanese snow is different."[28] There was even once a claim that foreign beef should be excluded from Japan because the intestines of Japanese citizens are a different length from those of foreigners and thus able to digest the meat of only local cows.[29]

Even the country's frequent and notorious import campaigns — which recently have come to include even such things as tax breaks for importers that mirror the tax breaks that used to be offered to exporters twenty years ago — have a double edge. At Narita airport, for instance, the baggage trolleys are marked with the slogan IMPORT NOW!, a legacy from the prime ministership of Yasuhiro Nakasone, who was keen to make sure the world in general and the United States in particular knew that Japan was opening up. The irony of the slogan is evident after only a moment's thought: putting it in English gives away the fact that the government's primary intention was to convince foreigners that Japan was opening, rather than to convince the Japanese to buy imports.

But Japan can surely be forgiven this. Unlike the countries of the European Community, in many of which exports account for a fifth or more of national income, Japan's dependency on trade is below 10 percent, like that of the United States. As the world's second-largest national economy, it has traditionally looked much more in on itself. And although the government's efforts to promote the sale of imported goods may well be sincere — witness the decision to parade around Tokyo the country's new emperor, Akihito, in a black convertible Rolls-Royce Corniche with a chrysanthemum on the doors, rather than in a Japanese car — there is no question that the buy-Japanese nationalism of the postwar generation will take some years to die away. At least things are moving in the right direction: in the United States, by contrast, a worrying symptom of the public feeling that the country has lost its economic leadership can be seen in the growing number of people who support buy-American policies. Both trends are a symptom of the fact that attitudes to trade tend to be closely linked with national confidence.

Foreign businesses face three key difficulties in selling in Japan. One is the *keiretsu* system, in which members of the same financial group tend to give preference to their fellow members for products as varied as electronic components, insurance services, and beer. Though it has its benefits (see chapter 2), the system is certainly anticompetitive to the degree that it prevents effective price competition. But it was not designed to keep foreigners out: domestic newcomers suffer from it too. Ironically, given the fact that American economists are increasingly suggesting that the United States should adopt a similar system,[30] the Japanese government has undertaken to remove the more egregiously unfair exclusionary practices and to enforce competition law more effectively.

A second problem for foreign firms in Japan is the simple price of establishing offices, factories, and sales centers from which they can do business. Even after the market crash of 1990–91, rents in Tokyo are the highest in the world and those in Osaka probably the second highest. The owners of commercial property in the two cities have done tremendously well as a result: a series of dozens of numbered Mori buildings in central Tokyo are a testament to the wealth of a billionaire property developer who started buying up land and buildings in the capital soon after the war. Foreign entities that have been long established benefited too. When Martin Sorrell's WPP group bought the American advertising agency J. Walter Thompson in a leveraged buyout, it was able to finance more than a quarter of the acquisition by selling the premises that were the site of its Tokyo office; and even a humble developing country like Burma[31] was able to make over $240 million from selling what in any other city would have been little more than a generous suburban garden surrounding its embassy. Many leading Japanese firms, such as those in the Mitsubishi group, can justify their stratospheric price-to-earnings ratios by property holdings that are valued on their books at acquisition cost.

Firms that were not already established in Japan have a much harder time. In the late 1980s, the securities companies that moved in to take advantage of the opening of the Tokyo stock market found themselves paying such high rents that each one of their employees had to cover astronomical annual rental costs for each desk before they could even begin to think about making profits. The result of these high costs is to deter foreign firms from entering the Japanese market: accountants tend to conclude that the high price of entry means that money spent on developing business in Japan is far less productive than money spent in Europe, the United States, or even in Southeast Asia. Even after clear evidence began to emerge that prices had begun to fall from 1991 onward, few analysts seriously expected Japanese urban property to shed more than a third of its value. Even then, it would still be the world's most expensive.

A third problem for foreign business is the Japanese distribution system, in which most big manufacturers sell their goods through a tree of first- and second-stage wholesalers and final retailers, which are often tied by shareholdings or by loans to the parent company. Only if they are lucky enough to find an enterprising Japanese partner who does not make a competing product can foreign companies get their goods easily distributed through the 1 million small shops up and down the country. Otherwise, they have to build their own distribution network, which is a slow and expensive business.

To Americans, this system has often seemed inherently unfair. But it is worth recalling that the Japanese system is only a more refined form of the sales channels that are common for plenty of products in Europe; it is only in the United States itself, with a concentrated and efficient distribution industry that is intensely interested in low prices and generally willing to give business to an unknown but promising supplier, that distribution is highly competitive. That is why American consumers benefit from the world's most favorable prices on most of the goods they buy — and why Europeans pay more, and Japanese more still. On the other hand, the Japanese system does have benefits: the distribution sector, which employs 2 million excess people, has cushioned the work force from mass unemployment during downturns; and firms learn valuable information about what their customers want from the closeness of their relations with their distributors.

Plenty of foreign firms have managed to overcome this obstacle — which incidentally affects Japanese businesses as well when they try to set up in a new line of business in which they do not already have friends. Procter and Gamble, for instance, has its toiletries all over Japan. The sparkling results seen by the German car makers when they switched to direct distribution have already been noted. Coca-Cola dominates the Japanese soft-drink market by virtue of a highly sophisticated distribution system including not only wholesalers and retailers but also the world's biggest private network of vending machines. The machines in Tokyo have just been connected up to an innovative system whereby each machine sends information automatically about how many drinks it has sold and which flavors need replenishing through a cellular data information network similar to portable phones. As a result, the delivery trucks that keep them stocked can be loaded with exactly the right mixture of products, and can avoid wasting time traveling through the Tokyo traffic to machines that need no attention.

What is more, the changes that are already taking place in the distribution system as a result of the sii negotiations are providing new opportunities. So far, U.S. firms have been the most aggressive at taking them up. Mail-order companies like L. L. Bean send an increasing flow of products across the Pacific to Japan, thus avoiding the costs of the distribution system altogether. And Toys "R" Us, the American discount toy retailer, has begun a program of opening toy superstores in Japan. Despite furious initial opposition from the inefficient and fragmented Japanese toy industry, which managed to get the local manufacturers to promise not to sell directly to the new competitor, the firm seems to have achieved a quiet compromise whereby it will be allowed to buy toys at factory-gate prices by acquiring a wholesaler of its own.

Despite these three difficulties, the firms that have gone to Japan have done surprisingly well. Government figures show consistently year after year that the Japanese subsidiaries of foreign firms are more profitable than Japanese companies are themselves, and foreign businessmen admit cheerfully that when they succeed in carving out niches in Japan, they are often more secure and more profitable than niches in any other market in the world.

The attractiveness of the Japanese market rose dramatically in the second half of the 1980s as the country's investment-led boom dragged consumer spending and share prices along with it, and created a gold mine for the financial industry and the makers of luxury goods. It then promptly fell again when higher interest rates, lower pay rises, and a 50 percent fall in share prices put a sharp stop to the more frothy kinds of consumer spending. The sharp rise in Japan's trade surplus that followed was a salutary experience: it was a reminder to the country's Western competitors that a recession in Japan might harm the ability of Japanese companies to export, but it would also reduce demand for imported goods in the world's second-biggest market. For many international businesses controlled in the United States or in Europe, a healthy and fast-growing Japanese economy now looks like better news than a stagnant one.

Michael Perry was not talking about the Japanese market just in his capacity as chairman of Unilever. He is also a leading light in a dramatic cooperative campaign organized by the British government but carried out with the help of British businesses to raise awareness of the world's second-biggest market. The campaign's first stage, known as "Opportunity Japan," spent three years just trying to wake up British businesses to Japan's existence. Seminars were held up and down the country. Firms that were too small to be listed on the stock exchange were bombarded with mailings. Opinion polls were taken to find out how much the business sector knew already about Japan. The top executives of leading firms were invited to breakfasts at which they were encouraged to set up task forces reporting directly to their company boards on how to get a piece of the gold mine at the other end of the world. The target was a striking one: to double British exports to Japan in three years. Luckily for the campaign's propagandists, the Japanese consumer boom lasted just long enough for the government to be able to claim that British business had almost met the target. From 1991 onward, a much more difficult process began: a new campaign, this one known as "Priority Japan," which was designed to concentrate on expanding British exports to the promising new market from just a few industrial sectors to a much broader range across the economy. Priority Japan is a daunting challenge; relatively easy though it may have been to persuade the Japanese to buy Aquascutum raincoats, Minis, and Peter Rabbit breakfast bowls, it is a great deal harder to make them take British machine tools or British electronic components seriously. A festival of British culture and technology in Japan in 1990 made valiant efforts but largely failed to dent the image of Britain as a country of history, old-style craftsmanship, gentlemen, and fog.

But the important thing is that the change has already taken place. After years of complaining about barriers in Japan, British businesspeople have begun to look in the mirror and wonder whether they themselves were doing all they could to succeed in the Japanese market. Opportunity Japan and Priority Japan are beginning to be flattered most sincerely elsewhere in Europe: the European Commission has given much greater prominence to Exprom, its program of export promotion, and to its annual scheme of taking middle-ranking but promising European executives out to Japan for an extended period to learn Japanese, work for a while with a Japanese company, and go back to Europe full of Japanese ideas and opportunities with which to shake up their former colleagues. France, too, has its equivalent. Germany has improved its already strong commercial presence in provincial cities such as Kobe. And in February 1992, Dr. Ruud Lubbers, the Dutch prime minister, addressed a conference in Utrecht on "Success in Japan" which brought together many of the country's leading businesspeople and management consultants.

Essential though such programs are, it would be idle to think that they can do miracles. The imbalance between Japan's investment overseas and overseas investment into Japan remains at a ratio of about fifteen to one. And the proportion of imports into Japan that are manufactured goods (rather than food or mere raw materials and intermediate goods to be processed and turned right around again as exports), although it has more than doubled from under 23 percent in 1980 to over 50 percent in 1990, remains much less than that of most other industrial economies.

If they are to bring trade with Japan into balance, European businesses will have to do more: they have to expect to devote great resources to competing in the Japanese market in the long term. Specifically, they have to be prepared to devote the time of their top managers to Japanese issues. They have to hire people who are familiar with Japan, and spend money to teach their existing employees competence in speaking and reading and writing Japanese. A British survey showed that 76 percent of a sample of companies that had already expressed an interest in Japan employed not a single person who could communicate in Japanese. It is no wonder that a purchasing manager in Osaka is likely to look askance at someone who flies in from outside for a few days and expects to sell him something — still more so at one who expects to be able to do the selling in English. Most Japanese businessmen who have worked for their companies abroad have had to learn English. They know all too well what commitment it demonstrates to speak a customer's language.

There is another reason for demonstrating a commitment to the Japanese market. Although patterns of loyalty are breaking down, male university graduates still often expect to spend all their career with the same company. They will therefore be extremely reluctant to take a job with a firm that may close down its Tokyo office five years or a decade from now, leaving them without work but unable to get back into the corporate hierarchies that their friends joined in Japanese firms. As a result, Western firms usually find that their first attempt to participate in the round of university visits in Japan yields a handful of job applications, if that. Once they have acquired the right reputation, however, foreign firms can draw in talented Japanese who like the idea of quick promotion and the chance to work abroad at the head office and are willing to put their trust in their new employer. Westerners may be tempted to dismiss this question of recruitment as unimportant, given that they can always poach workers from other firms using headhunters. It is significant, however, that Japanese firms themselves consider the number of university graduate trainees a firm takes on to be a key indicator of its managerial health. Tables giving the number of trainees hired, and the average age of a company's employees, are pored over by competitors and customers alike.

"So what?" a cynic would be forgiven for asking. Japan may be the world's second-biggest market. It may well be more open than the inexperienced outsider believes, and more profitable than he expects. The long-term rewards for getting in and staying in may even justify the unquestionably high initial investments in time, money, and effort. But there are other parts of the world that are less risky, less foreign, and certain to produce a quicker return. Why not try there first?

There are two simple answers. First, the Japanese market is not just big; it is also a market that tends to set trends, to be first to accept products and ideas that then spread abroad. A firm that knows what is happening inside the Japanese market is much less likely to be caught by surprise by Japanese competitors in its own. It will get an early warning signal of when a Japanese firm is doing better or more efficiently what it does. Furthermore, the very act of selling there allows a firm to put pressure on its Japanese competitors, to prevent them from making high profits in the home market that can be used to subsidize export sales. Second, working in Japan is invaluable discipline. Competitors there soon realize how uncompetitive and backward are vast swaths of the country's industry; but they also come to understand the methods of those Japanese businesses that are world-beaters.

In the year 1992, the persistence of recession in all three of the world's big markets — the United States, Europe, and Japan — displayed Japanese industry at its most vulnerable. Until then, with the exception of the oil crisis years, it had been unusual for economic conditions to deteriorate simultaneously in each of those markets. This had been a hidden advantage for Japanese industry. While American and European industry had invested extensively in each other's markets, and had thus been able to spread risk across the two, neither industry had a strong position in Japan. It was only the Japanese themselves, with their presence in all three of the great blocs, who could claim that their risks were safely hedged.

That was the position until the end of the 1980s. But when the Japanese economy — previously the apparently unstoppable engine that had always protected domestic firms against trouble overseas — began to turn down, suddenly everything looked different. Profits disappeared. Firms found themselves with excess capacity on their hands. Capital costs were high. The stock market obstinately refused to respond to defibrillation by the men in white coats at the Ministry of Finance.

The result was a great change in the popular view of Japan overseas. Newspapers and magazines that had previously been full of dire warnings of what would happen unless the Japanese bid for world conquest were stopped now began to point out that Japan was politically decadent, creatively stultified, financially rigid.

To be fair, one important thing had changed. In several industries, Japanese firms had ceased to be hungry newcomers, desperate to catch up with the leaders. Now they *were* the leaders, and it was hard to see what to aim for. The years of "reverse engineering" — taking apart a competitor's radically new product, and trying to come up with something that offered 90 percent of its functions for only 60 percent of its price — were over. The burden of market innovation was on Japanese companies. It was like being a violinist from the back bench, suddenly brought to the front of the stage and asked to play a concerto. The fact that Japanese firms had long yearned to be market leaders, and had long prepared for it, did not make them any less nervous when their time came. This was not merely a psychological point. A company that has a small market share can continue to prosper even as the market falls. For a company that dominates the market, doing so is a great deal harder.

But in other respects, it was quite wrong to see the recession that clouded the opening of the 1990s as a structural problem for Japan. True, a depressed stock market and high interest rates meant that capital was more expensive; but such was the spending spree that Japanese companies had carried out in the second half of the 1980s that their factories were already far more modern than those in the United States or Europe. Many companies were able to manage quite well with a slower pace of new investment.

Japan was certainly facing problems. Its shortage of labor at home was greater than could be compensated for by sending production overseas. Its workers were demanding better conditions, more free time, *and* more money. Big businesses — even those that topped the list of winners of patents in the United States — found that their research and development departments were more geared to the small incremental improvement than to the technological jump they now needed to make. But in all these three areas, Japanese business did not need to be told what to do. With a pessimistic introspection that was maddening to foreigners, it was already discussing the problems. Newspapers ran endless series of articles about them. Speakers at conferences wrung their hands at the imminent collapse of the country. And meanwhile, Japanese companies themselves were getting on with the job of remaking themselves once again in response to changing circumstances.

It may have been wrong to declare that Japan was doomed. But it was equally wrong to declare that it was invincible. For years, political and business writers have combed the country's companies, its government, and its society for "secret weapons" to explain its success. When subjected to scrutiny, however, few of the putative explanations stand up. If Japan's development is simply a matter of all-seeing bureaucratic controls, why are some of its most successful export companies those that have the weakest ties with the government? If

Japanese firms owe their long-term success to the revival in another form of the prewar industrial combines, why is it that they have continued to succeed when manufacturing in overseas markets where their traditional methods have to be abandoned? If it is an intrinsic racial quality of the Japanese themselves that makes their companies so strong, how can it be that Nissan's British workers are more productive than those at home?

There should be no mistake about one thing. The stability of Japanese society and the openness of its bureaucracy to pressure from business have certainly helped to create an atmosphere in which companies can succeed. One does not need to look even to the hyperinflationary countries of South America, or to the mass of red tape that used to be India, to see that the wrong kind of government or the wrong kind of society can stymie whatever business skills exist. American firms that find it hard to recruit people who can both read and write and do their jobs without taking drugs or Italian firms that have to win the agreement of recalcitrant trade unions for the smallest changes in their factories would agree with that.

But for the most part, this book has argued that it is Japanese business itself that is responsible for its success. The fads that have swept the West, from quality circles to egalitarian canteens, are in fact only manifestations of more basic virtues. As we have seen, Japanese companies are good at controlling their costs — not only keeping them down in general, but also knowing which bits of their operations, which products and which processes, take up money. They are also good at time: bringing out new cars or CD players those crucial few months before the competition, because the bulk of the profits of a new product come at the beginning of its life.

Underneath these, however, are things that are more fundamental still. Successful Japanese companies pay great attention to the question of how to get the best out of their work forces. In some ways, they fail spectacularly to do that: women and talented young workers, in particular, often feel that they are unable to make their mark in a rigid hierarchy. But by learning from the mistakes they made in the 1950s, they have avoided the Western trap of allowing relations to develop between unions and management that are so confrontational that even basic decisions cannot be taken for the good of the business.

And they have retained, even in some of the largest firms, an ability to change: to look critically at their operations for waste or for inefficiencies, and to try to remedy them. A measure of how far such an approach can be taken even in basic factory management can be seen in the experience of the American workers at Mazda's Michigan plant. They were given instructions in how the cars should be assembled, precise and specific even to the point of saying which tool a given worker should pick up in which order. That was not a sign of rigidity, as the workers first thought; it was proof that Mazda had already spent years subjecting to scrutiny every detail of the way its factories worked.

Perhaps it is this inclination for continuous improvement that has made the Japanese seem so depressingly unbeatable to Westerners. No sooner does the competition catch up with one idea or one way of doing things, it seems, than Japanese companies have already moved on to something else.

A book like this, which attempts to give the reader an impression of competitive position in a number of different industries, cannot hope to serve also as a step-by-step manual for industrial recovery. It can offer a single maxim, however. Its message, for both businesses and governments, is to stop asking what the Japanese are doing wrong and instead to ask what they are doing right.

One of the reasons the United States is responding better to the challenge from Japan is that public debate there has shifted away from accusing the competition of unfairness toward trying to understand it. In Europe, by contrast, that stage has not yet been reached. My research showed that across numerous industries and numerous borders far too few business leaders are ready to concede that one of the reasons Japanese firms are taking market share away from them is simply because they are better at what they do. Once the Europeans can do that — and once they are able to see Japanese behavior not necessarily as unfair but merely as different — they will be ready to respond.

NOTES

1. THE WORLD'S BIGGEST MARKET

1. Loukas Tsoukalis, *The New European Economy: The Politics and Economics of Integration* (London: Oxford University Press, 1991), p. 56.
2. He declined to be interviewed for this book. The information here has been assembled from discussions with those who worked with him and other employees of the company in Japan, the United States, and Britain.
3. To the dismay of Ohbayashi, the Japanese building contractor that bought it, however, the British government promptly added Bracken House to its list of buildings of architectural merit, thus preventing the new owner from knocking it down and building an up-to-date office block on the site to take advantage of its prestigious location in the City. In fact, Ohbayashi probably paid too much for Bracken House in any case. So did Mitsubishi Real Estate when it bought Rockefeller Center.
4. The first of these three — Britain's apparent openness to foreign investment — is by far the most important. Proof of that can be seen in the fact that the United Kingdom is by far the most popular destination for foreign investment in the European Community, not just investment from Japan; during the 1980s it received 40 percent of all inward investment into Europe, and

in the 1970s, 32 percent. Calculations made by Stephen Thomsen and Phedon Nicolaides in the study quoted below suggest that foreign investment accounts for 16 percent of Britain's GDP, compared with 5 percent for France, 3 percent for Italy, and 2 percent for Germany.

5. The Japanese were not fooled. Cresson's remarks having been seized on by the Japanese press, sales of French goods in Tokyo dipped after she became prime minister. Right wingers organized boycotts and marches to the French embassy; Peugeot cars and showrooms were vandalized with paint; and most spectacularly, a group of extremists organized for the benefit of the world's press a demonstration in a Tokyo park in summer 1991 featuring the ritual decapitation of an effigy of Edith Cresson, made from a tailor's dummy full of tomato ketchup.

6. Stephen Thomsen and Phedon Nicolaides, *The Evolution of Japanese Direct Investment in Europe: Death of a Transistor Salesman* (London: Royal Institute of International Affairs, Harvester-Wheatsheaf, 1991).

7. See, for instance, Clyde V. Prestowitz, Jr., *Trading Places: How America Allowed Japan to Take the Lead* (Tokyo: Tuttle, 1990).

8. Endymion Wilkinson, *Japan versus Europe: A History of Misunderstanding* (London: Penguin, 1983).

9. The SII talks were a direct result of Japan's failure to respond to the use of the so-called super-301 provisions of the 1988 omnibus trade law, which mandated that the administration take punitive action against countries deemed not to have opened their markets sufficiently to U.S. goods. Super-301 was an impressive stick when used against countries like India and South Korea, but the Japanese authorities, refusing flatly to be intimidated, simply declined to negotiate on the basis of the provisions. The United States faced a dilemma: such was the extent of trade and cross-investment between the two economies that it was far from clear that Japan would suffer more than the United States from the trade war that might result from a unilateral American imposition of punitive duties or sanctions. Happily, Washington chose the SII route.

10. Significantly, the Japanese side called the negotiations "structural talks," removing the implied criticism in the word *impediments*. This showed, perhaps, that the two sides did not see quite so much eye to eye as the Americans liked to believe.

11. This was quite wrong. Japan dominates the manufacture of

latest-generation DRAM chips and the CCDs (charge-coupled devices) that are the electronic eyes of video cameras, but U.S. missiles tend to use tried equipment that is several generations old and built to more exacting military tolerances.

12. Foreign residents of Japan have become so tired of hearing about the absence of muggers and violent criminals in Tokyo that a backlash has set in: it is now fashionable to issue reminders of how widespread organized crime and extortion are, and to deplore the absence of moral standards in Japanese political and business life. But the fact remains that although the Japanese may be regularly ripped off by gangsters, industrial conglomerates, and leading politicians, they are extremely unlikely to be mugged, raped, or murdered.

13. And to *The Economist,* which dreamed up this apt comparison.

14. The quotation is from Arthur Schlesinger's introduction to the English translation of Jean-Jacques Servan-Schreiber's *Le Défi Américain* (London: Hamish Hamilton, 1968).

15. Servan-Schreiber, *Le Défi Américain,* p. 12.

16. Good examples of this are the use of arcade-game technology in fighter planes, and of devices similar to those used in hand-held video cameras to direct "smart bombs."

17. Daniel Burstein, *Euroquake!* (New York: Simon and Schuster, 1991), p. 284ff.

18. Japan's excessive concentration on trade with the United States, which is only now belatedly being corrected, is a powerful reminder of this.

19. Such a sweeping statement must, of course, be an oversimplification. Europe's strengths in specialty chemicals and telecommunications are the two most obvious industrial gems it has to offer potential Japanese partners. But the first of these is a relatively discrete sector with few consequences for the rest of industry. As for the second, the recent rise to leadership in satellite and cellular communications of American firms such as Motorola has drawn the attention of many Japanese firms.

20. There is a copious literature and a vigorous political debate about the degree to which the exclusion of foreign business from Japan's markets is due to unfairness, rather than simply to the high costs of entry and the cutthroat competitors within. It is worth making two observations. First, the startling success of Japanese firms in Asia, where they fight on the same terms as American ones, suggests that the answer is much nearer to

the second than to the first. And second, the growing Japanese presence in two of the other four major markets of the world — the Asian market and the European market — threatens from the American point of view to render this argument sterile in any case.

2. A GLIMPSE INSIDE THE JAPANESE MIRACLE

1. Tokyo: Tuttle, 1989, p. 1.
2. Professor Johnson dislikes the label. "I am happy to be called a revisionist," I heard him say in a speech in Tokyo during 1989, "when the word is used in contrast to the word *fool*."
3. A recent book (John Woronoff, *Japan as* Anything but *Number One* [New York: Macmillan, 1991]) mines this seam more deeply than is possible here.
4. This is changing very rapidly. Pressure from employees in foreign subsidiaries prevents Japanese companies from providing only cramped accommodation overseas. And in the late 1980s the city of Tokyo saw a sharp increase in the building of prestigious office blocks; it is worth noting, however, that the owners of the new building are more likely to be financial and other kinds of service firms than manufacturers.
5. James C. Abegglen and George Stalk, Jr., *Kaisha: The Japanese Corporation* (New York: Basic Books, 1985).
6. A dynamic random-access memory chip whose capacity is about 4 million 1's or 0's.
7. Japanese use the unkind phrase *kurisumasu keeki* (Christmas cake) to refer to women who have passed the ideal marrying age. They are perfect on the twenty-fifth, you see; who wants them on the twenty-sixth?
8. A friend of mine at the Japanese Foreign Ministry is widely seen as a high-flier there. Why, I asked one of his colleagues — is it because he is so obviously intelligent and analytical? No, the reply came back; it's because he stays in the office until eleven every night.
9. They are known, somewhat chillingly, as *me-ue* (above your eyes) or *me-shita* (below your eyes).
10. T. W. Kang, *Gaishi: The Foreign Company in Japan* (New York: Basic Books, 1990).
11. Filofax later went bust, vindicating warnings that its runaway success in the Japanese market was due more to the skill of its

local distributor than to its own ability to provide what Japanese customers wanted.

12. The 2 percent estimate comes from Peter Tasker, *Inside Japan: Wealth, Work and Power in the New Japanese Empire* (London: Penguin Books, 1989).

13. The Pickens-Koito saga continued for many acrimonious months, during which there were rowdy scenes at the Japanese company's annual general meeting and its American attacker was stymied in his attempts to be represented on the board. Yet Pickens's successful attempt to portray his battle with Toyota as a fight between the open economic system of the United States and the closed one of Japan was tarnished when he was later forced to file information with the Japanese financial authorities that showed that the company from which he had bought the shares continued to hold a beneficial interest in them. Japanese nationalists felt themselves vindicated; Pickens had proved to be nothing but a greenmailer after all, they said.

14. It is interesting that although tens of thousands of English words have entered the Japanese language, particularly in discussions of trade, economics, and international affairs, *Miti* is not one of them. On my first visit to Japan, speaking no Japanese at all, I once had cause to ask for directions to this notorious institution in Kasumigaseki; no one understood at all.

15. There are many who believe on simple economies-of-scale grounds that it still has today. Yet it is interesting to observe how much more competitive in world markets the Japanese car industry is than the American, despite the fact that three American firms produce twice as many cars as nine Japanese.

16. The Large-Scale Retail Law of 1974 imposed a consultative process that often resulted in delays of a decade before a new supermarket or store of more than five hundred square meters could open. Under pressure from the United States, however, the government began the process of reform in 1990. Although local authorities continue to have the right to slow down new store openings, MITI has promised that in the future the consultative delay will not be more than a year.

17. Such arrangements have many faults; they are discussed more fully later in the book.

18. The UNIX operating system and radar were spin-offs from military R&D, but they cannot yet be described as consumer products. One of the most recent military-technology spin-offs is the

ability to identify one's position anywhere on the globe, accurate to a few meters, using a hand-held receiver that processes signals from the Pentagon's Navstar satellites. Although a number of American companies sell these gadgets, Sony introduced one in 1991 and Japanese companies such as Pioneer have taken the lead in using satellites to build in-car navigation systems.

19. "They overlook those who have been laid off, those who will be employed within a month, those who turn down a job offered by the labor exchange, those looking for work during the month but not the week of the survey, and some others. Moreover, 'unemployed' means not having done even one hour's work during that week, which is a bit restrictive," argues John Woronoff. I disagree, however, with his inference that underlying Japanese unemployment is no lower than in other OECD countries.

20. The use of *katakana* is fascinating. On the one hand, it is proof of a hunger for ideas from outside; every week, one comes across some new and puzzling *gairaigo*, or word from abroad. Japan has no equivalent of the Académie Française that sees its job as protecting Japanese culture from incursion from outside. On the other, the very use of *katakana* acts as a discriminating force, marking out foreign ideas from their context by the very way in which they are written.

21. The *meishi*, or business card, is used to identify the holder and his status not just to customers or suppliers, but also to people inside his own company. In 1990 the electronics company Matsushita discovered that its eighty thousand white-collar employees in Japan were handing out 4 million cards a year — and that 30 percent of those were given to other Matsushita workers. With the consciousness of costs that has helped it become the world's biggest electronics maker, the firm told its workers that they may henceforth dispense with the formalities inside the company.

22. The complaint is known in Japanese as *karoshi*; pressure groups have been trying to get the government to acknowledge its existence so that widows and orphans can receive state benefits or sue for compensation when a Japanese office worker falls ill or dies as a result of working too long hours.

23. Abegglen and Stalk, *Kaisha*, p. 51.

24. In one school I visited to research a report for *The Independent*, the teacher gave a long and erudite account of the history of the European Community. When he had finished, he turned to the

class to solicit their opinions on relations between Japan and Europe. They all looked at me and tittered nervously, apparently unaccustomed to speaking except in answer to a specific question.

25. This has become an increasingly vexed political issue in recent years, for textbook screenings have been used by the ministry to anesthetize accounts of Japan's recent past, in particular with regard to the Second World War. Textbooks have not gone so far as to suggest that Japan was the victim, though they tend to dwell on the tragedies of Hiroshima and Nagasaki without addressing the issue that at least some people in Washington saw nuclear bombs as a last resort for ending the war without the death of millions, rather than merely hundreds of thousands, of civilians. But they have glossed over Japan's invasion of China, its ruthless suppression of the Koreans, and the cruelty of its soldiers all over Asia. In one notable incident, the screening committee removed an account of how Japanese soldiers threw babies up in the air and killed them by catching them on bayonets, and replaced it with an episode from the English musical *My Fair Lady*. In 1991 the government decided to reduce the screening process to a single stage, and to publish some, but not all, of the details of the changes that had been made.

26. The case for this is argued in persuasive detail in Bill Emmott's *The Sun Also Sets* (New York: Simon and Schuster, 1989).

3. THE LONG MARCH OF THE JAPANESE BANK

1. *Manhattan, Inc.*
2. Not his real name.
3. Here is a sign of the significance that these lapel pins have in Japanese society. I was once invited to a drunken dinner with a leading member of the Yamaguchi-gumi gangster syndicate in Osaka, in which the gangster told me quite openly that he had murdered a dozen members of a competing gang, and described the different methods (shooting, stabbing, garroting) that he had used to get rid of them. One of the hostesses at the smart *ryotei* where we were dining handed me a record of a song he had written and had recorded which described the love of a gangster's moll for her man and her fear that he might not return tonight. He gave me a business card with the syndicate's logo on it in embossed silver and his own name in bold black calligraphic

strokes. But when I asked him whether I might have a syndicate lapel pin as a souvenir, the answer was clear. It was quite out of the question.

4. Of course, the money did not come out of thin air. Existing shareholders lose when a company issues a CB, because of the risk that a dilution of earnings will take place when the buyers of the CB convert into shares and demand that the dividends now given only to the existing shareholders be shared also with them. Such was the buoyancy of the Tokyo market, however, that a company's share price was often unaffected by a big CB issue.

5. "Mad Dogs and Japanese," *The Economist*, January 25, 1992.

6. Comparison from "Downbeat: A Survey of Japanese Banking," *The Economist*, December 8, 1990. Figures updated to reflect later market falls. This short paper, one of the best expositions of the problems of Japanese banks, predicted a fall in the value of the Nikkei to 13,000.

7. Margin requirements are the rules that govern what proportion of the value of shares a speculator must put up before he is allowed to ask a broker to lend him the rest. The arbitrage that the ministry most wanted to discourage was that between the stock market index and the underlying stocks that it consists of, and between cash and futures indices. Heavy program trading is believed by some, wrongly in my opinion, to exacerbate the swings of share prices.

8. Most big Japanese companies require their employees to hold a personal account with the firm's main bank. Workers say that there is only rarely a formal rule that they must do so; rather, the company says that it is convenient for the sake of paying salary for the employee to bank with the same bank. Employees are free to hold accounts elsewhere but usually do not; it is taken as a sign of disloyalty to ignore the firm's advice on this, as on so many other things. Sometimes, the personal accounts of the firm's employees are every bit as important as the business of the firm itself — especially if, like Matsushita Electric, the firm has more than 100,000 workers.

9. Lower share prices mean that a company issuing new shares receives less money for a given dilution of its future earnings than it would if prices were higher. That means issuing shares in a depressed stock market is a more expensive way of raising money than issuing shares in a booming market.

10. This section draws widely on a business cover story I wrote in *The Independent* on Sunday, June 30, 1991. I am grateful to the editor for permission to reproduce material from the article.

11. Gangsters were used at a shareholder's meeting to prevent T. Boone Pickens, the American corporate raider, from demanding seats on the board of a Japanese company in which he had more than a 20 percent shareholding.

12. London: Bloomsbury Publishing, 1990. This book is the only serious study of the firm in English, and the section that follows draws extensively from it.

4. KILL OR CURE IN THE CAR BUSINESS

1. Joseph Fucini and Suzy Fucini, *Working for the Japanese: Inside Mazda's American Auto Plant* (New York: Free Press, 1990).

2. David Halberstam, *The Reckoning* (New York: Bantam, 1987), p. 73.

3. James P. Womack, Daniel T. Jones, and Daniel Roos, *The Machine That Changed the World* (New York: Rawson Associates, 1990). This book, which reports the conclusions of a series of studies carried out by the International Motor Vehicle Program at MIT, has become a bible for change in the automotive industry. Top executives of car companies all over the world quote statistics from it, or devote painstaking arguments to explaining why they differ with its conclusions. The analysis of this section draws heavily on this book; further historical details are drawn from *Toyota: A History of the First 50 Years* (New York: Toyota Motor Company, 1988).

4. This was true only in its early days; more recently, Toyota and other Japanese car makers have been able to make use of temporary labor. The significance of the point, however, is to see how Toyota's production system was a cleverly thought-out response to a set of highly constricting circumstances.

5. Womack, Jones, and Roos, *The Machine That Changed the World*, fig. 4.7, p. 92.

6. Editorial page, January 17, 1992.

7. "Local content," defined loosely, is the proportion of components and services making up a product which come from the market where it is sold. The irony of the Honda controversy in 1991 was that when it came to exporting the same cars to Europe, U.S. trade officials dismissed claims from France that the

cars should be considered as Japanese and insisted on the contrary that they were 100 percent American.

8. "Survey of Japanese Automotive Industry," *Financial Times,* December 20, 1990.

9. In *The Enigma of Japanese Power* (New York: Knopf, 1989), Karel van Wolferen maintains nevertheless that "the fact that an imported car has its steering wheel on the wrong side for Japan is part of its snob appeal value; it marks the cars as foreign. Some imported cars like Mercedes have a lower resale value if they have the steering wheel on the right side" (p. 475). This used to be true, perhaps because at first the only available imported cars were left-hand drive. Recent inquiries, however, suggest that it is no longer the case.

10. Some of the details in this paragraph are drawn from *The Reckoning,* which provides a fascinating comparison of the histories of the Ford and Nissan motor companies.

11. Ben Hamper, *Rivethead: Tales from the Assembly Line* (New York: Warner Books, 1991).

12. *Financial Times,* June 7, 1991.

13. There were some abortive European attempts to globalize. Volkswagen, for instance, had a factory in the United States for a while but later closed it after losing money heavily for years.

14. It will take some time before the Japanese makers have spread their production sufficiently widely to overtake them. But that is part of a wider question that is addressed later in this chapter.

15. These claims are addressed in more detail in chapter 7.

16. An export restraint raises prices just like a tariff, but the exporter pockets the difference rather than the government of the importing country.

17. Britain and Portugal also restricted Japanese access to their markets; the market penetrations there were 11.8 percent and 14 percent respectively.

18. August 3, 1991.

19. Updated from Geoffrey Bownas, *Japan and the New Europe* (London: Economist Intelligence Unit, 1991).

20. Womack, Jones, and Roos, *The Machine That Changed the World,* p. 257.

21. My italics.

22. It is not clear whether it was political pressure from Paris, lack of takers in Japan, or the company's own reluctance that prevented Renault from establishing a direct joint venture of its

own. Whichever it was, the political establishment is likely to have made its views known: Louis Schweitzer, a graduate of the École Nationale d'Administration, was chief of staff for Laurent Fabius for six years up to and including when he was France's prime minister.

23. Adam Opel AG is a subsidiary of General Motors.

5. TOSHIBA, OLIVETTI, AND THE EUROPEAN COMPUTER

1. Marie Anchordoguy, *Computers Inc.: Japan's Challenge to IBM* (Cambridge, Mass.: Harvard University Press, 1989). The details of this paragraph are drawn from this important book.

2. Today, while both Europe and the United States impose tariffs on imported computers and machinery, Japan allows computers to be imported duty-free. One of the results of this has been that the distributors of American personal computers, who have deliberately kept prices high and sales low, are finding themselves overwhelmed by a tide of "gray imports" as customers buy machines cheaply abroad and import them. This gave rise in 1989 to an embarrassing case in which Japan's Fair Trade Commission investigated allegations that Apple Japan had put pressure on computer magazines and wholesalers not to cooperate with importers who were undercutting its high-priced Apples.

3. The creation of the PC "clone" industry was made possible when other firms succeeded in writing programs that imitated IBM's Basic Input-Output System (BIOS) without infringing on its copyrights — thus allowing other companies to produce machines that behaved exactly like IBM machines without having to be licensed by IBM.

4. Most Japanese-language word processors allow the user to type either in *hiragana*, one of the Japanese syllabaries, or in Roman letters on a standard QWERTY keyboard. Recent models come with sophisticated software that uses some limited context analysis to predict which Chinese character the user intends to use, and makes that one the first choice.

5. I heard this description first from Joichi Aoi, the president of Toshiba, in 1990.

6. Two months later, however, an article about the two models in *Foreign Report*, a confidential newsletter published by *The*

Economist, called "A Trade Row in Your Lap," predicted incorrectly that the battle for dominance of the portable computer market would result in claims of Japanese dumping and American demands for protection against imports. "Next year," the article said, "there will be a vicious domestic battle in Japan, as five other companies dive into the market and try to catch up with Toshiba. The five will be able to maul their competitors abroad in 1991 . . . Toshiba has no immediate plans to export the Dynabook to America . . . But eventually it will either export [it] to America, or make it there. Japan seems certain to take this market over from the Americans; importing countries seem certain to complain." Another consequence of Toshiba's achievement was that Zenith Corporation, the American consumer electronics maker that was the parent company of Zenith Data Systems, found itself unable to continue to invest both in consumer electronics and in portable computers. As it blundered into increasing difficulties, the firm made the bizarre decision to ditch the growing market and hold on to the stagnant one: it sold ZDS to the French firm Groupe Bull. This will be discussed later in the chapter.

7. Abroad, the machines are known more prosaically by numbers. The export versions of the original Dynabook JS3100SS-001 model bore the name T1000SE.

8. UNIX had actually been invented two decades earlier at Bell Laboratories, the New Jersey research center of AT&T, the American telephone company.

9. RISC processors have two other important advantages over conventional complex instruction set computing. First, they take advantage of the microprocessor's ability to do some operations simultaneously to save time — for example, they can perform a calculation on one number while the next is being taken out of memory (rather like the principle of drying one set of clothes while washing the next). Second, they remove an entire layer of command interpreting by doing without the sequencer that lies at the heart of many CISC processors. This, however, is an area for the technically minded.

10. Andrew Rappaport and Shmuel Halevi, "The Computerless Computer Company," *Harvard Business Review,* July/August 1991.

11. Their achievement reminds one of Talleyrand, the mischievous

cleric who managed to serve successively as Napoleon's foreign minister and then as one of the leaders of the government that restored the monarchy after his downfall. Asked much later what he had done during the French Revolution, Talleyrand replied simply, "I survived."

12. Quoted in *Financial Times*, March 11, 1991.

13. There is an irony in the fact that the spread of computers, as measured by the number installed or the proportion of companies who report that their work is computerized, has consistently been less in Europe and in Japan, both places where governments have been much keener to help suppliers, than in the United States, which has left them much more to their own devices.

14. Software is perhaps an honorable exception. Cap Gemini Sogeti, the Paris-based software house, is unquestionably a world-class firm. In some areas of software development, Europe leads both Japan and the United States.

15. A 16-megabit dynamic random-access memory is a memory chip with a capacity of over 16 million 1's or 0's that can store information only as long as it is electrically charged. SRAM, or static random-access memory, retains the data stored in it even after the power is switched off. Between them, the two kinds of chip constitute the key building blocks not just of computers but also increasingly of a host of other electronic goods; they are widely seen as essential to future generations of computers.

16. *Financial Times*, February 10, 1992.

17. Similar things are happening in the United States. Toshiba first started assembling computers there in order to get around the punitive duties imposed on it by the United States as a result of the *Toshiba jiken*, the incident in which one of the parent firm's subsidiaries was found to have contravened COCOM rules by selling sensitive submarine-screw technology to the Soviet Union. By the time the duties were lifted, however, the company had found that it made economic sense to assemble machines in the United States — and continued to do so.

18. This, I believe, was the first prominent case in which a European firm tried to play the nationalist card in selling a product against Japanese competition. U.S. car makers, of course, had been doing it for years.

19. For instance, a computer running Windows needs a 386-type mi-

croprocessor and a 60-megabyte disk drive to do the same sort of thing at the same speed as a much more basic 8086 machine with a 20-megabyte drive did without Windows five years ago.

6. A BATTLE FOR THE FUTURE OF DIGITAL AUDIO

1. Akio Morita, with Edwin M. Reingold and Mitsuko Shimomura, *Made in Japan* (London: Fontana, 1988), pp. 66–67. Parts of this section draw on Morita's account of the history of his firm.

2. Makoto Kikuchi, *Japanese Electronics: A Worm's Eye View of Its Evolution* (Tokyo: Simul Press, 1983).

3. Morita, *Made in Japan*, p. 112.

4. In five years, its place may be taken by Nintendo's Game Boy, the product of another Japanese leap of commercial imagination. Portable video games, however, are probably the only electronics products that have the dubious honor of engaging the human spirit even less than television. They are a reminder of a painful dilemma: do all these new gadgets make us better off?

5. An example of this love for novelties is the brief 1990 craze for *furawa rokku*, or "flower rock": plastic flowers that jerk and twitch in time to music, by means of a sound sensor in the pot beneath them. This spread outside Japan; a Sony product that did not, however, was the Movica still-video camera, which used the charged-couple device (CCD) at the heart of the video camera to store still-picture data digitally on a floppy disk rather than physically on light-sensitive film as in a traditional 35-mm camera.

6. The group also owns half of the Japan Victor Company (JVC), acquired in 1954, but it insists that JVC is independently managed. The two biggest firms in the Matsushita group are Matsushita Electric Company and Matsushita Electric Industries, Ltd. The word is a common Japanese name; it uses the two characters for "pine-tree" and "under," and the emphasis is on the second syllable.

7. Richard Tenner Pascale and Anthony G. Athos, "The Matsushita Example," in *The Art of Japanese Management* (London: Penguin Business Library, 1982).

8. The story of the development of Japanese word processors is explained in more detail in chapter 5.

9. The transaction raised a political storm in Berlin, however. Sony paid DM 100 million when it bought the 30,000-square-meter

plot from the city government. The rate was almost double than that paid by Daimler-Benz, the only other prominent company that the Berlin authorities had then managed to persuade to move its headquarters to the city, but the Green Party in the local assembly complained that Sony had been sold the plot at a knockdown price. Daimler-Benz, whose purchase was already under investigation by the European Commission, later paid more than triple the Sony rate when it bought another piece of property nearby from a private seller.

10. Read-only memory. An average CD-ROM, which is the same size and costs the same to produce as a standard audio CD, can store 500 megabytes of information — about the equivalent of six hundred copies of this book. That is capacious enough to bring to the desktop sources of information previously too vast to be accessible except by telephone to a mainframe computer.

11. *Quest for Prosperity*, p. 265.

12. The principle behind digital recording is simple enough: any sound, from a simple electronic hum to the overture of *Don Giovanni*, can be represented by a graph of amplitude (or volume) against time. The frequency of the different notes, and the quality of the instruments that make them, are all represented in the tiny imperfections on that huge graph. A digital recording consists simply of a long list of numbers that represent the amplitude every fraction of a second. In theory, it is therefore possible to make a perfect recording of a piece of music; in practice, however, everything depends on how often a sample of the amplitude is taken. Present CD technology samples the amplitude about forty thousand times every second — which means that only sounds whose frequencies are less than 20 KHz are captured on it. The nostalgic view that something is "missed out" in CD recordings is probably wholly mistaken; if it is correct, though, it is because the human ear can actually detect sounds of a much higher frequency than scientists are now aware of.

13. They called it precision adaptive subcoding (PASC).

7. THE PITFALLS OF EUROPEAN INDUSTRIAL POLICY

1. NTT, the partly privatized Japanese telephone company, has developed a new kind of color photocopier working by direct ion transfer which is likely to be on the market in 1993 or 1994. Doubling as a color fax machine, it will work out at approxi-

mately a quarter of the size and half the price of existing color machines.

2. This issue is discussed in more detail in chapter 2.

3. John Brooks, "Xerox Xerox Xerox Xerox," in *Business Adventures* (London: Pelican, 1971), p. 165. Looking back, it is tempting to believe that it was obvious even then that the technology needed to be refined and simplified if it were to reach a real mass market. But that was not how things looked: Brooks noted that Xerox was quite content with the machine's unpredictability, because it encouraged customers to rent, rather than buy, it. "Xerox ultimately makes more money that way," he explained.

4. *Normal value* is a technical term used by European antidumping experts. In the United States, the equivalent is *fair market value.*

5. *Official Journal of the European Communities*, p. 22.

6. "Getting the Best Out of European Industry: The International Dimension." Speech to the Japan-EC Association, Brussels, November 14, 1991, p. 6. The "anti-circumvention measures" that the commissioner spoke of were the so-called screwdriver rules, under which the commission sought to impose duties even on Japanese photocopiers that had been assembled inside the EC — a set of rules that were later declared illegal by a panel of international trade experts appointed by the GATT.

7. Private sources.

8. Cynthia A. Beltz, *High-tech Maneuvers: Industrial Policy Lessons of HDTV* (American Enterprise Institute, 1991).

9. "Research after Maastricht: An Assessment, a Strategy — Communication from the Commission to the Council and the European Parliament." Unpublished, 1991. It is worth noting just how significant Japan's R&D/GNP ratio is. Not only did it ensure that Japan spent more on research and development in 1991 than the United States did, it also helps to explain why, despite the recession-led decline in demand for Japanese goods across the world, Japanese firms are still certain to be in an immensely strong position in world markets during the course of the 1990s.

10. Japanese companies hire only very small numbers of foreign scientists: this is a microcosm of the broader management problems that make it hard for Japanese firms to offer a stable and rewarding career to non-Japanese citizens. See chapter 8.

11. "Research after Maastricht," p. 13.

12. *Adult Illiteracy and Economic Performance* (Center for Educational Research and Innovation, OECD, 1992).

8. THE RELUCTANT MISSIONARIES

1. Keidanren staff argue quite rightly that the greenback is still the world's reserve currency, and still the foreign currency in which more of Japan's exports are denominated than any other. Nevertheless, the use of the display seems to be taking dollar dominance a little far.
2. Jean-Jacques Servan-Schreiber, *Le Défi Américain* (Paris: Editions Noel, 1967; English translation, London: Athenaeum House, 1968). His italics.
3. Sources: company reports; author's information; D. and P. Barrett, *Motorsharp 1991* (London: Albert E. Sharp, 1991).
4. It is worth recording, however, that Nissan's Intelligent Body Assembly System, introduced in 1990 in Japan and spread later to its plant in the United States, raises the possibility of much more extensive final-assembly automation. The system works by combining welding robots, the numerically controlled jigs that hold together the body panels of the car for welding, and an integrated computer system to produce an assembly process that checks the accuracy of every car assembled, recalibrates itself after every car, and allows the equipment to be reprogrammed instantaneously at zero cost for a new body shape. Although IBAS has not yet been moved on from the welding process to final assembly, it clearly raises the possibility of much more accurate and extensive automation there too.
5. The operating system is different, of course, to allow machines in Japan to display Japanese characters on the screen.
6. It is not fair to say that the highest value-added is always kept in Japan, however. In Sony's case, the laser pickups of its CD players, arguably the key technology of the entire product, are made 100 percent in Europe for products sold in Europe. Since there was no other company that had the technology to manufacture them, Sony set up capacity on its own.
7. Richard Tenner Pascale and Anthony G. Athos, in *The Art of Japanese Management* (London: Penguin Business Library, 1982), p. 38; *Foreign Direct Investment in the United States*, p. 52.

8. General Motors press statement, August 15, 1991.

9. The Japanese name was *Saisho*, not to be confused with the San-sui electronics firm that was bought by the British firm Polly Peck.

10. It is more feudal still in Japan, where a sense of hierarchy pervades the head offices of big companies that is far more rigid than any visible in Europe or the United States, and where proposals often have to be stamped with the *hanko*, or personal seal, of scores of managers. It is one of the great mysteries of Japanese business that firms manage to remain flexible all the same.

11. The former is true of Japanese car makers, the latter of Japanese railways and its police force.

12. In Japan, workers often have an important safeguard: because the top executives of almost all manufacturing firms have been promoted through the ranks of the firm — often having worked on production lines themselves at the beginning of their careers — there is less of a danger that they will disregard blatantly the concerns of people farther down in the firm. In the West, where the freer market in executive labor means that managing directors and company presidents can easily come from an entirely different industry, from legal practice, from accountancy, or from government, the risks are higher.

13. The British Nissan assembly plant has a lower defect ratio and higher productivity than some of the firm's factories in Japan, a senior manager of the firm in Tokyo told me in 1991.

14. Trevor Bonner, managing director of Auto Drive Line System, GKN Ltd., at a conference in 1991.

15. Speech to the Boston University School of Management, October 25, 1991.

16. Conference, The Quality of Japanese Investment, March 1990, Gosforth Park Hotel, Newcastle-upon-Tyne.

17. This may well be a preemptive political strike by Toyota, however, in preparation for having to announce a lower local content ratio than originally planned for its factory.

18. In early 1992 there were rumblings that the French government might actually try to weaken the Volvo-Mitsubishi-Dutch axis by insisting that it was incompatible with Volvo's complex alliance with Renault, including exchange of engines and of shareholdings. This was despite the fact that Renault had had a chance to veto the Volvo plans with Mitsubishi before they were

fixed, and the apparent enthusiasm of Renault management to learn as much as they could from Mitsubishi via the Volvo venture.

19. Interview in *Nihon Keizai Shimbun*, reprinted in *Nikkei Weekly*, June 1, 1991.

20. Ben Hamper, *Rivethead: Tales from the Assembly Line* (New York: Warner Books, 1991), pp. 201–2.

21. See Pat Choate, *Agents of Influence* (New York: Touchstone, 1990).

22. See, for instance, Barry G. James, *Trojan Horse: The Ultimate Japanese Challenge to Western Industry* (New York: Mercury Business Paperbacks, 1989).

23. I once passed a trying two hours with a Western employee of Toyota when we were caught in traffic between the company's headquarters at Toyota City and the *shinkansen* (bullet train) station at Nagoya. The conversation turned to cars, and to idle remarks about the new models of the competing Japanese manufacturers that we could see around us. Not once, however, was the Toyota man willing to concede either a merit in a competing company's model or a fault in a car made by his own. His Japanese colleagues, by contrast, had no such scruples.

24. Not one of these Western employees at the heart of Japanese business has ever told his or her story in print. The nearest approximation is Gary Katzenbaum, an American computer scientist whose book *Funny Business* describes the baffling cultural traps into which a foreigner fell in a year at the head office of even so cosmopolitan a company as Sony.

25. "Binding the roots before moving a tree" — the principle, much beloved of writers on Japanese business, of consulting widely but informally inside the company before making a decision — a system that naturally excludes members of the organization who do not speak the company language, and who do not regularly go drinking with key colleagues from other departments.

26. See his book *The Japan That Can Say No.*

27. See chapter 1.

28. Nowadays, however, it must be said that no Japanese office lady can take to the slopes of the Japan Alps without her Rossignols.

29. The long-running dispute in the late 1980s between the United States and Japan over beef and orange imports has now been resolved, however. Quotas are gradually being replaced by tariffs, and although oranges and fresh orange juice remain shockingly

expensive (nearly two dollars for a good eating orange in the Yu-rakucho branch of Seibu, and almost nine dollars for a glass of squeezed juice in the hotels of Akasaka in late 1991), beef prices in Japan have fallen fast. Cheap cuts of meat are still hard to buy, and the Japanese retain their bizarre liking for beautifully packed gift boxes at stratospheric prices — but supermarket steak is now cheaper in Tokyo than in Brussels.

One interesting consequence of the beef wars has been that American cattle farmers have reversed their move toward raising leaner and leaner animals. Japanese customers eat beef rarely compared with Americans, but when they do they want highly marbled, fatty meat that makes excellent steaks and tastes good sliced thin for *sukiyaki* or *shabu-shabu*. U.S. farmers who serve the Japanese market have found that an increasing number of domestic customers, too, are turning away from frequent lean meat to occasional fatty meat. This is good business: the margins are higher.

30. For instance, Charles Ferguson of MIT, who believes that a *kei-retsu* is the best hope for the salvation of the United States' high-tech industries.

31. Now known officially as Myanmar by order of the military government that seized power in 1988.

INDEX